Addicted To My Ego

By Dan Cohen M.D.

First Edition, 2015

First Printing, 2015

Library of Congress Cataloging in Publication Data
ISBN 0-9777577-4-9
Published by One Red River, Inc.
Eden Prairie, MN 55347

Acknowledgements

I would like to give special thanks to my wife Jennifer Palmquist. Had it not been for her wise counsel over the past fifteen years this book would not have been written. I would also like to thank Frank Stucki for his observations during thousands of sessions together and all the fun we've had in the process. In addition I am very grateful for all of the editing assistance and suggestions provided by Jennifer Palmquist, Ellen Cohen, Tonia Galonska, David Campbell and Tracy Jo Hamilton.

Cover artwork and design by Barry McMahon (barry@deeperarts.com). Thank you Barry for creating such a well done caricature.

Preface

Growing up I thought I would become a medical researcher studying the mind using the latest scientific technology. I didn't realize then, that by the time I would be ready there would be so much scientific resistance to a different notion about the mind. Why not consider the possibility that the mind, or higher mind as some would say, is not the result of the organic brain, but instead is primarily of an energetic, spiritual nature? Due to this resistance the scientific community had not and still hasn't developed any technology to directly measure the mind, only the brain.

I became a neurologist, a brain doctor, and then a successful businessman. I worked on hi-tech and low-tech medical diagnostic and therapeutic devices. These included brain wave monitors, sleep disorders diagnostics and the Breathe Right nasal strip. When I was ready to begin my scientific research on the mind I couldn't. There were no tools. So instead I became an explorer.

This book, to a large extent, covers our seventeen years of exploration to better understand what we truly are as human beings. The scientific community has focused mainly on the physical body. We attended more broadly to our physical, emotional, mental and spiritual nature. Our understanding has been derived from both experience and observation, but not the types of observations that one can make using any existing technology.

However, as part of our exploration we developed technology. Although the goal of our technology was to boost our emotional, mental and spiritual experiences and enhance our capabilities. This dramatically enriched our understanding about the differences between our spiritual and egoic self in addition to advancing our own personal development.

What we learned is chronicled in this book. One of the more significant ideas that emerged was the degree to which we become bound to our egos, both in terms of our self-identification and our dependence on it for our gratification. Unlike our higher mind, the ego is a function of the organic brain. Unfortunately however, we unwittingly become addicted to our egos, despite the fact that, in our opinion, we are primarily spiritual beings. The reason that this is so significant is that this addiction to our ego is primary to all addictions and in general results in humankind's hardships and suffering.

Although this book is written primarily to impart this information, it is also written as a guide or workbook. Using the story and dialogue as examples, anyone interested can write their own story and work through the considerations and questions included to better understand their own ego. Through this process they may also experience and realize for themselves what they truly are. One learns that we needn't remain addicted to our ego or identified with this limited state of being. We are much more than that.

Contents

Part II - Considerations

Part III – My Story Continued

Part IV – More Considerations

Part V – The Technology, Applications and Instructions for Use

Part 1 – My Story

Chapter 1: Introduction

I have a problem. As a physician I've come to realize it's a disease, but it's not classified as a disease by the medical profession like an infection or diabetes. Although it is passed down from generation to generation, gene therapy will never produce a cure. If I had to classify my problem I would say it's an addiction, but not to alcohol, narcotics, sex, gambling, or food. My problem is that I'm addicted to my ego. This issue not only plays a role in the cause and recovery of all addictions, I believe it qualifies as our primary addiction.

You're probably thinking that of course he's addicted to his ego, he's a doctor and they all are. I generally agree, but most of my career has been spent in business. However, much of my business career has been spent as an entrepreneur and CEO so again, a big ego goes hand in hand with those roles. Regardless, a discussion about the size of my ego is entirely unnecessary. This addiction affects everyone with an ego irrespective of its size, although a bigger ego may result in a bigger addiction.

By now I hope you're asking, what is ego anyway? The simplest way to think about ego is how you tend to define yourself, since most of us are ego-identified. If someone wants to get to know a little about you it is common to introduce yourself by telling them your name. That may impart some information about your nationality or religion. Depending on the circumstance you may tell them about the various roles you play in life. You may say you're married with two kids and you work as a consultant. As you reveal yourself further you may discuss your beliefs in terms of what's important to you in life, the principles you stand for and the changes you would like to see in the world and maybe even in yourself.

Although your ego develops and changes over your entire lifetime, most of the fundamental beliefs that you hold about yourself were firmly entrenched at a very young age. Your fundamental beliefs about yourself and your roles in life compose the core of your ego. At some time in your life you may have even said, "I am my beliefs." Most people self-define in that way because when it comes to themselves that is all they are aware of. How could they define themselves any differently?

The problem is that this is absolutely false. That's not what we are even though many of us think that's what we are. Given what I've experienced and learned during my sixty-two years, I am convinced I am living a lie whenever I think that way. I am not my ego. But I am addicted to it so strongly that I have been unable to see past it without it blinding me to the truth.

I don't want to live this way anymore. Sometimes I think I would be better off if I was an alcoholic on the verge of death. With that type of addiction there is greater motivation to move past one's egoic issues. It is a matter of life and death. Almost all of us are addicted to our egos, but the common myth is that with a few tweaks we can fix ourselves and we will be happy, healthy and have abundance. I used to believe that. I have come to realize that I was as deluded as the alcoholic that thinks they can manage to have just one drink.

I've had periods in my lifetime when I was happy and healthy with plenty of money in the bank. That's not the answer, although people often strive for that situation believing it is. Sure, money doesn't buy poverty, but it doesn't buy happiness either. Happiness is fleeting depending upon the temporary agreement between one's expectations and their reality and health can change in an instant.

We judge our lives through the lens of our ego, but no matter how much we polish that lens, in the depths of our egoic psyche we will never be good enough or be worthy of love, because that is what the ego truly believes. Never being good enough or worthy of love fuels our addiction. That lie is the trap that keeps us striving for our brand of heroin, which is whatever it is we believe will make us good enough or worthy of love. That drives the hamster's wheel of our egoic addiction.

I understand my ego fairly well after decades of self-work. Furthermore I have remodeled and tweaked it towards egoic perfection, if there is such a thing. That path has left me at a dead end as far as realizing my goal, which is experiencing what I truly am. As I've moved, closer to that goal, I have come to recognize that I cannot discard my ego. We need our ego in life. However, its limiting beliefs restrict our conscious awareness. The key lies in accepting one's ego without limiting one's awareness so that we can perceive the truth about what we are.

When I started to write this book I had a thought that writing this book would help me cure my addiction. I'm not sure if it will during the writing of this book or afterwards, but it is providing sufficient motivation for me to wake up around 4 or 5am every morning to write for a few hours before starting the rest of my day.

What follows is my story.

Chapter 2: Early Childhood

I was born in Philadelphia in the summer of 1952. My birth took place in a hospital named after Albert Einstein. I suspect my mother thought that was a good omen and hoped that Einstein's mental prowess could somehow be magically imprinted on my brain.

Intelligence was highly valued in our family. My father and some of my parents' siblings had attended some college and became merchants, salespeople, and builders, but they wanted better for their children. They wanted us to become doctors, dentists, lawyers or some type of professional. I was the first child born to my parents, Sid and Betty who experienced the great depression as young children. They wanted me to have a profession that was respected, well paid and could weather economic downturns.

My mother was my primary caregiver. She was strong-willed and determined that I succeed in school. She actually asked my first grade teacher, early in the school year, if in her opinion I was college material. I have no idea what the teacher said, but I wasn't a good student until my second year in college. During grade school it was difficult for me to pay attention. I was a daydreamer.

When I was called on I would rarely have an answer. I would remain silent. Shame and anxiety were constant unwanted companions. I would feel tightness throughout my body and a prickly burning warm sensation in my face and chest when called on. I learned to fear that feeling and so I would never volunteer any answers in case I was wrong. Being wrong created embarrassment, shame's little brother.

I practiced invisibility; be quiet, make intermittent eye contact to appear reasonably engaged, don't move and shrink down into my seat. I got pretty good at it. School was misery. The object I was most focused on was the round black and white clock on the front wall. I

4

would often watch the red second hand as it clicked second by second. Time moved very slowly until 3pm and then I was free for the day. Friday was the best day of the week. Sunday night was the worst night of the week, with the dread of Monday morning constantly intruding into my thoughts. The last day of the school year was my favorite day of the year, even better than my birthday or any holiday.

Report cards were issued every six weeks. I could count on a two-hour lecture from my mother on those days. I was essentially a B- student through elementary and middle school. I could achieve C's and B's without doing much homework. I was only interested in getting by and staying unnoticed. I promised my parents I would do better when there was a reason to.

I understood at an early age that colleges didn't evaluate school performance during elementary or middle school. My cousin Lenny, who was highly regarded by my parents, was seven years older than me. He was my surrogate older sibling and my most trusted advisor, although we were only together infrequently. He told me that I could skate through school until I reached 9th grade and then I would need to produce better grades.

Lenny also gave me great advice regarding my mother. He would tell me to just agree with her and then do what I wanted. He became a doctor, specializing in Radiology, but he would have made an excellent Psychiatrist. He diagnosed my mother as an over-protective, nagging Jewish mother who wouldn't leave me alone until I became exactly what she wanted me to be, college bound.

Just as planned, 9th grade came and my grades improved. I volunteered more in class, as my grades depended on it. I did a little more homework and studied for tests. Lenny was in his 1st year of medical school. He had gone to a small college, as it was thought that entrance to medical school was facilitated by such a path. He realized that many of his fellow medical school students came from Penn State. Apparently, the Temple Medical school faculty liked students from large schools. They were forced to learn with little assistance from professors and so they became independent learners. As a result they did well in the medical school environment.

Lenny recommended that I do well enough in high school to get into Penn State and that's what I did. My major was pre-med, of course. I leveraged the learning I received from Lenny about college admission criteria and during my first year in college paid a visit to my pre-med advisor. I asked, "What do I have to do in order to be accepted to one of the four medical schools in Philadelphia?" He was an older man with a lot of experience. He seemed surprised by my question or maybe a little taken aback by my impertinence. Regardless, he was remarkably well prepared to provide an answer.

He opened the top center drawer of his desk and pulled out a single sheet of graph paper with a detailed chart neatly centered on the page. It precisely elaborated the range of GPA's from pre-med students at Penn State who had been accepted to medical schools in Pennsylvania, mainly Philadelphia. The chart revealed a relatively tight bell-shaped curve with a center point at a GPA of 3.6 bracketed by tails at 3.4 and 3.8.

Apparently medical schools wanted students that were capable of mastering the workload, but not so book-smart that they couldn't relate to patients. My goal was clear. I needed slightly more A's than B's and I had to do reasonably well on the medical college admission test. I graduated Penn State with a GPA of 3.64 and then followed in Lenny's footsteps and attended Temple Medical School.

I had developed an interest in things related to the body at a young age. Much to my mother's chagrin, when I was five years old I discovered something that little boys like to play with. My father who has always been a great joke teller remarked many years later, "We were so poor growing up that the only toy I had to play with was my penis." Unlike my father, I had plenty of toys growing up, but few boys would argue the value of that toy.

Growing up in our house we had a TV built into a cabinet in the corner of the basement just above the floor. Nobody but me used that TV, probably because it was so poorly positioned in the room. My mother had a built in desk in the same room to the left of the TV. I remember when I was five years old on a Sunday morning being downstairs watching cartoons in my pajamas. My mother was working at her desk.

The pajamas I was wearing had an open fly and protruding through it was my erect penis. I was fascinated by it and began to play with it, not much differently than if I were pulling on my ear. When my antics caught my mother's attention she screamed, "Don't you dare do that! Put it away." That was my first and only lesson in sex education from my parents. Needless to say, anything to do with that must be bad. It certainly did impact my views about sex for quite some time.

When I was very young polio was a big concern. My mother tended to keep me indoors in the summer as a small child until a vaccine became available. I remember the trip to the nearby elementary school where the vaccine was dispensed. We waited in line for quite a while. I could see the sugar cubes spaced neatly on trays as we approached the table staffed by a nurse. I was attracted to the pink fluid-stained blotch in the middle of the cubes. All medicine should taste so good. I thoroughly enjoyed it and wanted another. Maybe if I had greater awareness or been raised in a different family or society I would have sensed the relief my mother was feeling as I ingested the vaccine, but all I sensed was the sweet taste.

I had my tonsils removed at a young age and was besieged by severe allergies to certain foods, dust, trees, grasses and who knows what else. After the polio scare most of my play time was outside. In the spring I would sometimes sneeze producing a thick string of mucous extending from my nose to the ground. I couldn't imagine how all of that could fit in my nose. I remember at one point questioning whether some of it was my brain. Fortunately there were many trees in our neighborhood so there was always a leaf in reach to substitute for a tissue.

I wasn't the sickliest of kids, but I wasn't the picture of health either. I was very thin and predisposed to catching whatever was in the air. I was so skinny that my mother would have to take in my pants to the point where the pockets in the back touched. I had a small-boned frame and broke my wrist in 2nd, 4th and 6th grades and dislocated a knee cap in 8th grade. In 7th grade I developed a bad enough case of bronchitis to be hospitalized and missed a month of school. As I became a bit more engaged in life by 9th grade and was treated for my allergies my health issues abated.

My emotional health was a different matter, particularly when viewed using life's rear-view mirror. At the time it seemed well above average. However, our society does such a deplorable job of recognizing and fostering good emotional health that we don't understand what it really is. Our benchmark is set so low that if we truly understood what good emotional health can be we would realize that our current highest standards equate to actual states of very poor emotional health.

Growing up I was much better at assessing how other people were feeling than in knowing my own feelings. I generally felt fine, outside of my early school years, because my definition of feeling fine was not feeling anything. When I did feel emotions they were generally of a negative nature associated with fear and some of its many variations, although again, I wasn't well versed in many of those subtleties either. And positive emotional states didn't really seem to register to any great extent in my body.

I was taught as a child and for many years as an adult in medicine and business to suppress my emotional feelings. By doing so I lost touch with the most perceptive antennae we possess, our physical body. I've learned over many years and I'm still learning now that our ability to perceive with our body far exceeds what we have been led to believe. It also provides for a mode of operating as a human being that is far superior to being head-centered, despite our society's veneration for intelligence.

Living in a manner that fosters greater feeling and perceiving from the body is much preferable and healthier than living in a manner that encourages greater thinking and processing from the brain. And remember, these words are being written by a Neurologist, someone who really appreciates the brain.

I modelled my emotional feeling nature after my mother's. Although she would laugh on occasion, more often she was serious or worried. As a result I learned to be more serious and concerned, because as a child I didn't have all that much to worry about. Growing up in Philadelphia in the 50's and 60's as a male also didn't foster a lot of overt emotionalism. Boys, unlike girls, were supposed to be tough and not prone to showing emotions.

The best way to not show emotions is to suppress them so that they aren't felt either. Outbursts of emotions related to anger, although not well tolerated by my parents, were acceptable in the presence of male peers, especially if it was a shared feeling. However, since I wasn't exactly a high energy child and those types of outbursts tend to use up a lot of energy, I tended to be more placid and neutral.

A very strange thing happened to me when I was about five or six years old, although I accepted it as if it were commonplace. I was playing in front of my house with two of my neighbors. I heard a voice that came from inside my head that told me to pay attention to all of my friends and determine what about them I liked and wanted to adopt as my own way of being. I remember receiving the message and without question, I began to follow the advice.

From that day on I became a great observer of my friends and others and learned to quickly understand what they were thinking and feeling. In the process of doing this however I was developing my observational skills, but not my feeling nature, as I wasn't feeling in my physical body what they were feeling. I was simply learning to recognize what they were thinking and feeling through inference and deduction and then model those aspects to my liking. I used to think that this was providing me with greater empathic ability, but I was wrong. Empaths feel a lot and I didn't.

I became a keen observer of people's facial movements, particularly the subtle movements around the mouth. There are many more muscles around a person's mouth than there are around their eyes and all of those varied and subtle expressions reveal a great deal. I learned to relax the muscles around my mouth so as to not provide others with information about how I was feeling or thinking. I found myself so fixated on mouths that later I had to train myself to look someone in the eye when I met them or when I wanted to seriously engage them to add weight to what I was saying.

Although this observational and analytic process provided me with a great asset, it further distanced me from my feeling nature. All of this information about other people could have been gleaned from my feeling nature and more reliably so. I wonder if the advice-giver within my head had realized that I would adopt the methodology I used to learn about others. I would have been much better off if I had learned to feel more, but I guess it wasn't the right time.

Chapter 3: Later Childhood

My invisibility training from my early days, hiding in plain sight in the classroom, also aided me in my ability to observe adults in action. When my parents had other couples over, they frequently met in the kitchen or the living room. It was very easy for me to stay small and quiet. Since in those days children were supposed to be seen and not heard, it was easy to remain in the company of adults and go unnoticed or most likely, ignored. I would observe my parents and their friends for hours, like some alien presence gathering reconnaissance on a different species. What seemed even stranger to me was that after watching them for hours I felt as if they were a different species or more accurately, that I was.

I clearly understood that my parents were my biological parents. My friend Aaron from up the street schooled me in the facts of life at the age of six. He had just learned them from his older sister. Soon after hearing them I brought the matter up with my mother. She immediately confirmed the facts I had learned by emphatically denying them. I knew her well enough by then to realize that Aaron had just told me the absolute truth about baby-making.

Despite knowing that my biologic parents were my parents and I have no reason to this day to believe otherwise, I never felt like they truly were. I knew I had to listen to them or at least pretend to, but I generally believed that they were simply one source of information and often they provided no greater veracity than anyone else and often less.

I understood that I needed my parents because I was just a child and had no other means of support. I also knew that people were supposed to love their parents. My parents seemed lovable and they treated me very well and to the best of their abilities. They did everything in their power to help me and keep me safe and for that I will be forever grateful. By the standards of their generation, they were excellent parents and they shaped me in many ways that assisted me in becoming a successful person in society.

What they didn't teach me, they couldn't. It was of no fault of theirs. You don't know what you don't know and you can't teach what you don't know. In addition, you model what you are and you can't model what you aren't. My father was the fourth of six kids. He grew up in a household run by a strict and stingy father, who my father hated and a distant, overworked subservient mother.

My mother was the youngest of four. She had three older brothers. The closest one in age was ten years older. When my mother was five, her oldest brother and my namesake died of cancer at the age of twenty. My maternal grandmother shut down. According to my mother, her mother suffered so badly from that loss that overnight her hair turned white and she lost all of her teeth. Whatever truly happened I'll never know, but I do know that from the age of five my mother was essentially raised by her two remaining adolescent brothers. My uncle told me stories about how he even took her with him when he went on dates.

Who was there for my parents? How were they to experience and learn meaningful parental love? They modelled their love for me as best they could. They were there for me. They were supportive and encouraging. My mother was more critical of me than my father, but not harshly and I clearly understood her motives. It was easy for me to interpret her criticism as constructive, which I did. But who was there for me to openly demonstrate heart-felt parental love? No one.

I never cried about that until the time of this writing. Even now, the deep sadness that I experience while recounting this doesn't fully register in my physical body even while sobbing with tears streaming down my face. Maybe this is the best I can do in terms of experiencing the physical feelings associated with the emotion of sadness, but I doubt it. Why? Because I can feel so many other emotional feelings throughout my body, particularly those considered to be of a negative nature, like anxiety, anger, shame and guilt. How is sadness different?

Sadness affects the heart just like love. I don't remember when I closed my heart to love and sadness. I believe that I came into this life with an open heart, but I can't say for sure. I don't believe that my heart closed from some significant event buried in my subconscious. Like so many people it was most likely a more gradual, insidious process resulting from many smaller, even seemingly trivial occurrences and learnings. Despite my current shortcoming in this regard I do know one thing. If I continue to seek these physical feelings to a greater extent, which I actively do, they will continue to open up to me to a greater extent. That is the nature of things.

Just to be clear about this and not just because these people will be reading these pages, I love my wife and my kids and my first wife. But my feelings of love are largely emotional counterparts of love experienced in my mind and only partially experienced throughout my physical body.

For the most part I also loved my time as a child growing up in a relatively small neighborhood with twenty other boys that were about my age. My little neighborhood consisted of two streets with five houses on either side surrounded by a large circular street bordered by at least another thirty-five homes. All told there were about fifty-five homes and lots of kids. There were two smaller neighborhoods that bordered ours, but we rarely had to venture beyond ours to find kids to play with.

I lived on one of the middle streets that was the most populated with kids and so it was the most popular place to be. Furthermore, my house was the middle house on the street and so it was often the place to meet. Since the only cars traveling on our street were for the most part driven by the residents living there, it was a safe place to play.

The manhole cover in front of Randy's house was home plate and the crack in the sidewalk was first base. The telephone pole was second base even though it was not in line with home plate and the pitcher's location. Third base was someone's T-shirt. The houses were set back far enough so we didn't break any windows. On rare occasions our fathers would play with us on a Sunday afternoon. They would have to bat other-handed to avoid hitting the houses.

My father was very athletic and loved most sports. After dinner in the summer he and I would often have a catch. Some of my friends would occasionally join in. When Frisbees became popular my father opted out as, in his opinion, that wasn't a sport. By that time I was becoming an adolescent anyway and having a catch with my father wasn't so cool.

In our neighborhood we played a lot of baseball and basketball. Larry had a net mounted on his deck railing which hung above a square driveway in back of his house. It was enough space to play three on three, but we usually played two on two. All in all, I was an average athlete and fit in just fine within the mix of capabilities exhibited by my peers. Participating in sports was a great way to pass the time. It did not define me nor did it negatively impact my self-esteem. It was simply what we did together and we all had fun doing it.

There weren't many girls my age in our neighborhood, especially compared to the disproportionate number of boys. We tended not to mix too much, but a number of us had a crush on Julie and Susan had a crush on me. I always felt self-conscious around girls until later in my college years after becoming more experienced. I attended and participated in some make-out parties in middle school and dated in high school, but never had a steady or significant relationship until college. Before college all of my relationships with girls were fairly superficial in all respects. I had already been significantly impacted by my mother's way of being.

Although I was fairly observant as a child and I knew early on not to always believe what my mother had to say, I never realized how much I bought into her way of being. My only excuse is that I did it for love, which is why in most cases the apple doesn't fall far from the tree. Growing up we tend to emulate those who we seek love from in an effort to receive it. And how can we not, isn't that the force that drives us?

Unfortunately emulating another to receive love from them is a flawed premise. It seems to make sense that if we are like another person they will love us. However the scenario doesn't usually play out that way. That concept assumes that the person we are emulating loves themselves and therefore would and could love us. However very few people truly love themselves and as a result they are incapable of unconditionally loving other people, even those like themselves. In the end, all we accomplish is adopting their flaws, which usually prevents us from loving and being ourselves. The cycle repeats itself generation after generation.

My mother has since passed, but in many regards she lives on in me. Showing up to an appointment on time means arriving ten minutes early, always! Never hurt anyone's feelings even if you have to lie. White lies were not only sanctioned, but encouraged. Appearances are everything. She was not focused on physical beauty, but one should always be clean, well groomed and dressed nicely. Never show up under-dressed. Being over-dressed is acceptable, as it is a sign of respect. One's home should always be clean and tidy, everything in its place.

Appearance was more important than function. My mother worked as an interior designer. She took pride in our furniture. We had this awful pink and white silk covered sectional couch in our living room. It was pretty, but because it was silk and my mother wanted to protect it, it was always encased in plastic slip covers. During spring and summer, if you were wearing shorts, your bare legs would stick to the plastic and even if you were dressed in long pants the plastic was uncomfortable and stiff, precluding any ability to sink into the couch and get comfortable.

It was a formal couch meant for formal upright sitting. My mother hadn't anticipated that the drapes behind the couch wouldn't block out the harmful UV rays from the morning sunlight. Soon after I moved out of the house, so did those couches as the silk fabric facing the windows deteriorated into shreds. I would have liked to have been there to waive goodbye to them.

Unfortunately, I was there to waive goodbye to Sean, my Irish setter when I was fifteen. I only had him for a year. He had been effectively house-broken soon after I got him, as I had a month to work with him during the summer. However, when the school year began and my mother had to let him out and retrieve him, his house training began to deteriorate. She feared that his barking would disturb the neighbors, so with his first bark she would bring him in before he had a chance to poop.

When my Irish setter became my Irish shitter and brown spots began to appear on the pink carpets, my protestations couldn't win the day. I gave him to a farm that had another Irish setter. I'm sure he was happy. Although I really enjoyed having a dog I was surprised that I did not experience much of a loss, as I gave him up.

Having good manners and respecting one's elders was a firm rule in our house. One of my maternal Aunts through marriage viewed herself as far superior in status as compared to all of my other relatives. Presumably it was because she came from money. She paid us a visit soon after my sixth birthday after returning from a trip to Hawaii. She said that she wanted to visit because she had a special birthday present just for me that she had brought all the way from Hawaii.

16

She was making a big deal about this gift and her reason for visiting. She opened her purse and pulled out a trinket that she called a keychain. What six year old living in a safe neighborhood in the suburbs in the 1950's needed a keychain? Our door was always open or if it was locked I was asleep in bed. I didn't own any keys.

The keychain was one of those small square bi-reflective surfaces that displayed a dancing hula girl as the viewing angle shifted back and forth. There was a small hole in one corner with a cheap, brass three-inch ball chain running through it. The .25 cent price tag was still affixed to the paper backing. After elevating my expectations about this gift from Hawaii she added insult to injury by saying, "If you're not going to use it please don't take it, as I can give it to somebody else." I don't know if she mistook me for a moron or just simply didn't realize that six-year olds are a lot smarter than that, even back in 1958.

I'm not sure I would have behaved any differently even if my mother wasn't watching. I remember feeling insulted and angry. As I looked at my Aunt I recalled my father's description of her, which was an arrogant pompous bitch who looks down on everyone. Even I knew that one doesn't give a gift with a price tag on it and then ask the recipient if they are going to use it as a requirement for handing it over. I would have loved to have been honest, as I really did feel insulted by the buildup and the conditional offer, but instead I simply said, "Thank you Aunt Bea. I'll use it." I took it upstairs and threw it in a drawer. It didn't see the light of day until years later when I cleaned out my desk. The keychain was discarded with the rest of the junk I had accumulated as a child. I shook my head as I recalled the memory.

My other maternal Aunt and Uncle, Jean and George were exactly the opposite. George was the brother who became my mother's surrogate mother. They always gave me what I considered to be extravagant gifts. More importantly they treated the gift giving as relatively inconsequential, almost an afterthought and instead made a big deal about me. They made me feel special. Since I was shy, their attention caused me to retreat into myself, which in no way diminished my affection for them. They passed their loving ways onto their children Sandi and Lenny, who also treated me extraordinarily well. I think they all felt the same way about Aunt Bea, but probably wouldn't have described her using my father's words.

My father, Sidney, saw the world more clearly than did my mother, but he kept most of his thoughts to himself. As a child I did not understand nor appreciate my father to the extent I did later in life. Regardless, I did adopt a number of his ways. Lenny never commented about my father. For that matter nobody else did either. In my neighborhood, fathers played less of a role in our lives. My father was a merchant, a store owner. When he got out of the army he worked for my uncle who owned a men's clothing store. After a few years he opened a women's clothing store a block away from my uncle's store. The store was named after my mother, The Betty Shop. He worked six days a week and generally played golf on Sundays when the weather permitted.

Sid was very bright and loved interacting with people. My mother had wanted him to go back to school and become a physician after the service, but he wouldn't hear of it. Before enlisting in the army in 1943 he attended one year of college. He was an excellent student. After enlisting he scored high enough on the entrance exam to be assigned to the Engineers Signal Core and sent to school in Missouri to become a radio operator. He was then stationed on a number of islands in the South Pacific including Nukufetau, the Cook Islands and the Philippines. He was part of the radio communication chain in the Pacific theater. While others in the army were fighting, my father figured out a way to turn wartime into a poker tournament.

He volunteered for the night shift. The radio operators that transmitted messages to him knew to send them in batches unless there were any that were urgent. He rigged the equipment to wake him when incoming messages were received. As a result he was able to get some sleep. During the day he would play poker. When he returned home from the war he bought himself a new car with his winnings. Just before returning home he was stationed in Japan as he was part of General Macarthur's Japan invasion force. Fortunately for my father, the A-bomb was dropped ending the fighting before they arrived.

As a child I considered our home's attached garage to be part of my domain. It was a one-car garage, but there was a rear extension with a raised concrete floor, one step high. It provided for a nice storage area, about eight feet by ten feet. Shelving units on either side held various boxes filled with odds and ends that belonged to my parents. Since I cleaned the garage every year I considered those boxes and their contents to be part of my domain. The most interesting box contained my father's war memorabilia.

When my father wasn't playing poker in the army he and his buddies were helping the local natives. Sometimes that involved fishing for sharks. I inherited some very interesting shark-toothed artifacts that the natives gave to the servicemen for their help. Of even greater fascination were pictures of some natives that had elephantiasis. This parasitic condition causes extreme swelling of the legs and testicles, because the parasite blocks lymphatic drainage. Some of his pictures contained testicles the size of melons and legs that were disfigured and swollen, double or triple the size of their normal counterpart.

Although less striking, but more significant to me were the pictures of my father. His arms were very muscular, much more developed than his torso. He resembled the cartoon character Popeye, but with big biceps too. He also had a full head of wavy black hair.

Probably the most striking difference between what I saw in those pictures and what I saw in life was that my father looked so vital and truly happy when he was in the army. At that time in my life, my father was about forty years old, twenty years older than he was in those pictures. Still enough time had passed so that his physical appearance had changed. But even more noticeable was his present-day muted demeanor. He certainly looked different when he would come home for dinner from work dressed in a nice suit or sport coat. He would take off his coat and tie and sit down for dinner. After taking off his coat he didn't seem more relaxed, nor did he appear nearly as happy as he did in those pictures.

Until my brother arrived when I was seven it was just my mother, father and I together as a family each evening. Although my grandmother lived with us, she kept to herself in her bedroom and didn't tend to eat dinner with us. There was a little small talk during dinner and afterwards we usually watched TV. Watching TV as a young child with my parents are my only memories of close physical contact.

Our main TV was in my parent's bedroom. It sat atop my father's tall dresser in the corner of the room. The rabbit-ear antennae sometimes scraped the ceiling when they were adjusted. My father sat against the headboard facing the TV with two pillows propped up behind him. The pillow in the back was laid sideways and the pillow closest to him was upright, just like I arrange them now. My mother was stretched out on her side of the bed.

She usually read or was doing her interior design plans for clients, while we watched TV. She used only one pillow. She leaned on it with the underside of her upper arm, while propping her head up with her hand. Although she could see the TV most of her attention was focused on her interior design plans or more often her design magazines. Her version of multi-tasking was reading those magazines while paying a little attention to the TV. Her posture afforded me a nice comfortable nook to nest in. I sat facing the TV leaning up against my mother's belly. She was my backstop. That was pretty much the extent of my physical contact with my parents.

Not only did we watch TV, but we also ate candy. Both my parents had healthy metabolisms and both were thin. In those days as long as you didn't have any illnesses and weren't overweight you were considered healthy. Very few people paid any attention to diet. My father had a bag of sugar-coated green jelly candy by his side of the bed. We also shared a bag of Bridge-Mix, which was an assortment of chocolate-covered peanuts, raisins, and other tasty stuff. Since I was so skinny there were no limits placed on what or how much I could eat. However, since it was readily available without much restriction I tended not to overindulge.

My father usually chose what we watched. I was content to sit in my makeshift womb, eat candy and watch whatever. There were three of us in that bed, but we were each in our own little world with little overlap. Except for passing the bags of candy back and forth there wasn't much other memorable interaction. My bedroom was directly adjacent to theirs. After being sent to bed I rarely remember hearing much other than the TV and afterwards, if I awoke, my father's snoring.

There was one night of the week were I would awake to yelling. On Thursday nights my father had friends over to play pinochle. They played until midnight. I think they usually played at our house probably because of the yelling and the fact that my father was the biggest offender. Quite honestly, I couldn't figure out how he maintained his friendships the way he yelled at the other men. They were probably happy to play at our house, as I'm sure they didn't want their wives hearing how stupid they were, at least according to my father.

21

Listening to my father it became clear that you could express anger if you were playing cards and watching sports or if you were playing sports and you did something that had a bad outcome. What I didn't realize until later in life was why his angry outbursts were so out of proportion to the event. These were his outlets where he could blow off steam. Clearly he wasn't happy much of the time and he suppressed that, until in a situation in which a display of anger was acceptable. He would then let it rip with his over-the-top outbursts. Fortunately, and to his credit, he was never like that with me or my mother.

I can't remember my parents ever holding hands or touching other than a token kiss when my father would leave in the morning and return in the evening. There was no hugging in our family. Their conversations mainly centered on their respective work or what was happening with the neighbors or their friends. My father rarely asked me about school. I think he figured that I had been nagged enough by my mother.

My maternal grandmother lived with us from as early as I can remember. Her husband died when I was 2 years old from a surgical complication. She had emigrated from Russia as a teenager. She spent most of her time in her bedroom, probably to give my parents their privacy. She spoke primarily Yiddish, as she grew up in a Jewish household. We were Jewish too, but for the most part we weren't very observant of the customs. My father attended synagogue during the high holidays. I did too if it got me out of school. My parents also spoke Yiddish, but mainly to say things they didn't want me to understand. It worked for the most part.

My grandmother was very kind to me. Her English was passable so we could effectively communicate, but I appreciated her nonverbal communications more. During my growth spurts I would have growing pains particularly around my ankles. She was very quick to massage my ankles and feet with rubbing alcohol. Her hands were warm and fleshy, which felt very soft against my bony legs and feet. She had a lot of empathy for ankle pain as she had a previous ankle fracture that by all appearances hadn't healed very well. It was chronically swollen and painful and she couldn't stand on her feet for very long.

She cooked breakfast for me from the time I was two years old until I was ten. She made oatmeal with lots of milk, butter and brown sugar. Due to her inability to stand by the stove she would only stir it occasionally so my oatmeal was always served with lots of lumps. When I was older and I ordered oatmeal at a restaurant I couldn't believe that it was served without lumps. I hated it.

Every morning after breakfast I would go back to my bedroom, pull up my shirt and place my cold pillow up against my belly. Nobody realized for quite some time that I was allergic to cow's milk. The cold pillow against my belly allowed my daily stomach ache to pass with less discomfort. Despite the stomach ache, I loved my grandmother's oatmeal.

Every once in a while for dinner she would cook a cow's brain for herself. She would boil it in water. I never tasted it, but I spent a lot of time staring at it as it sat in the pot. It was a whole brain, fully intact sitting in a pot of water. I was absolutely mesmerized by it. I don't think that watching my grandmother cook cow brains influenced me in becoming a neurologist. However I do feel that at a deep subconscious level I knew that becoming a neurologist was part of my path and that seeing those cow brains did trigger something deep inside of me that really registered. As I watched, I remember sensing a somewhat unusual feeling that seeing the cow brain in a pot of water was somehow wrong. It just didn't belong in that pot of water on a stove top.

When I was fifteen, my grandmother left our home to live in a senior living facility. She was becoming demented and she needed more care than my mother could provide. It was an upscale nursing home and a pleasant place to visit during our weekly visits. I remember one trip when she complained that the nurses were stealing her dresses. My mother and I checked all of her drawers and she was correct, they were all missing. We checked everywhere, in and about the room and we couldn't find any of them.

Finally my mother took a closer look at my grandmother's neckline and she realized that my grandmother was wearing all 6 of her dresses. My mother and I couldn't contain ourselves and began laughing. What was even more fun was that my grandmother joined in on the laughter. Visiting a happy demented person had its benefits.

On a later trip my grandmother seemed more with it and was also more serious. She told my mother and I about the prior night when she was visited by some dead relatives. Although she seemed more lucid she couldn't differentiate between her waking state and dream state, as she was adamant that they came as visitors to her room. Not surprisingly, she died soon thereafter.

When my grandmother moved out, I inherited her bedroom. I had been sharing a room with my brother. When my brother was born I was seven. Randy's mother next door called to our house and congratulated my parents on the birth of their new child. She knew that the new baby must have just arrived home as I was playing outside in the rain without a raincoat. She figured that there must have been a life-changing event in our house for my mother to have allowed me to be playing outside in the rain.

I had been an only child until Cary arrived. His arrival meant greater freedom for me. My mother had a new baby to worry about and as he became a little older, boy did she worry. When he began to talk he had a mild speech defect. It turned out that he had fluid in his middle ears and so his temporarily impaired hearing caused a mild speech defect. It self-corrected after he had tubes inserted in his middle ears to drain the fluid.

In addition, it was discovered that he was legally blind with 20/200 vision in one eye, but the other eye was normal with glasses. It was clear to me playing Frisbee with him that his impairment was minimal. As an adolescent he actually moved gracefully and exhibited great athletic ability while playing Frisbee. His physical impairments were inconsequential.

In the scheme of things his mild impairments should in no way have prevented normal childhood development provided he was allowed to develop normally. But my mother was determined to find any and all potential issues that he might have in order to get to the bottom of his difficulties or more likely, avoid her own. In fact, he really didn't have any difficulties in my opinion. I believed, then and now, the problems that developed were of her making.

My father tried to intervene on many occasions, but she wouldn't allow him to participate in my brother's care. She took Cary to doctors and psychologists until he was finally diagnosed with a vaguely characterized emotional disorder proving her point that he was deeply damaged. Earlier she wanted to have our family physician declare him mentally retarded, but there was no evidence.

I think his disorder should have been named Betty's disease. She convinced everyone that Cary had issues that required special care and a special school, which he attended. He was always made to feel different and so that is what he became. In addition to Betty's disease, he had a bicycle accident with some head trauma and loss of consciousness when he was about twelve. The head trauma didn't seem to worsen his existing condition however he did develop a post traumatic seizure disorder about a year or so later. His seizures only occurred during sleep and they were well controlled with medications.

When you have an excuse to behave in any manner of your choosing and avoid most responsibilities and consequences you tend to choose the easiest path through life. My mother paved the way and my brother did exactly that. He learned to manipulate my over-protective mother which created his inability to cope with life.

When it came time to get a job and participate in life as an adult, he failed time after time and as best I could tell, his failures were all of his making. He either didn't like the job or didn't like his boss. He was argumentative and always out to prove that he was right. Everybody else was stupid. He either quit or was fired from countless jobs.

When Cary was thirty years old he and my mother were having such severe arguments resulting in physical battles that I insisted he come live with me and my family in Minnesota. After several years he was living in his own apartment. He decided, on his own, to stop taking his anticonvulsant medications. He died as a result of a seizure in his sleep at the age of thirty-two.

From my perspective, my mother had used my brother as an excuse in life. She channeled the majority of her energies in crusade-like fashion to fix a problem of her making. She needed him to be sick otherwise she couldn't focus on his dilemma. In her later years she would watch the CNN news channel incessantly, despite the fact that they cycled the same stories repeatedly. She would obsess over the problems of the day. Some people worry superstitiously because what they worried about yesterday hasn't come to pass. They worry, thinking it will avoid the potential problem. My mother worried to avoid her life. She would have welcomed the problems.

Sometimes when my father would attempt to discuss my brother's issues I would chime in too. I realized that my opinions wouldn't be seriously considered as I was just a child or adolescent during those times. It was all in vain. She would become very emotional and tell my father that he had no idea what was going on. She ignored me. She would rant about what the psychologist, Dr. Green would say about my brother's condition. I didn't have great faith back then in my own convictions, but I doubted that Dr. Green or my mother had any clue about what was really happening. I knew how easy it was to manipulate my mother and I could see my brother becoming a master.

Chapter 4: Adolescence

Watching the interactions between my mother, brother and father only distanced me further from my nuclear family. I remember thinking they were all nuts. My mother definitely seemed crazy about this whole issue. My brother seemed like a victim during his early childhood, but later there seemed to be times when he could have changed the path of his life. It wasn't entirely clear to me why my father never stepped in more forcefully. I felt as if I would have if I were in his place.

What was holding him back? Why didn't he stand up to my mother? I never asked. I didn't want to know because I didn't want to know that my family was more dysfunctional than I already thought them to be. My mother held to her position with tremendous righteous indignation. It was as if the world was against her. She knew she was right or at least she needed to think that. She must have felt all alone. In a sense she must have always felt that way. She effectively lost her mother when she was five. She was in a marriage that seemed very distant. I as her first born only gave her lip service and although she had some relatives that seemed close, she didn't appear to have any real confidant. She really was an island.

By the time I was a teenager I opted out psychologically and became an island too like my mother and my father, from what I could see. I decided that I wasn't really a part of this deal. Whatever injustices were occurring, it seemed to me that all of them were implicated and I was a bystander with only a small part to play and poorly equipped to impact the situation. I felt like an outsider. The only reasonable path I could see was to proceed using my own wits. I was about sixteen years old and it was clear to me that I needed to make my own path in life.

I didn't feel totally alone. Although I had been very dismissive of my religion I did hold a belief in God. The concept of God wasn't discussed much in our home, but the topic must have been mentioned enough and in meaningful enough ways that caused me to create a belief in God's existence. I had also attended Hebrew school Tuesday and Thursday afternoons after school and Sunday mornings until the time of my Bar-Mitzvah at age thirteen.

I spent the last year of Hebrew school in the candy store down the street or the convenience store two blocks away. My report card from Hebrew school during my fifth and final year was all E's so clearly I didn't learn much. If I wasn't given a recording of my part to learn in Hebrew for my Bar-Mitzvah service I wouldn't have been able to participate at all.

My belief in God was reinforced by a nightly prayer. I did take that prayer to heart as I said the words silently. Saying that prayer – now I lay me down to sleep I pray the Lord my soul to keep, if I should die before I wake I pray the Lord my soul to take – every night was the single most important factor in fortifying my belief in God, because it was the only God-related action I took.

In addition to my poorly informed understanding of God, I also received a number of books from my mother that allowed me to develop a broader belief system. They influenced me to a great extent. My mother had developed an interest in psychics and the paranormal. When I was fifteen a variety of books began to appear on my bureau. The first was *An Autobiography of a Yogi* by Paramhansa Yogananda. Then I read the books about Edgar Cayce that had been published by that time and other books on reincarnation and energy fields associated with living matter.

The material in these books resonated very deeply within me. When I was reading one of the Edgar Cayce books I remember thanking God for finding a way to get that book into my hands because I knew it had set me on my life's path. I felt very strongly that what I was reading was true, yet I didn't feel the need to share it as my mother did. She had real missionary zeal, but it was evident to me that despite what she read and said she still held to her own insecurities more tightly. I felt changed by what I had read, but she seemed the same. Her childhood programming was her final truth and despite all of our efforts and example, for the rest of her life she changed very little if at all.

My last two years in high school couldn't have been more schizophrenic. I did well enough during 9th and 10th grade that I could start to coast a bit and still retain a high enough GPA to get into Penn State. My old hatred of school reappeared like an addiction by the middle of 11th grade. During my senior year I was absent every Friday. Fortunately I was accepted to Penn State by mid-year and all I had to do to attend college was to graduate high school. I was diligent enough to call the admissions department and check for myself.

I was more interested in reading books about yogi's and paranormal phenomena than in reading my school assignments. I had also developed a keen interest in playing pool at a pool hall, the Cue and Cushion, a few miles from home. I started playing pool when I was about fourteen. By the time I was sixteen I was reasonably competent.

When my friend Marty and I would cut school we would make our way to the Cue and Cushion. It didn't open until noon, but we had developed a relationship with the manager, an old pool bum named Lew. Lew would let us in at about 8:30am on Fridays and we would clean the tables and vacuum in return for a lesson and free time at the tables for the rest of the day and evening.

Lew used to play with the likes of Willie Mosconi and could run 80 balls without breaking a sweat. He taught us the proper use of english, when and how to put spin on the cue ball. He also taught us how to see and make creative shots when the balls were bunched in packs. All of these tricks are necessary if you want to learn how to position yourself for the next shot and keep the run alive.

In addition to reading books about the paranormal I also read books about pool. I enjoyed a book written by Minnesota Fats, the most well-known pool shark of his era. I went to see him at a local exhibit in Philadelphia. Afterwards I approached him with his book and asked him to autograph it using his real name, Rudolph Wanderone. He looked at me, laughed and remarked, "I don't know if I can spell it" and then accommodated me.

I loved wagering and playing pool at the pool hall, but I think I loved the rule of the jungle environment even more. There were a few of us skinny Jewish kids that played there in the midst of drug dealers and addicts, prostitutes and pimps and a variety of other petty criminals. Everyone there was trying to scam or game the next person and we all knew it, so the playing field was as level as the professional Brunswick tables. In pool people of different skill levels can play and wager with one another by giving or receiving different advantages. It was termed weight. How much weight are you going to give me and how much are we playing for was often the extent of the conversation.

Typically the weight would be negotiated at the onset provided each player had an understanding of the other player's skill level. If not, it didn't really matter, as weight could be adjusted on subsequent games. Hustling occurs over time as you pretend to not be as good as you are and then when the stakes go higher you ratchet up your game. The trick is not to ratchet your game up too abruptly otherwise your opponent realizes that he's being hustled.

Although everyone knows what's happening, nobody likes it to happen to them. Sometimes when it happened toward the front of the room a fight would break out and someone would be thrown through the large plate-glass window. The police were regular visitors as a result. It was fun to watch all of the drugs quickly move back into hiding in anticipation of a police visit after a fight erupted.

As in all social systems there was a hierarchy. Lew imposed a system based upon talent level. He would work the cash register at the front. Since he liked to watch the best players and since he couldn't leave the register unattended with all the hoodlums present, he established table one as reserved for the best player in the room. On Friday nights a guy in his twenties named Berkowitz would come in. He always played at table one. His game was straight pool. They would play to 50 to keep the games short and the bets flowing.

One Friday night Berkowitz came in early to warm up. He asked me to play a game with him for five dollars. Since he knew I was a player at table four or five he gave me 15 balls to start with. Lew had taught me well. I was nervous, but I had a steady hand and head. I knew how and when to play a safety to keep Berkowitz from having a good shot. I won 50 to 10, took my five dollars and happily retreated to table four. Berkowitz laughed and claimed he was hustled. Everyone knew better.

I wasn't quite so fortunate during Christmas break of my senior year. A heroin dealer called Bird came in and asked me to play nine-ball with him. It was early in the day and the place was empty. He wanted to play at table six, which was at the back of the room by the water fountain and bathroom. A friend of his came to watch. I was better than Bird so I had to give him weight. He could win if he called and pocketed the eight-ball or luck in the nine-ball by pocketing it anywhere without calling the shot. In return I had the break regardless of who won the last game.

When you know another player pretty well it's hard to hustle them, but sometimes even when you don't intend to hustle another player it appears as though you are. Bird was impatient and wanted to play at higher stakes early on. I was resistant because I didn't have much money. We started at fifty cents a game, but

32

quickly escalated to five dollars a game. Nine-ball is a game that can be played very quickly when the players are competent. Soon after we escalated to five dollars a game I ran off four games in a row without him ever lifting his cue. I had hit a hot streak at just the wrong time.

At the Cue and Cushion the rule was that you paid after each game. There wasn't a lot of trust and loans were never repaid. I learned to pocket the money very quickly once paid and to never show my winnings. After winning the fourth game in a row, Bird handed me a twenty. I had to give him fifteen dollars back. Those were the days of ultra-tight fitting jeans. I had been stuffing bills in my pocket and now I had to retrieve and unfold them in order to give him change. When I pulled out a handful of bills he grabbed at them.

I pulled my hand back still holding the money. He bent down, encircled my waist in his arms and hoisted me up in the air. Bird was 6' 2" and weighed about 220 pounds, while I was 5' 10" and 135 pounds. What was more frightening was that the bathroom door opened before we got there and Bird's friend was standing inside with a knife drawn and ready. Talk about an adrenalin rush. Instinctively, as I had no training, I raised my hands up and out and then buried them into the sides of his fat neck.

He collapsed and dropped me in the process. We were both on the ground. I stood up first and should have just run to the front of the room, but I was too shocked to move. Bird got up and pushed me hard in the chest with both hands. I knew the force would propel me backwards over the pool table behind me. I also knew there was only one viable solution to my predicament.

I let go of the money and did an involuntary back somersault over the table landing on the floor on the other side. Bird and his friend collected the money and walked out telling Lew that I would pay for the hour's use of the table. I was broke, but alive and unharmed. Bird was banned from the Cue and Cushion, but even knowing that I wasn't going to venture anywhere near the place ever again. My pool hall days were over.

I didn't tell my parents what had happened until years later. I was in the habit of keeping them uninformed, particularly when it was to my advantage. Years later I learned that was a lie of omission as they really did have a right to know what I was up to. I had become very well practiced at not only lies of omission, but also bold outright lies. Usually I did so to protect myself or more accurately, my ego, which is why we tend to lie anyway.

When I was eleven, my friend and I were caught shoplifting at a store in our local mall. We were stealing paperback books. First we had gone to one store and made an inexpensive purchase that justified a paper bag. We then stole some books in the same store and went to another store to steal some more. That's when we were caught, trying to stuff too many books into too small a bag. We were taken to the manager's office in the back.

The manager looked like a marine with the military style crew cut of that time. Each hair on the top of his head stood upright at attention. He looked very fit. As an eleven year-old in an already bad situation this intimidating character was the last thing I needed. Why couldn't he be an understanding, warm sympathetic mother figure? When he began to bark questions at us, my friend broke into tears. I looked at my crying friend disbelieving that he was leaving our defense entirely in my hands. In that moment a brilliant fabrication emerged in my mind.

"The big kids made us do it." The manager's utter look of surprise made me realize how effective the lie had been. He wanted more information about the big kids, which wasn't hard to furnish as I had a number of neighbors that I could draw on for descriptive purposes. I sealed the deal by asking the manager if we could take the books we had stolen from the other store to get us off the hook with the big kids.

"They won't beat us up if we give them the books", I said. He wouldn't let us have them. I didn't think he would, but I thought that line would convince him that the lie was true.

He had taken our phone numbers and told us he was going to call our parents. My friend manned his phone for two weeks, to avoid having him speak to his father, a former Major in the army. The manager never called. We'll never know if the lie worked or if he ever intended to do more than scare the crap out of us. Either way, he succeeded. We didn't shoplift again.

That same year I was arrested by the police. I couldn't lie my way out of this one. Another friend and I were throwing rocks at a local greenhouse that was located at the corner of our neighborhood. The greenhouse had been in a terrible state of disrepair for many years and all the windows were already broken. We were throwing rocks at it from far away just to see which of us could throw it far enough to hear some already broken glass break some more.

We were so preoccupied that we hadn't noticed a police car hiding in the connecting driveway with the street on the other side of our neighborhood. When some glass broke two policemen got out of the car and began to chase us. It was our neighborhood and we knew all the best hiding places. By rights, we should have never been caught. Unfortunately, although my friend found a good hiding spot he wasn't patient enough to sit still. He vacated the spot too early and one of the cops grabbed him. I watched in vain.

I figured he would rat me out. I went home and sure enough the police car pulled up to my house with Jake in the back seat. That was the first and only time my father slapped me across the face. I'm not sure if he was more annoyed at what I had done or the fact that he had to take me to the police station on his bowling night.

We had to stand in line waiting to see the police captain. I was surprised at how many people were in line.

We were by far the youngest. I leaned over to Jake and said, "We're starting young."

My father overheard my remark and wasn't pleased. The police captain said that we could be fined for every broken window in the greenhouse. I protested and made my argument to no avail. We actually hadn't done anything wrong and probably shouldn't have run from the police. I guess this made up for my unpunished shoplifting episode. We were fined $5 each. That cost me twenty weeks of allowance.

Chapter 5: Penn State

I learned that it was even more fun to tell the truth and have people think it was a lie. I enjoyed doing this with my mother. She was such an easy target. On one break from college I was in the back seat of the car going out to dinner with my parents. I was sitting behind my father who was in the driver's seat. I could see my mother's profile, as she was the front passenger. I told them that Marty and I had been evicted from our apartment a week before finals. Actually we vacated without notice and then they changed the locks.

I reassured my parents that they had no financial risk regarding the damage that we had caused in the apartment or the parking rent that we hadn't paid. I had checked with the legal affairs office at Penn State and since my parents hadn't been cosigners, they were off the hook. My mother asked, "Where did you and Marty stay?"

I replied, "Marty stayed at his brother's frat house and I stayed with my girlfriend Jane in her dorm room."

That was the truth, but my mother turned to me and ended the conversation by declaring, "No you didn't." I could see my father smirk in the rear view mirror. Unlike my mother, he had no problem hearing the truth.

I had little remorse when lying to others until later. However even early in life I never developed the ability to effectively lie to myself. Lying to oneself is an interesting concept. Who is actually lying and who is being lied to? It implies a dialogue between two parties occupying one mind.

I've wrestled with this issue for many years and have concluded that there is really only one party, but that party expresses itself in two flavors, filtered and unfiltered. The unfiltered me is who I truly am, my authentic self. The filtered me is still the authentic me, but filtered through my egoic beliefs, fears and conditioning.

The filtered me also holds the belief that I am these beliefs, etc.

The filtered me has self-identified with my ego even though the ego is nothing more than a collection of beliefs, conditioning, fears, and memories, stored in my brain. Lying to myself is essentially believing, feeling and acting as if I am the filtered me without the awareness that I am not. These personas, unfiltered and filtered, real and imagined, are the players of our inner dialogue.

I couldn't lie to myself when Marty and I were driving up to Penn State to begin college. I had been accepted to start in the fall, but Marty had to begin in the summer. I arranged to start with him so we could begin college life together. We both had strong independent streaks and the thought of having our parents accompany us to college produced feelings that we wanted to avoid. We rented a U-Haul van, loaded it up and left Philly for Penn State.

I had just turned eighteen. I had mastered the look of calm and control, but it was just an appearance, a well-crafted mask. By the time we reached Harrisburg I began to feel queasy. I didn't know how my first grade teacher responded to my mother's question as to whether or not I was college material. But I did know how I was feeling. What was even worse was the sense of knowing I had deep within. I wasn't well prepared for college. I knew it and I couldn't convince myself that I was. I was keenly aware that I was likely to fail unless I dramatically changed.

I had rallied in 9th grade and performed well enough through the first half of 11th grade to be admitted to Penn State. I had lots of doubts about doing well enough in college to gain admission to medical school. At that time medical schools were receiving 100 applications for every spot. I certainly didn't feel as if I was even close to being in that 1% category. Furthermore, since the middle of 11th grade I had fallen back to my childhood ways. I was becoming invisible again. The only thing I had going for me was a taste of what my life would be like if my college career was unsuccessful.

During the summers of my sophomore and junior years in high school I worked in a sweater warehouse picking, boxing and shipping orders to Sears' stores nationwide. It paid well for a kid, $3 per hour and I worked 40 hours per week. The warehouse was old and cockroach infested, not air-conditioned and poorly ventilated. Summers in Philly are hot and humid.

The cartons of sweaters were housed on shelving units up to twelve feet high. The job consisted of a lot of climbing and retrieving individually packaged sweaters from different cartons in order to fill specific orders. Every day we had to pick, pack, box and ship all the orders that had to leave at 4pm. We also had to hoist the large cartons onto the shipping trucks. It was hot, sweaty work all day long with a 30-minute lunch break.

That job was just what I needed. It provided me with a real life taste of a possible future I wanted nothing to do with. Unfortunately, experiencing a potentially undesirable life path didn't help me feel any better about my lack of preparedness. However, it definitely provided me with the motivation I needed.

Marty and I were very comfortable with one another. We didn't need to fill silent space with idle chatter and the U-Haul van was noisy and not conducive to conversation. I don't know what he was thinking about during the last half of that trip, but I was changing with every mile, leaving my childhood farther behind. Eight weeks later I returned home for a weekend visit. My mother remarked that I was a child when I left and a man upon my return. I had not yet become a good student, but I was committed to becoming one. The commitment must have showed.

The only comment my father ever made about my grades was when my first semester grades arrived from college. All he said was, "That's not going to be good enough."

I knew it, but hearing him say it out load, which only took ten seconds, was more impactful than all of the two-hour lectures I had endured from my mother during elementary and middle school. There certainly is something to be said for less is more. All I could say was, "I'll do better." to which he replied, "Okay."

Penn State was on a trimester system, three ten-week semesters per year, each followed by a week of finals and a couple weeks of vacation. Marty and I and another friend, Ben, stayed during the summer semester as well. Ben had to because he was part of a five-year program that included medical school during the regular school year. Marty and I liked college better than being home and a pass to play golf all summer long only cost $25 with no additional greens-fees.

By the fifth semester I was an A-student and my grade point average climbed steadily. I was spending hours and hours working at it, but at least it was paying off. A year later I became sufficiently adept so that I didn't have to work nearly as hard and I could still do very well. There was now time to have a girlfriend.

I realized when I went to college how important a few years of hard work could be in determining my future. That became my primary concern. Everything else was a distant second, including girls. Despite my preoccupation with my coursework I did have a girlfriend during my first semester. There were other girls that were more than willing to enter into a relationship during my freshman year. The fear of failure in school however caused me to keep my distance and avoid the temptation. It wasn't too hard to do given the training by example I had received from my mother and father.

My college career was compressed into three years of actual time since I stayed during the summer semesters. During the last half of my middle year I had a girlfriend who was serious as opposed to a serious girlfriend. The next semester I developed a serious relationship with a girl who was full of life. She was a newly entering freshman.

Our relationship persisted throughout my last year of college and during most of my first year of medical school. We probably would have married if not for her need to first experience more relationships. I wasn't really ready either, although I thought I was. We finally went our separate ways. This was the first time separation left a mark upon my heart that I could consciously feel.

I received my acceptance letter to Temple Medical School during winter break of my senior year of college. I no longer had to worry about returning to the sweater warehouse. Obviously there would have been many other vocational opportunities had I not been accepted to medical school, but I had created a binary scenario in my head, primarily for motivational purposes. It was going to be one or the other; either become a doctor or pick, pack and ship sweaters for the rest of my life.

There was one other significant factor that provided for some real-life motivation. It was 1973 and the Vietnam War was still ongoing despite years of protests. The draft was alive and well. My draft number was 61, a winning number if you like army boots. Attending medical school provided me with a free pass, a stay out of jail card that I really wanted. I had transformed into being college and now med school material, but transforming into a soldier was way out of my comfort zone. After my acceptance to med school, my only obligation was to provide the letter to the local draft board and my name was off the list. Done!

The only thing left to do at Penn State was to graduate. Since I had become a good student that wasn't much of a challenge and my remaining course load wasn't all that difficult. The pressure was off, the courses easier, and my girlfriend still had her college career in front of her so she was busy much of the time. I actually had some free time. Marty and I were still very close. We shared an apartment with another friend of ours, Ritchie.

It was a two-bedroom apartment, but upon moving in we immediately built and installed a wall to carve out a 3rd bedroom from the living room. All three of us had girlfriends, who frequently stayed in our apartment, so having three bedrooms was a necessity. Each semester we would swap rooms. If we didn't the apartment would never have been cleaned, other than the bathrooms and kitchen, which we actually did clean every week. If we didn't, I'm sure our girlfriends wouldn't have been willing to stay over.

By the spring, Marty, Ritchie and I had all been accepted to medical school. Marty was finishing up a double major in pre-med and philosophy. I had been on track to major in both pre-med and psychology, but a bad case of mononucleosis in the fall of my senior year caused me to reduce my course load and switch my pre-med major to science. I still took extra courses in psychology, but not enough to obtain an additional degree. Given our common interests Marty and I started to visit a local ashram.

I had read about meditation and briefly tried it during high school. Now I could learn from some experienced meditators. They were followers of Guru Maharaj Ji. After we began visiting the ashram, Guru Maharaj Ji was on a speaking tour through New York and Boston. We were told that if we followed him and sat in meditation we may be able to receive knowledge, whatever that meant. And so we did.

After only a week of following around his entourage and sitting in meditation we were selected to receive knowledge. The process consisted of sitting in a lotus position meditating, while one of the Guru's disciples pressed his thumb and middle finger against our eyes, while his index finger was placed on the location of our third eye or sixth chakra. The pressure on our eyes was sufficiently strong to stimulate our optic nerves producing a colorful visual sensation. As for knowledge, there was none other than the jokes on us. Fortunately we had the time to waste and it didn't cost us anything other than some minor travelling expenses.

I never went back to the ashram. Marty continued to visit there for another month or two. There must have been some attractive young woman that kept his interest, but if so I never heard about her. I continued to meditate for some months, but I never liked sitting in the lotus position. I had no problem with hip or knee flexibility, but I had no meat on my butt. The few rules around meditation reminded me of the kind of religious dogma that I disliked. When my bottom became too sore I decided to quit. It was time to move back to Philly and get ready for med school.

Chapter 6: Medical School Training

I had strong doubts about my ability to succeed before entering college and now I was joining a much more elite academic group, the 1% of students accepted to med school. Although I felt as if I could achieve reasonable grades in medical school, I still had an unshakable feeling of inferiority when it came to school performance. It was a holdover of wanting to stay small and invisible and not be noticed.

I liked Penn State for that very reason. I was anonymous, just a number as the class sizes were often very large. The nice thing about medical school was that the entire class of 1977, our year of graduation, sat in the same classroom. There were 180 of us, so we too were a large class.

Despite our large class size, invisibility was not an option. All the anatomy professors knew all of our names on day one. I shouldn't have been surprised. Learning anatomy is all about memorization and they had our pictures as part of our applications. It was actually quite impressive. On our first day they called us Dr. Collins, Dr. Cohen and so on. We obviously hadn't earned the degree yet, but they probably wanted us to get into the habit of feeling like doctors. Or maybe it was because it allowed them to only memorize our last names.

Our medical school curriculum began with gross anatomy, histology and embryology for ten weeks. I had such a good histology course in college that I took the histology exemption test and passed, so my days were a bit shorter and I had more time to study anatomy. I frankly didn't need the extra time. I scored 96% on the final anatomy exam. By that time and after ten weeks exposure to my classmates, I realized that they were all about as dumb as I was. None of us knew anything and we were all there to learn. My feelings of inferiority were beginning to wane.

Students who excelled in anatomy were asked to be preceptors the next year. Preceptors did the anatomy dissections on half the cadaver for the first year students. Supposedly it was an honor to be selected. I turned down the offer. Although I enjoyed learning anatomy I had no interest in spending extra time carving up cadavers. I don't think the staff was particularly pleased that a first year student refused the honor.

Despite my early academic successes in med school and my new-found feelings of greater self-acceptance I returned to my old ways of cutting classes. Although there was some lab work during the first two years of med school, which I generally attended, most of the time was supposed to be spent in a large lecture hall. Typically, lectures began at 8am and ended at 5pm, with an hour off for lunch.

Medical school books are expensive and there was virtually no time to read them. The professors provided copious handouts before the lectures and we had a note-taking service that provided type-written notes a couple days after the lectures. What was the point in attending the lecture? I decided my time was better spent going to the library and reading the books, which few of my classmates ever did. It wasn't hard to review the handouts and notes before the tests and so that became my process. After a semester of missing classes I was invited to visit with the Dean.

The Dean wasn't pleased. I began to feel a little bit like I did after I was caught shoplifting, although the Dean wasn't as imposing a figure as the store manager. He wanted me to attend classes as he thought it was a bad precedent for students to not be in attendance. I explained to him that I learned best by reading as my visual memory far exceeded my auditory memory. Furthermore, I was a slow reader and in order to read all of the assignments in the books and keep up with the handouts and notes I had to read all day and into the evening. Otherwise what was the point in having us purchase all of those books? He didn't have an answer and he didn't threaten to call my parents.

We agreed that as long as my grades remained high I could spend my time in the library rather than the lecture hall. I gave him an out and for all I know, he may have placated the offended professors by labelling me as learning impaired. We were never given class rankings, but the graduation booklet revealed that I had been an honor student, top ten percent of the class. Not bad for being learning impaired with an inferiority complex.

I thoroughly enjoyed learning the medical sciences. Every aspect of it was fascinating. Although it took me a long time, none of it was difficult to comprehend. I was finally becoming much more comfortable in my role as a student. I made a couple of new friends as Marty and Ritchie attended a different medical school. One of my friends also spent less time in the classroom and accompanied me to the library. I don't remember if he had to visit the Dean.

The first two years of medical school provided me with a nice educational foundation on which to proceed and a confidence level that I had never experienced. The last two years of our medical school curriculum were hospital-based. We spent the first two years learning how the body works and what goes awry during disease. The next two years were spent seeing patients with signs and symptoms of disease, making the diagnosis and learning how best to treat them.

The mental approach that a third year student uses to diagnose a patient's illness does not integrate well with how or what we learned about diseases in years one and two. The transition between years two and three was very confusing and frustrating. It made me wonder why they taught us what they did. Most of the students simply thought of year three as a reboot and started from scratch with a different perspective. The new approach was to create a differential diagnosis, a list of possible disease states that the patient might have, given their symptoms and findings on examination.

Creating a list of potential diagnosis seemed like a task that was better suited to a computer. I felt like I was being trained like a robot. With all of these lists occupying all of our headspace, how did they think we would have any capacity to develop compassion and have a reasonable bedside manner?

I refused to abandon what I had worked so long to learn in the first two years. I spent time with patients trying to understand them and relate their symptoms to their underlying pathology and pathophysiology. The process I undertook provided me with greater insight as to how the patient was responding to their illness as all people are different. It may not sound like a big difference, but adopting that attitude when evaluating patients helped me to appreciate greater subtlety in terms of cause and effect. It also allowed me to think of the patient as an individual, not a disease.

This is particularly helpful when considering the mind-body interaction, which has slowly been creeping into greater prominence in medicine during the past forty years. Unfortunately the business of medicine rarely permits physicians enough time to spend with their patients, which is essential if the mind-body connection is going to be explored clinically. The business of medicine has a lot to say about how medicine is practiced to the detriment of making significant progress on this front.

Chapter 7: Hypertension or Hyper Tension

The process I used to evaluate patients during my training reminded me of a three-year old who is always asking, why? Why does that manifest in this way. After you have an answer, keep asking why until you get to the real cause. A simple example is hypertension or high blood pressure. During my years in medical training it seemed to me that the medical profession couldn't make up its collective mind as to what to call it.

The name given to most cases of hypertension shifted from idiopathic, meaning we don't understand the cause, to primary, meaning that there is no identifiable cause other than itself, which makes no sense whatsoever. Most cases of hypertension didn't and still don't have an assigned causation according to modern medicine, regardless of the fact that something is causing it to go up. The prevalent name of the disorder, Primary Hypertension reflects that.

The key point is that hypertension is a physical sign of a deeper problem or problems. There are a number of established causes of hypertension. These include kidney disease, obstructive sleep apnea, hyperthyroidism, adrenal disorders and others. When patients with those disorders have hypertension, the high blood pressure is always considered to be secondary to those disorders and not primary.

When I was in med school the cases of high blood pressure without an assignable cause were considered and labelled as idiopathic, meaning that the underlying causation was unknown. As a result, those patients were appropriately diagnosed by calling it Idiopathic Hypertension. That was an honest diagnosis reflecting the state of medical knowledge back when I was in training.

Most of you non-medical folks are probably reading this and saying to yourself, "Are you kidding? Do you mean to say that the medical profession today doesn't acknowledge stress as the biggest cause of hypertension?" Believe it or not, the medical profession has not been able to design studies linking stress to chronic hypertension.

However studies have shown the link between stress reduction techniques and reducing or eliminating Primary Hypertension and the need for prescription medications. Typically when medical science encounters conflicting data that could upset the status quo it tends to find ways of discrediting the unwanted results.

This is when it's important to pretend you are three-years old and ask the question, why haven't we investigated this further? After all, the stress response was discovered in 1949. We've had a long time to figure this out.

The bottom line is that the bottom line would suffer if the status quo changed. The medical-industrial complex and its seven lobbyists for every person in Congress, is quite satisfied to treat hypertension with medications. In 2013 in developed markets, $40 billion were spent on drugs to treat hypertension. It takes very little physician time to prescribe medications.

On the other hand, if stress, meaning anxiety, anger, frustration and a range of other psychological issues, were considered causative and required various forms of talk therapy, countless man-hours would be required. This would result in massive patient backlogs and much lower profit margins.

It was simply more expedient and profitable to rename Idiopathic Hypertension as Primary Hypertension implying it is its own causation. In this way we don't have to look any further. We also don't have to consider treatment options that tend to be objectionable to doctors and patients alike, and instead just write prescriptions. Let's sweep the dirt under the rug and move on.

All the stakeholders seem to be fine with the system as it is. The drug companies are making lots of money. The doctors don't have to spend more time with their patients and the patients don't have to evaluate their flawed psychology. So much for exploring the mind-body connection.

From the mid 70's to now, the approach to hypertension is about the same. After my training and learning more about the mind-body connection it was clear to me that arguing for a different approach would have been like arguing with my mother about my brother. I understood that there was no point in getting invested in this kind of healthcare system, especially when I knew deep down inside that I was never really going to participate in it.

Chapter 8: Credibility

I went to medical school to gain personal credibility not because I was interested in becoming a practicing physician. Somehow that point was lost on my father. He thought I would make a great doctor because I could get along with people so well. I told him that he should have become a doctor for that very reason, but that path is not for me.

When I started medical school I assumed that my medical career was only going to be a stepping stone. I would continue through internship followed by a residency program in neurology and then move on to whatever lies beyond as long as it wasn't actually practicing neurology with patients. I enjoyed working with patients and I enjoy being with people, but I couldn't see myself in that role, day after day and year after year. From my perspective it wasn't particularly challenging, but more importantly it wouldn't allow me to pursue my real interests.

The books my mother gave me as an adolescent had sparked an unquenchable desire to understand things of a metaphysical or spiritual nature. Throughout the 70's and early 80's during my training, mind-body medicine began to emerge as a discipline. A small number of doctors and scientists began to explore the mind-body connection. That was considered to be cutting edge in the medical sciences.

Unfortunately for me, what they considered to be cutting edge seemed like a dull blade. I have no doubt that many of those in this new field had the same sentiment. They probably feared that they couldn't push the envelope any further due to the resistance it would trigger in their peers who were more entrenched in practicing mainstream medicine. I give those souls a lot of credit. I didn't have that much patience or tolerance.

This new field was interested in the relationship between the mind and body with a caveat that the mind was generally considered to be a function of the physical brain and nothing more. I was interested in the relationship between spirit, mind and body. Furthermore I was convinced that the mind was definitely not restricted to being a byproduct of neural processes. The question for me was much broader. How does the spiritual realm, including what we truly are, interface with the world of matter.

Science, by its very nature, deals with what it can measure. As far as science is concerned, if something can't be measured, it doesn't exist, because it can't be subjected to scientific testing. During my training period, the field of medicine was already past the point of no return in terms of becoming a field of science rather than an art.

Medicine used to be considered the medical arts, but it had already begun to morph into the medical sciences with the advent of antibiotics and anti-hypertensives in the 1950's. In my opinion that step was taken too soon. There was still too much unexplored territory to assume we knew enough or could measure enough to be exclusionary in our thinking. Moving from the abstract arts to the concrete sciences limits creative possibilities and creates rigid standards.

To make matters worse, medical schools were siphoning off some of the brightest minds because becoming a medical doctor offered good pay and high esteem. These factors in a society that valued such things led to inflated egos for many of us who chose and mastered this discipline. There's a well-deserved joke about what MD stands for. The punch line is Medical Deity. Our successes fuel a bigger ego, which is what most doctors have, me included. Big egos generally don't allow room to consider what we don't know. After all, aren't we the experts? If we don't know about it, it probably doesn't exist or at best, it's not important and has little relevance.

Before medical school, my doubts and insecurities kept my ego in check as far as anyone outside of me could observe. It wasn't my nature to develop and display the false bravado that some people employ as a form of coping strategy to mask their insecurities. My psychological tendency was more aligned with suppression as opposed to projection. I would stay small and go unnoticed if I could. I was a counter-puncher and more passive-aggressive rather than taking the lead and being bold.

However, every success emboldened me further and I became less and less likely to swallow my pride and stuff my feelings and thoughts. I began to express myself more. This is commonly referred to as, coming into one's own. In my case it signified greater ego fortification. I was becoming more comfortable playing the role I had chosen. I was modelling the persona that society expected given my role in the play.

The question I wasn't asking was, "Am I becoming more authentic?" I have a tendency to be too hard on myself, too self-critical. In truth, I was becoming a little more authentic, but I was also developing a bigger ego. It was as if all of me was getting bigger, both sides of the coin, my ego and authentic self were beginning to express themselves to a greater extent.

Chapter 9: Broken Bridges

During medical school, something else inside of me began to express itself, the need for companionship and greater intimacy. Intimacy may be too strong a word for that stage of my life. Probably the need for sharing one's experiences would be a better description, especially since I was still pretty much an island. I met Ellen during my first year in medical school. Our parents knew each other. She was two years younger than me. I had vague recollections of her from high school, although we had never really met and talked.

She was easy to be with and we shared many of the same values. We were raised in a similar fashion and under similar circumstances. Ellen was the oldest of four kids and very responsible. She had two younger brothers that were about two and three years her junior, but her sister arrived when Ellen was thirteen. Ellen swooped in and became the mom, not because she needed to, but instead because she wanted to. Her maternal instincts were in full bloom at an early age and her sister became the beneficiary.

After my days in the library I would visit Ellen at her parent's home. She was in college studying to become a teacher with an emphasis in special education. I still had more studying to do on many of those evening visits, so some of my time with Ellen consisted of more reading, but she also had studying to do. We spent more and more time together. During one long evening of sitting and talking we both reached the conclusion that we should marry. I was absolutely certain that this was the right path. Everything about it felt right.

Both our parents were excited about us getting married. Soon after our engagement I approached Ellen's father, who was planning to pay for the wedding, about dramatically scaling it back or not having a wedding party at all. Ellen and I would have been very happy to have a very small wedding consisting of only family. It was like pushing a rope uphill. There was no way our parents would consider our request. Our mothers began collaborating almost immediately on all of the details.

They tried to rope us into the planning. Finally I put my foot down and told them that as far as we were concerned this was entirely their party. We weren't going to participate in its planning. My last remark was, "Just tell us when and where and we'll show up."

Our lack of participation in no way dampened their enthusiasm. Our mothers were like two young girls getting ready for prom. Our involvement was minimal and during the summer of 1975 we attended a big party in honor of our marriage. It was actually very nice although we were so busy meeting and talking with all of the guests that we didn't even have time to eat. I left the affair hungry.

We immediately encountered a few bumps in our married life. We left the wedding party by cab to stay at a hotel before departing the next morning on our honeymoon. A ride that should have taken thirty minutes lasted about two hours. An eleven-alarm fire erupted at the then owned Gulf refinery earlier in the day. Eight firefighters lost their lives and fourteen more were injured.

The refinery was located just northeast of the Penrose Avenue Bridge, which we needed to cross. That bridge was renamed in 1979 and became the George C. Platt Memorial Bridge in honor of George Crawford Platt, a Civil War hero. Platt had nothing to do with bridges, although he did fight for the Union.

As the fire enveloped much of the refinery, several explosions put a large crack in a smokestack next to the bridge. At about the time we needed to cross, officials closed it for several hours, fearing that the stack might collapse or the fire might damage the bridge. We checked into the hotel about three hours before we had to head to the airport to fly to Bermuda. It was a good thing we had consummated the marriage before the fact. We both needed sleep.

The beaches in Bermuda were beautiful. We spent some time in a rocky alcove where the water was clear, warm and shallow. We could watch the tropical fish as they swam between our legs. Sitting on the beach we could see the oil freighters heading north. They came close enough to shore to see their flags and names. They were from Venezuela. We hadn't realized that the Venezuelan oil tanker *M/T Afran Neptune* was responsible for the refinery fire that we had seen in the distance during our cab ride to the hotel.

The cause of the fire was attributed to the overfilling of Tank 231, which resulted from a failure of the tanker's personnel to properly monitor the quantity of crude oil being pumped to the tank. At approximately 6:02 a.m. in the wake of the first explosions and fire, the tanker terminated its pumping operations. It took several days for the fire to be extinguished.

Seeing those oil tankers heading north in no way signaled any future mishaps, although they did peak my interest. A day or two later we rented motorbikes to tour the island. We headed out early in the morning. We were driving over a narrow bridge when oncoming traffic forced Ellen into the side wall. Another bridge incident. She was pretty banged up so we spent the next few hours in the local hospital, having her looked over. Nothing was broken, but she had lots of scrapes and bruises.

During my medical training it always seemed as if things happened in sets of three. What was next? A couple of days of rest allowed us to resume doing what people do when they're on their honeymoon and that's when it happened. Crack, "That really hurts", she exclaimed.

She must have partially fractured a rib in the accident, which was now complete. Fortunately, her lung wasn't punctured. Ribs are like bridges. They bridge an expanse creating a space for the lungs to expand. Bridges, like marriages are unions. I guess ours was precarious from the start. As a young medical student I couldn't read the tea leaves and even if I could I wouldn't have done anything differently.

We lived very frugally on the small income Ellen made working for a bank. I was two years away from finishing medical school as I was beginning my third year and then I would be paid as an intern, but not much. My medical school tuition was being paid for through a student loan program. Fortunately in the mid-seventies, my medical school tuition was very inexpensive. In total it only cost about $8,000, but every year it was escalating, tripling between my first and fourth years. It was a bad sign for future medical students.

The last two years in medical school consisted of mandatory six-week rotations on different clinical services, such as surgery, internal medicine, pediatrics, etc. There was also time to take some electives. That provided us with the chance to sample some other specialties. Even though I wasn't slated to take neurology until later in my fourth year I knew that's what I was going to specialize in. That meant four more years of postgraduate work following medical school, including my internship.

I also knew, quite consciously, that I wasn't going to become a practitioner, although I really didn't know exactly how my life was going to unfold. That left me in a peculiar situation. I felt like an idle wanderer amongst seekers. The other students were actively considering the different types of medical specialties as potential career paths. I was drifting along, biding my time.

Early in our fourth year we were given three weeks off to visit different internship and residency programs that we were considering. Fourth year medical students participated in a matching program that matched our rank-ordered selections with those of the programs. Later in the year we were told where we matched. It turns out to be a pretty important decision, because it was common for residents to stay where they trained after their residency training. It made sense as they develop medical contacts throughout that community and those people doing the hiring could develop first-hand knowledge about the local crop of prospects.

Ellen was willing to move away from Philadelphia and family. She viewed it as an opportunity to experience something new as well as give us space to learn and grow without family pressures. I agreed and felt it was best that we pick up roots and experience a new geography. As a result there were excellent residency programs on the east coast that were excluded from consideration. We both felt that the west coast was a bit too far. Neither one of us liked the heat, so southern programs were ruled out as well. That left the Midwest.

Chapter 10: Internship

Neurology training requires a large patient catchment area. This is necessary in order to encounter patients with both common conditions in large quantities and those with rare conditions at all. That meant we needed to consider the programs in Chicago and St. Louis primarily. Ellen decided we should also consider the Twin Cities in Minnesota. I was looking for a program that offered both an internship and residency program so that we didn't need to move after one year.

Most people I talked to in Philadelphia had a misconception about Minnesota. Geographically they thought it was located where Montana is. Furthermore they had this notion that it existed in a time warp and that we would be transported back into the Wild West if we moved there. All I knew about Minnesota was what I learned from watching the weather on the 11pm news. The weatherman would regularly point to International Falls, Minnesota as the cold spot in the nation, which was nowhere near Montana.

During our three-week drive to and throughout the Midwest we visited programs in Chicago, St. Louis and the only program in the Twin Cities, the University of Minnesota. We spent about one week in each of the cities. To avoid a future trip we found potential living spaces so that once we knew where we matched we could simply mail back the leasing documents.

Chicago and St. Louis seemed a lot like Philly. The Twin Cities had a totally different feel to it. At any moment I expected Opie and Andy Griffith to appear with fishing poles in hand. As far as I was concerned the Twin Cities did exist in a bit of a time bubble. It seemed about twenty years in the past.

That sealed the deal for me. I was more interested in finding the right place to live than the right program. We wanted to raise our children in a time more reminiscent of when we grew up and the Twin Cities seemed just right. I had developed such a high confidence level in my ability to learn what I needed to know that I figured I could learn anywhere. It also turned out that the staff in Minnesota was huge and very dedicated to training.

My only disappointment was that the main person I was supposed to interview with had to leave emergently, as his father had just passed away. Upon my return to Philadelphia I called him and told him that Minnesota was my first choice and that I would gladly fly out for an interview with him if it would improve my chances of being accepted. I could tell he was smiling. He assured me that another visit wasn't necessary. Programs, or students for that matter, are not supposed to disclose their intentions regarding ranking preference. Although he played the situation entirely by the rules, I felt as if I saw him wink through the phone line.

In the spring of my fourth year of medical school I was accepted to attend the University of Minnesota Hospital and Clinics for internship and residency in neurology. I also became a father for the first time. My start date for my internship was June 24th. The three of us left Philadelphia in late May soon after graduation. Jason was only six weeks old. His grandparents were not pleased. They thought we would be away for four years and even that was far too long. I didn't tell them that graduating residents typically remain where they train. It is thirty-seven years later and I'm still in Minnesota with no thoughts of returning. This is home.

Before my internship began at the Hennepin County Medical Center in Minneapolis, I read, underlined and partially memorized the Washington Manual of Medical Therapeutics. My medical school training in Philadelphia led me to believe that interns essentially functioned as full-fledged doctors with little reliance on anyone else, especially when they were on call at night. As a medical student on call in Philadelphia, I would evaluate my assigned patients and recommend tests and treatments. The intern would then approve or change my orders. I typically only saw residents during rounds with the attending physician during daytime hours.

During our fourth year in medical school we had a six-week externship during which we functioned essentially as interns. This occurred in hospital wards that served mainly the local indigent population, who clearly received a different standard of care. That was really scary and we did the best we could. There was an intern available to us, but he or she tended to be overworked and occupied elsewhere in the hospital. We all carried the Washington Manual in the pockets of our white coats for quick reference. It was our surrogate intern.

During my first night on call in Minnesota, as an intern, I had four admissions. One of them was a diabetic with a blood sugar of 600. He didn't have diabetic ketoacidosis, which is much more of an emergency, so he was admitted to the floor and not to the intensive care unit. Using my Washington Manual I calculated his insulin dose. Having too little experience with this type of case I didn't realize that I had prescribed too much insulin.

Due to my level of uncertainty and anxiety I spent much of the night sitting by the patient's bedside closely monitoring his blood sugar level. It was a good thing as it dropped precipitously and he required the infusion of glucose to maintain normal levels, which I did. As far as I was concerned, no harm, no foul. That patient and the three others that were admitted to my service that night were all doing well by morning.

Chapter 11: Respect

Being an intern in Minnesota was entirely different than being an intern in Philadelphia, but no one had informed me of the rules. In 1977 interns in Minnesota functioned more like medical students did in Philadelphia. The chief resident found me in the morning and gave me quite a chewing out. He couldn't believe that I had taken care of four patients without consulting my supervising resident, which was standard practice.

I told him that where I came from interns do the work and residents sleep, only to be awakened in case of emergency. My resident was standing behind the chief out of his view. She was working hard to suppress her smile. She greatly appreciated the full night sleep and complimented me on my night's performance.

I had to admit that the protocols for interns led to far greater supervision than I had been accustomed to. They were very appropriate and in the best interests of all concerned. Patients were given excellent care and interns were less stressed. Still it was a teaching hospital and one unwritten rule in particular was impossible for me to follow.

I couldn't get used to the idea of treating patients just to keep their bodies alive when their quality of life was virtually nonexistent. In my view, we were using these patients to learn how to treat their bodies irrespective of how family members wanted them cared for.

In all fairness, it wasn't as if we treated the patients against the will of their family. That wasn't the case. My concern was that we were treating these patients without asking the family how they wanted us to treat their loved ones. There was no rule preventing me from contacting the families before I initiated treatment, so that's what I did when I thought it was in everyone's and societies best interests.

At night in a county hospital there were lots of admissions from nursing homes due to suspected pneumonia or other infections. The evaluation and treatment regimens are fairly routine and as a result there really isn't much to be learned from these patients. So, did it make sense to treat the infection and return a severely demented patient who has no remaining cognitive functioning, back to the nursing home without the family's consent? I thought not.

I would call the closest living relative with a nurse serving as a witness on the phone with me. In almost all if not all of the cases, the family thanked me profusely for calling. They couldn't understand why they hadn't been called during previous admissions, as this type of admission was commonplace. They were more than happy to let nature take its course. With their consent the patient was declared DNR and DNT; do not resuscitate and do not treat, respectively and respectfully. The patient was placed in a room and allowed to pass peacefully. At one point about half my patients were in this state.

As a result, at least one attending physician reproached me in regards to my tactics and my fellow interns nicknamed me Dr. Death. The simple truth is that so many physicians either consider a patient's death as a failure on their part or are so afraid of death themselves that they can't stand encountering it. Fortunately I had a relatively thick skin and felt very comfortable with my position.

Twenty years later I ran into the same dilemma with Ellen's grandmother. The hospital literally refused to allow her to die. She was in her late 90's and severely demented. What did they think they were saving? After threatening to talk to reporters about their lack of compassion they quickly relented.

My internship was co-sponsored by the Hennepin County Medical Center and the University of Minnesota Neurology department. The neurology department wanted us to have more exposure to neurology during our internship. So in addition to spending two of our twelve months on the neurology wards we also spent two afternoons a week in the neurology clinic seeing outpatients.

I was in clinic Monday and Thursday afternoons. There were several of us interns and residents in the clinic at any given time. We were supervised by neurology staff. In my case there were two staff physicians, the Chief of Neurology at Hennepin County Medical Center and a junior staff person. The protocol was for us to evaluate the patients and then present the case and treatment plan to a staff neurologist.

The Chief of Neurology resembled Buddha. He was also very wise and was tremendously respected. During clinic he would sit in his office. The junior staff person was scurrying around the clinic supervising most of the case load. As such, most of the interns and residents would present their cases to him. There was rarely anyone waiting to present to the Chief. I think he was generally feared by many, which was very surprising to me as he had a very welcoming and pleasant countenance.

The Chief was the person who was supposed to interview me during my first visit to Minnesota and the person who reassured me that another visit was unnecessary. I always believed that was why I was assigned to his hospital and why I was assigned to his clinic days. It would have been foolish of me to not present my cases to him. In addition, it allowed me to complete my work load early as the Chief was readily available and almost always agreed with my assessment and plan.

He would ask if he needed to see the patient, to which I regularly replied, "No that won't be necessary." Only on very rare occasions did I request that he see the patient and that was usually if there was something of interest to see.

In the days of clinical neurology, when hi-tech scans weren't available, the clinical history almost always informed the diagnosis. It was said that if you didn't know the diagnosis after listening to the patient you weren't going to find it on exam. The physical exam was essentially performed to confirm the suspected diagnosis made during the history taking. The Chief was considered an armchair neurologist. He never had to get out of his seat to make the diagnosis.

I always felt that the junior staff person resented me for presenting my cases to the Chief. I'm not sure if his job was to shield the Chief from being bothered or whether he thought I was challenging his authority, by going over his head so to speak. He was silent about his resentment, but it was readily apparent.

Chapter 12: Ego Inflation or Authentic Confidence

After internship the real residency program in neurology began. The University of Minnesota Neurology program was the largest program of its kind in the world. We had eight residents in our year and two more in a sister program specializing in pediatric neurology. There were sixty staff neurologists, so experiencing a variety of opinions and approaches was an everyday affair.

The first of those three years was spent on the neurology wards of four different hospitals for three months each. The four hospitals that we rotated through also provided us with varied patient populations. Hennepin County Medical Center was a county hospital that served the Minneapolis area. There we encountered very few if any private patients. At the University Hospital and what was then called St. Paul Ramsey Hospital we saw a mix of private patients and referrals from many sources and at the VA Hospital we saw veterans.

A first year resident or a G2 as we were more commonly referred to, as it was our second post-graduate year, was supervised by a G4 or chief resident. My G2 year began at the University Hospital. Two G2's were assigned to a staff neurologist. Mine was particularly uptight and rigid, a by-the-book kind of guy that I never wanted to emulate. I did my job and stayed out of his way as much as possible. Most of my interaction was with my G4 and we got along exceptionally well.

My second rotation was at HCMC, where I spent my internship. We were one G2 short. That meant that our G4 would have to evaluate half the admissions to the ward himself without a G2 to do the write-up and orders. My G4 from the University Hospital followed me to HCMC as my chief resident. He was widely regarded as the best

66

in his year. I was very fortunate to learn from him during his six months of service as chief resident.

It always pays to learn from the best so I volunteered to see all the patients rather than just my half. He was happy as it cut down on the menial work he had to perform each day and I benefited by twice as much instruction. What I didn't realize at the time was that he was pretty much going to be the only chief resident I received instruction from in my G2 year.

My next rotation at what is now called Regents Hospital was the beginning of a transition for me. My G4 came down with a very bad case of mono during the first month of the rotation. It was his job to not only supervise the neurology ward, but to also do all of the neurology consults in the emergency room. Even though there were a couple of us G2's I was assigned the extra task of ER neurology consultant. The supervisory activity for the ward vanished and we simply reported directly to the staff neurologist.

The lack of supervision continued during my last rotation as a G2 when the G4 was demoted and not replaced. By that time I felt very competent and not in need of a G4. My staff neurologist was very junior and somewhat insecure. He was studying for the board exams in neurology so he was filled with esoteric book knowledge that generally didn't pertain to the wards at the VA Hospital. He would sometimes want me to order tests that were in my opinion a waste of taxpayer dollars and totally unnecessary. We argued a fair amount. I refused on a number of occasions to comply with his requests, which infuriated him.

As a result I was asked to meet with a senior staff Neurologist at the VA. He asked me to go easy on the junior staff person as he was studying for the board exam. It was clear that I was no longer being treated as a resident. Amongst the staff neurologists it seemed I had developed a bit of a reputation. During the prior rotation I had another encounter that added to my reputation as a person with strong convictions and a sharp tongue to match.

I was working alone on call one night and had four pretty sick admissions and four additional consults that also required a lot of attention. Normally I worked fast enough to get some sleep during my on-call nights, but this night had maxed out my capacity. It was about 5am and all eight patients had finally been stabilized. I was really looking forward to an hour of sleep when the phone rang. It was the ER. They wanted a consult on a patient with a migraine. As it turned out, the patient had been discharged from the neurology ward the day before, so I knew him well. He was a known substance abuser and his strategy was to complain of migraines in order to get more prescription narcotics for pain relief.

I informed the resident in the ER of the facts of the case and instructed him to discharge the patient with a follow-up appointment to the neurology clinic and no additional prescriptions. The resident called back and told me that his staff person insisted I come down for the consult. I refused. Then the staff person called and insisted and I refused again. He then called the head of neurology at the hospital to complain about me. Finally I fell asleep only to be awakened by a call from the head of neurology. He said, "Don't worry about it, you did the right thing." By then it was too late to go back to sleep, although I did feel relieved.

During my last two years in medical school I felt like a journeyman. I clearly believed that I wasn't going to become a practitioner. I sampled the different medical specialties with as much concern as selecting candy from a box of chocolates. I had somehow lost that attitude during my internship and first year of residency. The work load was so intense that I got sucked into the role of a practitioner in training and I lost my elevated perspective. Living those very busy years caused me to forget.

I had been molded to excel and placed in circumstances that were challenging. I was forced to rise to the occasion. The real surprise was that I was enjoying it all. I was thriving in this environment and developing a standing in my little world. I stood taller and was no longer invisible. I was happy to be seen.

I began to value my childhood experiences and east coast roots as they provided me with some street smarts that seemed uncommon in the Midwest. It was clear that I was different amongst my peers, but in a fun way and we all got along well. I also was learning to value their friendship and adopting some of the Midwest values of greater respect and work ethic.

Early on, the quiet cunning I had developed in childhood caused me to feel like a wolf in sheep's clothing. But later, my Midwest surroundings allowed me to relax and fit in easier. I felt I was changing in a good way. Certainly my ego was becoming more solidified. However, I also felt more authentic and comfortable in my skin.

Chapter 13: Bluff

My G2 year was only my second year in Minnesota and I had been very preoccupied with work. I was only beginning to realize what the phrase Minnesota nice really meant. It was remarkably different from the attitude I brought from Philadelphia. Philly clearly isn't the city of brotherly love or at least it wasn't while I lived there.

Minnesotans by contrast were far more respectful and also more passive. However, as I got to know Minnesota nice better I liked it less. I perceived it as an acceptable form of lying, by omitting the truth. Minnesotans often worked hard to avoid conflict, even if disagreement seemed appropriate. I preferred Philadelphia straight talk to Minnesota nice, but I learned to play both roles effectively.

In a more passive culture it is easier to be in control by exhibiting more forceful behavior. That can take a number of forms, such as outright bullying, being critical or even just standing up for your convictions. I wasn't a bully and in general I was very optimistic so holding a critical attitude was a stance for me that was difficult to maintain. On the other hand it was becoming easier for me to be certain of my convictions and be sufficiently vocal in order to make my views heard. In general though, I was happy to go along to get along as long as I was treated fairly.

Each class in the neurology program elected a representative to serve on the Staff Relations committee. The committee met quarterly. It consisted of the heads of the neurology and pediatric neurology departments, the chiefs of neurology from each of the four participating hospitals, a couple of other staff neurologists and the resident representatives from each class, G2 through G4. I was the representative for our class.

As the G2 representative I was the most junior person in the room. I don't ever remember receiving a formal agenda in advance of the meeting, but any topic of interest to my constituency would have been heard through the grapevine far enough in advance anyway.

A little more than midway through our G2 year we began to hear rumors about a change in policy that was very problematic for us soon to be G3's. G3's spent their time in rotations such as EEG, neuropathology and pediatric neurology. It was generally a soft year that allowed for more reading and most importantly some let down time without night call so we could feel like normal people again. During the first two years of the program we worked 80 to 100 hours per week, every week except for two weeks of vacation.

Traditionally there was no night call duty during the G3 year, which was extremely valuable. That was about to change. Many of us had plans to do some moonlighting to supplement our rather pitiful incomes. More night call would mean that those of us planning to moonlight would not only have scheduling difficulties, but would also have to spend even more time away from home.

The G3 year was supposed to be easier, not harder. When I heard about the change in plans I convened a meeting of all of the G2's. I was amazed to find that the group overall did not feel as passionately disadvantaged as I did. Although they were not in favor of the change, they were willing to abide by it.

My plan was simple and was derived from my many nights of playing poker as an adolescent. I proposed, "We can bluff our way out of this. They'll never call us on it."

My statement was met with a collective inhale and look of wide-eyed fear. Despite their trepidation, they really didn't want to do more night call. They were willing to hear more. "If we stick together they will have no choice but to back down from their proposal." I said.

The idea was for me to attend the next Staff Relations meeting and inform them that we wanted to know immediately if they were planning night call duties for us as G3's. If so, we would have time to find positions in other residency programs throughout the country, which would also give them some time to replace us.

There was no way they could ever replace us and they couldn't possibly deal with our absence when it came to finding a sufficient number of G4's a year later to act as chief residents. Without chief residents some of the staff neurologists would effectively be on night call. The thought of that and the damage it would do to the reputation of the program was an untenable position for them. We clearly had the upper hand. The G2's gave me permission to put forth our bluff at the upcoming Staff Relations meeting.

With as calm an appearance as I could muster I informed the staff of our position. One of the staff neurologists went ballistic. He was the chief disciplinarian in the department. The more senior staff with greater authority looked on to see how this level of intimidation would play out. I reiterated in a dead calm voice, "It's simply in all of our best interests to figure out how best to proceed."

The disciplinarian was red-faced with saliva collecting at the corners of his mouth when the head of pediatric neurology intervened by saying, "Look, he's just the messenger for the group. There's no reason to take it out on him."

The head of pediatric neurology was as intelligent a person as you could find on the planet. He also spoke with a very deep voice and formulated his words slowly with great precision. He was not a person to be trifled with. The senior staff person immediately backed off.

I made sure to not engage anyone with direct eye contact for fear that they would recognize that I was more than the messenger. It was time for me to retreat to my invisibility mode as if I were back in grade school. I sat quietly for the remainder of the meeting, but deep inside I was rejoicing. In my gut I knew we had won. About a week later we were informed that G3's would not be required to perform any night call duties.

In reality we hadn't won anything. We simply had avoided being taken advantage of. Compared to other residency programs we were underpaid. The University of Minnesota justified this by claiming our salary was a stipend. They advised us to declare 99 deductions and not pay any taxes, which I'm pretty sure we all did. Several years later we discovered that the IRS took a dim view of that practice.

I distinctly remember many of the details of our meeting with the IRS. Ellen and I and the auditor met in a very small cubicle. The auditor was a very young woman. Given the setting and her youth, it appeared that we were not exactly being considered a high profile case.

When she reviewed our tax filings she also accused us of not declaring all of our income. Ellen and I looked at each other in disbelief. We had done no such thing and we informed the agent of that fact. She responded by saying, "No doctor makes this little money. In 1977 your income was below the poverty line."

Before I could respond Ellen jumped in and said, "Yes that's right. We were poor." I had started my internship at the end of June in 1977 and so we only earned about $5,500 from my stipend during that calendar year.

Ultimately, the IRS decided that although we had been poor, we were not entitled to declare our salary as a stipend. Nor were any of the other interns and residents. All of us owed back taxes. The University of Minnesota silently shrugged its shoulders, as if to say, "Oops." We never received any back pay or even an apology. By that time it was of little consequence. I was making enough money in my G3 and G4 years moonlighting such that my salary as a resident was the smaller part of our income.

We needed the added income. Our second son, David, arrived Christmas day in my G2 year. We moved into a three-bedroom house and had a bigger mortgage payment. Fortunately, the house purchase included an assumable VA loan at a reasonable interest rate and we could handle a small second mortgage. Having a house as opposed to a really small townhome also gave Ellen enough room to offer daycare services. At one point she was taking care of ten children. By the time we were audited we didn't have a problem paying the back taxes.

Chapter 14: Wake Up or Join a Practice

Normally residents begin to figure out their future employment opportunities in the G4 year. I received several offers as a G3, which was very unusual. It also produced a fair bit of discomfort on my part.

I was sitting at home in my bathrobe on our hand-me-down, living room couch. It was a Sunday morning during the end of my G3 year. It was as if someone had just shaken me and woke me from a dream. "Yes, that's right. I was never going to become a practicing Neurologist", I remembered. It dawned on me that I had so effectively played the role of neurologist wannabe that even I believed it. The illusion of living this life is extremely potent.

Apparently I had convinced many others too. The job offers I received were very flattering. Not only did they come so early, but they came from sources that were unexpected. I received offers from a prestigious large local clinic of neurologists and from the former head of the entire neurology program. He had to retire from the neurology department due to his age and then went into practice with his son. I also received an offer from the University of Minnesota Neurology department itself. It had been so long since I had given any serious consideration to my career path that I was at a total loss.

In those days the thought of being part of the medical fraternity was very comforting. As a practicing neurologist I would continue to do what I had been doing and get paid a lot more. There are local and national meetings that I would attend to keep up with advances in the field. In addition I would have partners to consult with for guidance. As a physician in the community I would be respected and be able to meet my material obligations without any difficulty. What's wrong with this picture? There was nothing at all wrong with this path, but was it the right path for me?

It was only natural for those people observing me to assume that becoming a clinical neurologist was my path in life, but they didn't live inside my head. It was not difficult for me to put pen to paper and make a list of pros and cons concerning this decision. That exercise tends to focus one's mental faculties on the issue at hand unless one also asks themselves how they feel about each item on the list. In that way each item can be explored more deeply, bringing our feelings into play and accessing more of what we hold subconsciously.

Most medical people were head-centered like me. They lived in their heads. They experienced life more by thinking about what was happening as opposed to feeling what was happening. It isn't that people are entirely one way or the other, but each of us has a tendency to be more one way or the other.

I was pretty much a thinker, since I had learned to suppress my feelings a long time ago. In addition, thinking was more valued than feeling in our society. Allowing ourselves to feel more also allows us to feel our negative feelings. These tend to be uncomfortable feelings that we experience in our bodies associated with negative emotional states. This is one of the reasons that many of us prefer to live in our heads most of the time. We get to avoid those feelings. All neurosurgeons know that even an awake patient doesn't feel anything when the scalpel cuts through brain tissue. Similarly, when we live in our heads we are not feeling our bodies.

So what are we actually doing when we live in our heads? Our conscious awareness is focused on our thought processes. It is easy to describe such a person as being head-centered, given the fact that our main thought processor is the brain. As I would come to learn later, this is only the main processor for the lower mind, the mind of the ego. We are much more than that, but unfortunately most people rarely access more of what we truly are.

Although I was principally head-centered I had always been a good daydreamer. I've come to regard daydreaming as a form of meditation in that our awareness drifts away from our egoic processes. It opens us up to infinite possibilities as we allow ourselves to dream without constraints. I had learned to be a good daydreamer as a means of escaping classroom boredom as a child. It was probably why I never knew the answer when called on by the teacher. Even as I became a good student I would often take breaks to daydream and let my mind drift. It would allow me to recharge and then I could resume studying.

I remained on the couch all Sunday morning considering my list of pros and cons. On face value the decision was clear. There were many more pros in terms of becoming a practicing neurologist. By society's standards it was a no-brainer. Although many outside observers would have pegged me as a conformist, I was anything but. In all of my daydreams I never saw myself as a practicing neurologist. Although I couldn't derive any feelings in my body that could inform my decision, I had a strong sense of knowing that defied rationale thought. It was clear that becoming a practicing clinical neurologist was simply not my path.

What was probably more disconcerting was that I didn't have any clear vision about my path. It's one thing to turn away from one path in favor of another, but I didn't have another path in sight. Or at least another path hadn't yet presented itself. Still, I owed three parties an answer and there was no reason to delay. I simply informed them that I've decided to go back to school after completing the residency program so that I would be better equipped to move into research. I saw a few raised eyebrows, but fortunately nobody threatened to lock me away.

When I informed the current head of the neurology department at the University of Minnesota, he presented me with an alternative path. "If you want to go back to school we can accommodate you", he said. He began sharing one of his hopes for the department. He wanted to reestablish a joint M.D., Ph.D. program. "If you commit to obtaining a Ph.D. in neurology in addition to becoming board certified in neurology we'll continue to pay you, cover your tuition expenses and in the process you will have no other responsibilities", he continued.

My alternative path just appeared. I would have had to be an absolute idiot to refuse this opportunity. I really did need to pick up some additional course work to outline and perform the research I had in mind. They were willing to pay for it and pay me to do it without burdening me with any clinical responsibilities. In a somewhat dumbfounded state I gratefully responded, "Thank you very much, I accept."

Both my grandfathers died by the time I was two years old. Dr. R., the head of the neurology program had become the grandfather I never had. How he was able to pull this off was beyond my comprehension, although I didn't have a clue regarding department finances and my salary was still pretty small so in the scheme of things it probably wasn't that big a deal. Still, it was an incredibly generous offer as far as I was concerned. I think that most beneficiaries of these types of offers expect the other shoe to drop revealing some malevolent motive. That never happened and I never expected it to.

Dr. R. was hoping that other students would join this type of program, beginning as an intern or G2 resident. I was ready to start my G4 year, so I would soon be qualified to take the board exam and then still need to continue with course work and a thesis. I was given an advisor in neurophysiology, as my Ph.D. work was more aligned with that discipline. As a result I had to comply with their basic requirements in order to obtain a Ph.D.

So much of what they wanted me to take in terms of coursework was material I had already covered in medical school. They wouldn't allow me to take an exemption test in its place, but they would allow me to substitute higher level coursework. Unfortunately, the higher level coursework was so esoteric and tangential to my interests that it made no sense to make the substitutions. After a year of getting all A's in the classes and learning what I needed to, I was not inclined to comply with additional required coursework.

I informed Dr. R. of my decision to leave the Ph.D. program. His immediate comeback was, "I thought that was going to happen. Just continue working on your project and that will be fine." Only a grandfather would be that accepting.

That gift was a little more than I could take. I offered to staff the consult rounds in return. He viewed that as a very generous offer. Every weekday I met with two G2 neurology residents at 3pm and they presented the cases that they evaluated at the University Hospital. It was actually a lot of fun as the cases were usually interesting and I enjoyed teaching. The arrangement seemed like a good deal for all concerned.

During that year I passed the board exam in neurology and psychiatry so I had become a board certified neurologist. Although the clinical work was of some interest I was not passionate about it.

I had hired a tutor in engineering to help me better understand the various mathematical techniques used in signal processing. I was interested in developing a new computerized technique to evaluate the brain waves we recorded using the electro-encephalogram. Most clinicians would find this type of work to be extremely boring and tedious with an uncertain outcome. I was thoroughly intrigued.

After six months of studying signal processing techniques with my tutor I had a better idea about how I needed to proceed. It was going to cost a fair bit of money to develop the technology I wanted to create. I was a junior staff person at a University Hospital. The likelihood of obtaining a large grant was very low, especially in view of recent funding cuts to the National Institute of Health during the early years of the Reagan administration. Fortunately, venture capital firms began to pop up in the Twin Cities to fund start-up businesses that had potential.

Chapter 15: Starting a Business

During the time I spent with my chief resident Ed, during my first six months as a G2 we had spoken of one day possibly getting together and starting a company to design and manufacture medical equipment. We both thought that the assessment of the brain using the electroencephalogram (EEG) was underutilized. In the spring of 1982 we formed a partnership to explore our ideas. We each kicked in about $10,000. On December 10, 1982 we incorporated CNS, Inc. I had left the University and Ed stayed in his group practice. CNS stood for central nervous system.

Ed was three years older than me. Before medical school he spent a year working in business. So between the two of us we had one year of junior business experience. Growing up I remember my father discussing business matters at the dinner table. It never seemed like rocket science, but still I knew very little about it.

I also appreciated the fact that I didn't know what I didn't know. Fortunately we hired an attorney who knew a lot. Peter was a senior partner in his firm and very well connected. His older brother was a physician and as a result he gave us credit for being intelligent people. His attitude was that if we were smart enough to become doctors we could learn to become good business people.

Still, I felt as if I was standing on shifting sand. It wasn't as if I could just read and outline a book about all of this stuff and know what I was doing. There are many aspects to business and I knew none of them. We were talking about designing new medical equipment and getting it cleared through the FDA and who knows what other federal agencies needed to approve it. We had to be able to manufacture it under the appropriate guidelines. After all of that we had to figure out how to market and sell it. We needed to raise lots of money and we would need to hire lots of people to do all of these tasks. This was a lot different than listening to my father talk about his women's clothing store around the dinner table.

Our combined $20,000 didn't last very long. It was time to raise money. I was way out of my comfort zone. The idea of reconsidering a neurology practice was sounding better and better, but I knew I had to move forward. What made matters worse was that Ed had a practice, was earning a nice income and was busy all day long with that practice. I was the one with no business experience who was left to run the show. Ed had promised that once the business was up and running he would come in and run it, as I had no desire to perform that function. That was a promise he never kept.

Fortunately he was around when I needed him during those early days. Rarely does anyone truly know their role in life before they live it out. Ed's role in hindsight was to be there to support me. As a chief resident he was my mentor and was as good a friend as he was capable of being. As a business partner he acted as my big brother and his presence bolstered my confidence. He took the lead in our early fundraising efforts and participated in every meeting with me during the first round of financing. After that he mainly acted as an advisor during our once a week business dinners at Pizza Hut.

Peter, our corporate attorney was invaluable to me. He was book-smart and street-smart and he loved to teach from his many experiences. I was a sponge. I used to think that my auditory memory wasn't very good, but I quickly learned to record in my mind everything he had to say. At the time I didn't realize it, but this was the beginning of my business training and it was going to be done on the job and include almost every aspect of business.

I learned more about fundraising from Peter than from everyone else combined, which is saying a lot since all told we did nine rounds of financing, five private and four public. He specialized in corporate affairs including

82

overseeing and writing much of our many offering documents. My early learnings about fundraising included the simple fact that there are two types of investors, sophisticated and unsophisticated.

Early money typically comes from unsophisticated investors that are generally part of one's current acquaintances, which is why that round of financing is termed friends and family. These are the people in one's life that are the most supportive. Some of them are hoping to make it big by getting in on the ground floor. What they don't realize is that it's a long way from the ground floor to the penthouse and even in the best of cases, the elevator ride takes a very long time. Typically the cables break and the elevator crashes through the basement floor never to be seen or heard from again.

Don't invest in this round of a company's financing unless you can afford to lose your entire investment. Consider the money gone for good as soon as you write the check. These statements are generally true. In our case the early investors didn't lose their investment. An investment of $25,000 in 1983 returned $1,000,000 in 2006 when the business was sold. That's not too bad if one had considered that money lost when the check was written, however it actually looks better than it is.

A sophisticated investor would calculate the compound annual growth rate, which in this case equaled 17.4%. They would compare that to the growth rate of one of the major public stock indices, such as the S&P 500. They would then make a determination if the gain was worth the risk, assuming there was a gain. The compound annual growth rate of non-dividend yielding S&P 500 stocks in that same time frame was 9.6%. More than 50% of new businesses end in bankruptcy. Therefore a sophisticated investor would claim that a first round investment in our company was a poor decision that happened to work out reasonably well. Chalk one up for friends and family.

We raised $348,200 in our friends and family round. Peter was impressed that we could raise our start-up money without the help of an investment banker. Even though we raised the money we learned that we couldn't predict who would actually invest and who wouldn't. It was a real crap shoot that became a numbers game. We pitched the deal to everyone we knew and many people we hadn't known. After about four months and many meetings in my living room we closed the deal.

Our first workspace was my dining room. We had purchased a used EEG machine from the Mayo Clinic. These machines use a lot of ink and when the EEG is very active the ink can spray several feet away. We had plastic covering the drapes, furniture and carpeting. When the EEG wasn't in use our computer programmer worked at the dining room table. We had hired a hardware design engineer from Medtronic, a well-known pacemaker company located in the Twin Cities. He worked at home since I didn't have any more space available in my home.

After closing on the $348,200 we moved into a small office space. Running a start-up business of this size was nothing more than running a small engineering project. Since the engineers knew much more about what they were doing than I, it was mostly a matter of checking in on their progress. Whenever I could, I acted as a sounding board for them to work through their issues.

After about a year it became evident that we were going to need a lot more money to complete the project. Peter recommended a local, well respected investment banking firm to assist in raising the capital. We needed to raise about $3.5 million, which in those days was a respectable, but far from outrageous amount of money to seek from venture capitalists. Our project seemed interesting enough and in a community that had done well with hi-tech medical deals it wasn't too much of a stretch to get the funds.

Chapter 16: Brain Wave Monitor

We were creating a sophisticated device to measure brain waves and analyze them in real time. We could display the results on a screen in a simple way that surgeons and anesthesiologists could understand without any training. The display included automatic warnings if there was a problem with the patient. The device was intended for use with patients undergoing two different types of surgery. One was open-heart surgery, where the patient was placed on cardiac bypass equipment. The other procedure was called a carotid endarterectomy where atherosclerotic plaque or fat deposits were removed from the carotid artery in the neck. The carotid is the major artery supplying the brain with oxygen and nutrients.

Both types of surgery sometimes result in stroke. We could provide enough warning to avoid that complication. After we developed a prototype of the device we took it to the Mayo Clinic for a side by side comparison with a traditional EEG machine run by a technician trained to analyze the paper output. The Mayo Clinic routinely used EEG to monitor carotid endarterectomy cases. Our device, with its automatic warnings matched Mayo's manual results in 50 consecutive cases. We had actually produced a device that could automatically warn of impending stroke, thereby allowing the surgeon or cardiac bypass technician to avoid the complication.

We and our venture capital investors believed we were poised for great success. Without too much difficulty we were able to get the device cleared through the FDA and our fledgling company was able to build the product so that it reliably worked. We hired a small direct sales force and by 1985 we were attempting to sell it. After three months travelling with the salespeople doing product demonstrations in hospital operating rooms around the country I was 100% convinced that it was going to be a complete business failure. Although the surgeons and anesthesiologists were generally polite it was easy for me to see that it wasn't going to sell.

At our small company we held Board of Director's meetings every three months. When our first venture capital offering had closed we added several venture capitalists to our Board of Directors. I insisted that we hire a real business guy to run the company, which we did. That made the VC's, venture capitalists, very happy. One of them said, "It's great to work with an entrepreneur who doesn't need to pretend to be the business leader."

About a year later, our business leader was causing enough employee dissent in the company that we fired him after he asked for a raise at a Board meeting. The Board asked me how I wanted to proceed to which I replied, "Given what he was doing I could assume his duties and continue mine without the need to hire anyone else. We should save the money." They agreed.

Still I was viewed as more of a scientist with a medical background. It was an honest and comfortable position for me and although I was running the business, no one thought of me as the business guy in charge of the business. I had managed to be invisible in that role. As a result, when I informed the Board of my opinion about our business prospects after three months in the field, they felt justified in telling me that I had too little business experience to come to that conclusion this early in the selling process.

Flashback to my adolescence when I spoke up and said my brother's problems are of my mother's making or when I told my parents I spent two weeks living in Jane's dorm room. I was absolutely certain that what I was saying was the truth, but they didn't want to hear it. They weren't even ready to consider the possibility. They dismissed my information as though it didn't exist.

I had spent three months observing our prospective sales opportunities crash and burn and I knew what I saw. That level of apathy and resistance wasn't going to be overcome by a little company with a new product. Even though we had something of benefit we had insufficient clout to change the status quo.

As I sat in that Board meeting after giving my opinion, I observed all of their interactions while remaining quiet. I felt just like the invisible child watching the alien adults in my childhood kitchen. This episode allowed me to see my fellow Board members in a new light, as viewed through the lens of childhood innocence. I respected them enormously. They had great experience and intelligence. But when confronted with new information that was unexpected and unwanted they quickly adopted an attitude of denial.

I knew better than to argue. I learned that from my dealings with my mother. I consciously decided to sit back, watch and weigh my options. I was the counter puncher again. I had already declared my truth quite openly so remaining silent on this issue from this point forward was no longer a lie of omission. Anyway, I wasn't the business guy in their eyes.

As a Board we decided to recruit a sales executive from a big company. Several months later we hired a very well qualified candidate from American Hospital Supply. He was an extremely nice person and seemed more than qualified to be our sales and marketing executive.

As far as I was concerned it didn't matter. I thought that he would have to walk on water in order to bring this business opportunity to life. Regardless, I was happy to have him join the company. He became our VP of Sales and Marketing. Since our VC investors fully endorsed this hire and the direction we were taking as a company I felt secure in the knowledge that we would have twelve to eighteen months of continued support and funding. However I was convinced that our operating room brain wave monitor would never become successful in the market.

When we started the company Ed and I had two different product ideas. His contribution was the technology behind the brain wave monitor. My idea was considerably more complicated and would take years of research, which is why we attempted to commercialize Ed's idea first. The hope was that if the brain wave monitor was successful we would then have the time and resources to explore my idea. Now we needed a third idea that could be commercially viable quickly. Again it was necessary to put my idea on the shelf.

Chapter 17: Sleep Disorders Diagnostics

Our best sales person, Rita, had an idea. She had been talking to a neurologist at the Marshfield clinic in Wisconsin who was running their sleep disorders clinic. In 1985 the field of Sleep Disorders Medicine was in its infancy. A treatment for obstructive sleep apnea had been developed in 1982 and so it made sense to diagnose and treat the significant population of patients that existed. Awareness of the disorder and its treatment was very low, but about to grow substantially.

Sleep clinics or sleep labs as they were frequently called used EEG machines with some additional measurement devices and transducers. The assemblage of equipment resulted in the practice of polysomnography. A patient would come to the lab to be monitored during their normal sleep time. The process resulted in a very large paper record that was a third of a mile long. It required four hours for a technician to analyze the recording and then the paper record needed to be stored.

Rita understood the technology we had developed for our brain wave monitor and thought it could somehow be adapted for use in sleep labs. It wasn't quite that simple, but with the incorporation of some new digital storing devices that were on the horizon and with entirely new software to display and analyze the data we could probably create something of value to sleep labs. This would allow us to fulfill a need that sleep lab personnel already acknowledged. This situation was preferable to attempting to convince surgeons and anesthesiologists that they had a problem that needed to be fixed. They like my Board preferred denial.

I had become a competent computer programmer. I also had a good sense about developing computer algorithms to analyze all the various types of data we would get from the polysomnogram so I took the lead in that area. In addition to a local lab, we found a great lab to work with in Oklahoma City with some sleep disorder specialists that were well known and exceedingly helpful. I spent many nights in the lab and ultimately several years analyzing our algorithms. After eighteen months we had a working device that could analyze the sleep recordings and provide various reports.

During our development effort I kept the Board informed of our progress. I had positioned our efforts as working on the next technology that would follow the operating room monitor and allow us to expand our business. All businesses need new products in different markets in order to expand.

In reality I was working on the new technology to save the company from bankruptcy after the operating room monitoring business was finally deemed to be a failure. This was an eventuality that I thought would definitely happen in the not too distant future. I knew the VCs wouldn't continue to fund us if we had nothing viable to sell. I also feared that when that day came they would be decisive and be gone the next day without ever looking back.

The Board felt that what I was doing would take ten years to develop. They seemed satisfied that I was busy at work and not interfering with the existing business strategy. I purposely didn't appear overly enthusiastic about what I was working on and I was openly supportive of our VP of Sales and Marketing in his efforts.

I quietly recruited two of our engineers and changed Rita's position to allow her to focus all of her efforts on the sleep diagnostic market. I wanted her to scout out potential prospects throughout the US so that we could begin discussions with them before we were actually ready to sell product.

By 1987 we needed to sell the new product, but it wasn't quite ready. I felt as if our days as a company were numbered without more significant progress. In essence, our cash was running out and we needed to show more progress to get more funding. This is usually the case in start-ups.

What we were developing for the sleep market was in a demonstrable form by January 1987 so that potential customers didn't have to have much of an imagination to perceive the benefits. We decided to sell it to customers in an incomplete form. Our pitch was, "You can buy into this technology now and we will incorporate your ideas into the platform. This is a one-time offer. We are only willing to work with twenty labs this year so it's now or never."

We outfitted nineteen labs that year, our first year in that market. Those sales brought in more revenue than we received from sales of our brain wave operating room monitor, which was in its third year.

The promise of a new technology and market in combination with an existing small, but growing operating room monitoring business allowed us to do an IPO, initial public offering of our stock in June of 1987. It wasn't as if we were doing well and it was time for investors to cash out of their investment. It was more that we needed the money and the best deal we could get was from the public market. As a person who still preferred to be invisible much of the time, it was becoming increasingly more difficult.

As we entered 1988 it became clear that the sleep disorders diagnostic market held much more promise for us than the market for brain wave operating room monitors. We stopped selling them all together that year and let our VP of Sales and Marketing move on to bigger and better opportunities elsewhere.

Rita became the new VP of Sales and Marketing. By 1991 we were still a small company with about $8 million in revenue and generally operating at about break-even. We were able to sustain ourselves, but our prospects seemed very limited. I couldn't see how we were going to create a financial return for our investors without a more dramatic change in our prospects.

I had learned enough about business by that time to conclude that a small capital equipment business model is not well suited for a publicly held corporation. Every quarter we started with zero sales and had to sweat to deliver the sales and profit numbers by quarter-end. Without any recurring revenue it was easy to miss our projections.

I began a project to create a device that would help train consumers with high blood pressure to lower their blood pressure and reduce their medications. That would provide us with a much larger market. One of our Board members wanted me to diversify the company and move us into the field of cardiology as that was becoming a very hot market for a number of new devices.

Instead, by January of 1992 I had licensed what one of our Board members called a nose band aid and had ignored the advice of one Board member and shut down my own project.

Chapter 18: Daddy's Nose Thing - The Breathe Right Nasal Strip

On October 11, 1991 the inventor of the nose band aid came to see me. It was arranged through a mutual friend who happened to be our VP of Operations. Bruce was very genuine and I liked him the moment we met. We were the same age and of the same demeanor. I had not entertained many inventors, but as I was one I was familiar with his reticence at showing me what he had developed. It was clear that he had shown his invention to some other people without a very positive response. As it turned out he hadn't shown it to too many others, but when he did, it had provoked some laughs. His children referred to it as Daddy's nose thing.

Bruce had a nasal breathing problem. He had a deviated nasal septum and allergies so his nose was stuffed much of the time. Furthermore he had developed bruxism, teeth grinding at night, which made it difficult for him to breathe during sleep. He had become addicted to nasal sprays, which aren't indicated for chronic use, as that causes rebound congestion after the effects wear off. After weaning off of sprays he became so desperate that he resorted to inserting bent paper clips into his nostrils to widen his nasal passages making it easier to breathe. That didn't last very long as he developed sores from the sharp ends.

As a native of St. Paul he would go to the Minnesota State Fair every year. Earlier that year he was standing across the street from the state fairgrounds waiting for the street light to change. His gaze was fixed on the archway to the fairgrounds when his big idea came into focus. "Rather than shove stuff up my nose to open the airway, why not build an arch over my nose that would pull the airway open", he thought.

He returned home that evening and taped a collar stay across the bridge of his nose and down on both sides. The stay wanted to spring back into its normally straight shape from its arched position. Therefore, as long as the tape would hold the stay in a bent shape against both sides of his nose it was acting as a lever spring. The sides of each nostril were being pulled outward with the bridge of the nose acting as a fulcrum. It was a brilliant design given the intended function. He had applied for patent protection in June of 1991 before we met.

Normally all the air that moves into our lungs must pass through the nasal valve area of one or both nostrils when we breathe through our nose. That space is only one-tenth of an inch wide. Bruce's contraption widened that space enough on both sides to make it much easier to breathe for anyone that had a deviated septum, allergies or the common cold.

Since it was drug-free it could be used every night without the concern of developing rebound congestion the next day, typically experienced with nasal sprays. That also allowed it to be used for snoring relief as many snorers are mouth breathers, which worsens or causes snoring. Many mouth breathers are able to relearn nasal breathing when using this device and therefore, reduce or eliminate their snoring.

When I asked to see his invention he reached into his briefcase and took out a band aid with a piece of plastic glued on top of it. Rather than handing it to me he placed it on the table right in front of him and across the table from me. That is when one of the strangest events in my life occurred.

I had heard about people in life-threatening situations who suddenly have a vision of their life's events flash before their eyes. If they lived they could talk about it. When Bruce placed his invention on the table I had a vision about what was in store for his invention and what it would mean for me and CNS if we were to license it.

Nothing like that had ever happened to me. It was as if I was shown an entire documentary about the product in half a second. Some people refer to these occurrences as downloads of information. According to a study out of MIT, our brain is only capable of processing about 60 pieces of information per second. I saw much more than that, but could only retain fragments. What I could retain was more than enough information to construct a business plan for his product.

After two months of negotiations Bruce and I signed a license agreement. As CEO I had the authority to license products without Board approval. Our Board of Directors knew nothing about the product until several months later after we were able to produce a finished product.

At a Board meeting in late April of 1992 I had them all wear the nasal strip, which I had named Breathe Right. It was fun to look at these sophisticated, serious businessmen in suits all wearing what looked like band aids across their noses. It reminded me of when I was a five-year old and had gotten a package of face stickers and wore them all over my face. I looked goofy in those pictures and so did our Board members.

They acknowledged that they could breathe better. We reviewed the terms of the license arrangement and I gave them a rough idea of the plan going forward. One of them asked, "What do you think this can do for us financially?"

I replied, "If we do a good job with this product I believe it can result in a $100 million annual business for us." A lot of eyebrows went up. After all we were only doing about $8 million in annual sales. Our Board members were all good poker players. Just like their cards, they kept their opinions to themselves and didn't reveal what they were really thinking.

That was evident as they held another meeting without me soon after our Board meeting. Some of them thought that I had lost my marbles. We were a hi-tech medical equipment company that had just licensed a nose band aid. We were presently selling into a small well-defined vertical market and now I was considering launching a consumer product. At 8am about a week after our Board meeting two members of the Board, both VCs, showed up at my office.

I had told them during our Board meeting that I had begun a search for an executive to help us launch the Breathe Right nasal strip. Our recruiter already had four finalists from large pharmaceutical companies that expressed interest. I was now being informed that the Board wanted me to change the parameters of the search. They wanted me to replace myself. I was instructed to hire a President that would run our sleep disorder diagnostic company and my duties would be limited to launching the nasal strip.

Essentially it was an ultimatum. Either make Breathe Right a success or there won't be any reason for me to remain at the company as I would have already replaced myself with a new executive. I informed them on the spot that I would do as they ask, although in my opinion a new executive to run the sleep products would probably not do as well as I would. I also told them that I knew nothing about launching a brand new consumer product. Obviously they understood my limitations and were counting on them so that they could finally have a more traditional businessman running the company.

I was still under the influence of the one-half second documentary that had been shown to me six months earlier. Of course I never told my Board about my vision. They would have had more grounds to consider me a lost cause. When one receives that type of information, provided in that manner, one's sense of reality changes, especially for a neurologist.

The brain simply doesn't work that way. There was no YouTube back then and I didn't have a smart phone implanted in my head. Furthermore, the information I received was transmitted with such perfect clarity and speed that it was hard to forget. What was even more radical was the fact that all the information pertained to future events. The brain stores memories not possibilities in the form of a short documentary film.

Fortunately I was a believer in spiritual phenomena. The only way I could incorporate that occurrence into my world view was that I was being provided with some very much needed information about my future. Since I had never been clairvoyant I often asked myself why I was given that gift of insight on that occasion.

I concluded that I was given that information in that way in order to give me the confidence and courage to proceed down a path that otherwise would have been too difficult for me. I probably would have taken a more conventional approach had I not received that other-worldly assistance.

Regarding more worldly financial matters, I had learned from Peter that there are two really good times to raise money. One is when the company is already successful and it doesn't need the money. We weren't there yet. The other is when the company has a lot of blue sky to point to. In other words, there appears to be great potential ahead with no reason to believe that we won't be successful. We had this patent pending, unique, new product and everyone on the planet has a nose.

We were already a publicly held company. We were going to need a lot more money. It was time for us to become more visible, which meant that I needed to become less invisible. I was now ready. I felt as if I knew something about the future that nobody else on the planet knew. This redefined insider information as far as I was concerned. I began passing out lots of samples to stock brokers that followed our company. They in turn gave them out to current and potential shareholders. Not surprisingly our stock price started to climb significantly.

We were able to interest a larger investment banking firm to do another stock offering for us. We raised $10 million in 1994. We had received FDA clearance to market the Breathe Right nasal strip in October 1993 and we were early in our efforts to secure distribution, which proved challenging.

Retail drug stores need to purchase product from wholesalers, as they rarely will purchase direct from a manufacturer they've never dealt with before. Wholesalers won't purchase product from manufacturers until they have orders from retail stores. As a result we couldn't get product on the shelf without first creating some level of demand.

My plan to overcome this obstacle was convoluted and tedious, but I saw no other approach. I hired a small public relations firm to secure radio interviews. I paid them every time they got a booking. I talked about the product on air and gave out our phone number. I had a full time person man the phone.

He took names and numbers of interested purchasers and the pharmacy they used. We called the pharmacist and informed them that their customer wanted to purchase Breathe Right strips from them. In turn we received information about the wholesaler that supplied them. We called the wholesaler and told them that one of their pharmacy customers wanted to order Breathe Right nasal strips from them. After they agreed to purchase product from us we called the pharmacist and then later called back the consumer.

We connected thousands of consumers across the US with their pharmacists in this manner during late 1993 and early in 1994. By the spring of 1994 all ten major wholesalers carried the product so virtually every retail store could easily obtain it.

We had done a good job of starting to penetrate independent pharmacies, but we needed to get into the large retail chain stores. To be in good distribution means we needed to be in not only the large retail chain drugstores like Walgreens, Rite Aid and CVS, but also in the food stores and larger mass merchants, like Walmart,

Target and K-Mart. Large chain stores were even more challenging. I had visited Walgreens headquarters in late 1993 and despite telling the cough-cold buyer our grand plan he wasn't prepared to put our product on the shelves of their stores until we had proven ourselves.

The regional managers of Walgreens had the authority to purchase product from wholesalers and place it in the stores they managed even if headquarters hadn't approved the product. In January of 1994 we approached the regional manager in our area after we began to have some success in local independent stores. He decided to give it a try. Since product placement on retail shelves of chain stores are all dictated by a corporate planogram there was no room on the cough-cold isle for our product. That turned out to be very good news for us. The only place the manager could place it was up at the cash register.

Our product sold so well that other regional managers began to hear about it very quickly. After five regional managers were selling product in about 200 Walgreen stores we got a call from the cough-cold buyer at corporate wanting another meeting. I thought he would be conciliatory, as we had proven ourselves in his own stores. I was wrong. He was annoyed with us. As far as he was concerned we had proven nothing. He exclaimed, "You can sell shit at the register."

We were causing him added work as all of these nonstandard orders from the regional managers had to pass through his hands. He decided to purchase product directly from us, but not because it was selling well. He wanted to make his bookkeeping easier and to do that it was best to consolidate the orders and have the product pass through their distribution centers. We received a very large stocking order from Walgreens in April of 1994 for all of their stores.

Now we were only one step away from having broad national distribution, but to get that we needed a broker network that could get us into more chain stores.

Since we had Walgreens we met with the premier broker in the Chicago area as that was where Walgreens was based. We offered them the Walgreens account if they would take us on. They were so surprised by our offer that they volunteered to connect us to the best brokers throughout the country, which they immediately did.

We spent the spring and early summer visiting brokers and their large chain store accounts. By the fall of 1994 Breathe Right nasal strips were on the shelves of about 25,000 stores nationwide. Getting product on the shelves is only part of the equation. Getting consumers to look for it, find it and purchase it is an even bigger undertaking.

One of the regional managers for Walgreens that decided to jump the gun and place Breathe Right nasal strips by the cash register was located in Cincinnati. One of the early purchasers of a box of nasal strips was a product manager who worked at Proctor & Gamble. P&G was widely regarded as the premier consumer products company in the world. That product manager and a market manager, both working on new respiratory products, paid us a visit in the summer of 1994.

They were willing to share their early market research data concerning Breathe Right nasal strips if we were willing to share our research data. I sheepishly smiled and said, "We don't have any."

They weren't really surprised and they decided to share some of what they had learned anyway. They also invited us to Cincinnati to meet with a larger group. About a month later we met with about a dozen people in their business development area. They wanted to license the product from us. That made no sense at all, as we already licensed the product from the inventor. If we were to sublicense the product, then contractually the proceeds would all flow to the inventor and we would see nothing as a result of our efforts.

During our discussion with them they pointed out that it costs them about $50 million to launch a new consumer product. I told them that we had only raised $10 million. In a very nice way they let us know that our chances of success were very low.

I said, "In all sincerity, you guys know more about launching new consumer products than I'll ever know. However, our shareholders expect us to try. In addition we have an unorthodox plan that if it works will not require a lot of money to gain a lot of awareness. If on the other hand it does not work, we'll be back and maybe we can work out a deal." We parted on good terms.

Chapter 19: Hail Mary and the NFL

My unorthodox plan was so unorthodox that by the time it came time to pull the trigger on the final element of the plan even I thought the plan was ridiculous. It hinged on what seemed as remote as a successful Hail Mary pass at the end of a football game. A Hail Mary pass is a long forward pass that is typically made at the end of the game in a desperate attempt to win.

Almost three years had passed since I met Bruce and had my vision. I remember going home that evening and telling Ellen all about it. She was in the laundry room folding towels when she asked, "How are you going to get people to know about this product?"

I told her that I saw football players wearing it in my vision and that I was going to generate awareness by having them use the product during their games. My wife was generally a skeptical sort of person, but she was usually fairly reserved and rarely caustic. Her response was, "That's the dumbest idea I've ever heard." Despite her negative response, when it came time to pitch in and help she did so in a big way, much to her credit.

While we were trying to get distribution it was her job, unpaid, to contact every medical, business and sports writer working for a newspaper in the US and get a press packet in their hands. Her pitch was, "We want you to take this press kit and file it, but not in the trash can. You're going to need it when the NFL players start to wear Breathe Right nasal strips during their games. I'm not asking you to do a story about the product now, but I want you to have this information on hand when you decide to do the story. If I send it to you will you keep it?" To those that responded affirmatively she sent press kits. In total she sent out 700 over nine months.

Seeding press kits with all of the information about Breathe Right nasal strips and samples was the foundational element of my strategy. My plan was that when reporters saw the product on the noses of NFL football players they would be forced to write about it since tens of millions of people watched pro football every weekend and during some week nights. When they wrote about it they would want to give their readers information that was pertinent to them, not just that football players were wearing a nasal strip. They could tell their readers that it could be used for allergies, snoring relief, etc. and that it was drug-free.

In late September I sent out a carton of nasal strips to every professional team's head trainer. Carl, who had been taking calls from consumers, was now instructed to touch base each week with every NFL head trainer in an attempt to get them to have their players use the product. He was fabulous over the phone and was actually able to reach these guys.

Unbeknownst to me in mid-October, Otho Davis, the head trainer of the Philadelphia Eagles kept kicking the carton of product as he paced in his office. He finally decided to open it. He placed a box of ten strips in his shirt pocket and forgot about it until later that evening when he was watching TV.

When he applied one to his nose he was shocked at how well it worked. He realized that players wearing mouth guards are obligated to breathe through their noses. Since this widens the nasal passages and makes it easier to breathe, less energy is used during the act of breathing. That leaves the player with more energy during the fourth quarter. Finely tuned athletes can appreciate the difference.

At about that time I had exiled myself at a conference for choir singers in Reno Nevada. I went alone as only one person needed to attend this conference. In truth, nobody needed to be there as choir singers didn't materialize as much of a market for this product. I was desperate to get away. I was anxious and agitated and didn't want to be near anyone. My whole plan hinged on having football players wear the product during the game. That visibility would cause a

104

tremendous number of news stories to appear which would fuel consumer purchase and launch the product overnight.

What I should have done was to contact some of the player's agents and paid the players to wear it. That would have guaranteed the visibility. But I wanted it to happen spontaneously for the right reason. I wanted them to wear it because it actually worked and was beneficial.

At this point, feeling as anxious as I did, I had wished I wasn't such a purist. If the players didn't wear it we wouldn't have any visibility. Nobody would know about it or purchase it. The stores wouldn't keep it on their shelves for long before they got rid of it. The entire opportunity would implode.

It was now or never and the anxiety I was experiencing was intense. While I was at that conference I received a message to call my father who lived in Philadelphia. He had been watching the news. During the sports segments he could see some of the Philadelphia Eagles behind the reporter wearing nasal strips. He thought I would want to know. Was it really happening? Was my vision of three years ago actually coming true?

During that week, right after Otho Davis had discovered the product; Herschel Walker entered his office complaining of a cold. Herschel didn't like taking medications. Otho said, "I've got the perfect solution."

Herschel was impressed after Otho applied one to his nose and said, "If I can breathe this well with a cold, imagine how well I can breathe wearing one during the game." He scored two touchdowns that Sunday while wearing the strip. There was a small picture of Herschel crossing the goal line on page six of the sports section of the Philadelphia Inquirer in Monday's paper.

Another reporter for the Inquirer saw the strip in the picture and decided to investigate. On Friday on page one of the sports section there appeared a six by nine inch color photo of Herschel Walker wearing the strip.

The article entitled, *Bandaged beaks breathing better* followed.

I had copies sent to every NFL head trainer with a letter stating that other players were using the product and obtaining an advantage. I suggested that they post the article in their training room for their players to see. The head trainer of the San Francisco Forty Niners did just that.

Jerry Rice, the most prolific wide receiver in the history of the NFL read the article. He had a nasal breathing problem and the strip was an excellent fix. Jerry wore the product during his next game, which happened to be on Monday Night Football with thirty million viewers.

The following day we received phone calls from many of the NFL head trainers requesting more product. The message was, "If it's good enough for Jerry it's good enough for our players."

We were more than happy to oblige. NFL strip usage climbed throughout the season and the playoffs. During the Super Bowl fifteen players wore the product. None of them were paid. My kids and I watched the game and using a stop watch we timed how much free exposure we received. In total the strip was clearly visible for six minutes and two seconds. After the season we did conclude a very reasonable endorsement deal with Jerry Rice.

During the first quarter of 1995 we had $16 million worth of orders for Breathe Right nasal strips. I had lobbied for as large an inventory as the Board would allow me to accumulate, but we could only fill orders for $7.5 million. Breathe Right sales totaled $60 million for 1995. Much to their credit, the folks at P&G called us after the Super Bowl to congratulate us.

They told us that we had rewritten the book on how to launch a consumer product. Of the $10 million we had raised, we had only used $1.5 million to keep our business going and launch the product. Needless to say, our investors were ecstatic. So was our Board of Directors. As for me, my job was no longer in jeopardy and I could breathe easier too. More importantly, a vision I had received three years earlier proved to be prophetic.

I had been focused exclusively on launching Breathe Right strips. Our President was responsible for our sleep disorders diagnostic business, since joining the company in 1992. Sales had declined steadily from $8 million to $5.5 million in 1995. We decided to divest that business and focus exclusively on consumer products. Meanwhile, we only had one person, our VP of Marketing who had any consumer product experience and that was only four years of working for an agency.

As an adolescent I used to play with model rockets. I once made a two-stage rocket, but I didn't get the timing right between firing the stage one and stage two propellant. The rocket took off just fine, but the second stage didn't ignite until the rocket had already turned back toward Earth. The rocket accelerated to its demise, smashing into the ground and bursting into flames. During 1996 I felt as though I was riding that rocket.

Our sales in 1996 climbed to $85 million, but $25 million came from international sales. Therefore our domestic Breathe Right business was dead flat. I knew we were in trouble towards the end of 1996.

Fortunately that spring we did another stock offering. I lobbied hard for this offering as it didn't appear that we needed the money. My gut was telling me that we would and as Peter said, "The best time to raise money is when you don't need it because everyone is willing to give it to you when you're doing well."

It was by far our most lucrative offering. We raised $35 million selling shares at just under $25 per share. This was by far and away the best financial deal I ever struck. After the offering we had $60 million in the bank.

When the sales rocket was falling our share price dropped all the way to $3. We were able to buy back about five million shares for about half of what we received from our last offering and in our last offering we had only sold about 1.5 million shares. For the shareholders who decided to hold their stock it was a huge windfall. In essence, during those several years we had added about $17 million to our cash reserves and retired about 3.5 million shares through our stock transactions.

At the end of 1996 I informed each of our Board members that we needed to replace our President with someone who understood the science of selling consumer products. The Twin Cities, with Pillsbury and General Mills headquartered here had lots of folks who knew how to make it happen. It wouldn't be hard to recruit some very capable talent.

"Here we go again" they thought. Collectively they thought I was nuts. We had just had our best year and I wanted to replace our President. They were concerned about the optics of replacing him; how it would look to the outside world. Had they forgotten that he was hired exclusively to run our sleep disorders diagnostic business, which no longer existed?

Our President had little to no responsibility for our early Breathe Right success. However after the sale of the sleep business he participated nicely in the Breathe Right business, but we needed help. Unfortunately, he knew very little about consumer products. We needed people who had decades of consumer packaged goods experience. After our sales began to visibly decline in 1997 I was able to replace him with a Pillsbury executive who was a gifted marketer and operator. Michelle joined us in 1998. She modestly claimed to be a very good business operator, but her marketing skills and instincts were exceptional.

After several years of hard work, during which she recruited the necessary talent, she reversed our declining sales trend and ultimately grew the business to about $130 million by year end 2006 when the business was sold to Glaxo-Smith-Kline. That transaction completed my vision from October 1991, fifteen years earlier. That vision had included what the Breathe Right nasal strip looked like after it was redesigned, generating public awareness by utilizing NFL exposure and an eventual sale to a large pharmaceutical company, amongst other things.

Chapter 20: A New Beginning

Psychologically I had already moved on by the spring of 1996 when we completed our last stock offering. Management was able to sell some of their own stock in the transaction. I sold some and we actually had some money in our bank account. Up until this time we had stock that was worth something, but now we could actually use it. I wasted little time.

Although I continued to work full time at CNS, I wanted to get back to my adolescent dreams. However there didn't appear to be any path for me to follow. I only had to wait six months for one to appear.

One day at work I received a call from Frank, an acquaintance at the time. He asked, "You're a neurologist right?"

After I acknowledged I was he asked, "I have a question I need to ask you, can I visit you now?"

"We're talking right now, why don't you just ask your question?" I replied.

"No I need to see you in person" he said. His office was close so he arrived about ten minutes later.

We met in our conference room. Frank seemed wary, looking around as though he suspected I was filming him with a hidden camera. He was about fifty at the time and an observant Catholic with no knowledge of spiritual phenomena other than some of the bible stories that were of a more mystical nature. He had a big heart and was quick to smile and make jokes, but he could also be serious. On this occasion he was serious and appeared a bit shaken. He didn't appear to be himself.

He had met a friend for lunch several weeks earlier who looked very relaxed. Frank wanted to know why. His friend informed him that he was using some technology that he acquired from a man in Georgia. Frank decided to take a trip to meet the inventor. The man in Georgia was an engineer who was experimenting with sound and vibration. Frank entered a geodesic dome structure with a suspended platform. There were sound speakers everywhere. After lying on the platform, the inventor, Paul who was an engineer by training, started to play music through all of the speakers, some of which were also mounted on the platform that Frank was lying on.

"The next thing I knew I was looking down at my body" Frank said.

"Where were you?" I replied.

"I was lying on the platform" he said.

I gently reminded him "You said, 'I was looking down at my body.' Who was the I you are referring to?"

With halting speech and a sudden look of surprise he replied, "Oh, I was up at the ceiling; that was me. How can that be when my body was on the bed?"

I asked Frank if he had ever heard of an out-of-body experience. He hadn't. This was entirely unexplored territory for a conventional thinking Catholic guy. He was wondering if he was going crazy, which was why he came to see me.

I assured him that he was fine and that his experience, although generally not very common, has been well described and was nothing to worry about. I had read a number of books on the topic and I relayed to him that his experience fit very nicely with those descriptions. After he realized that he wasn't going crazy he felt much better. I asked for Paul's phone number.

Most engineers are very logical and conventional, while a few can become quite eccentric. Paul could have been the poster child for the latter category. He was also gregarious with few boundaries and was prone to actions that most people would consider reckless. When I arrived he immediately ushered me into the room with his equipment. He physically guided me through the entry into the geodesic dome, had me hop up and lie down on the suspended bed-like platform. He then turned on the music with no explanation. I decided to go with the flow even though the music was deafening, playing at volumes far exceeding safe sound levels.

I didn't have an out-of-body experience, but I was relaxed. I didn't realize how relaxed until I got off the platform and fell to the ground. My muscles were so relaxed that my legs didn't properly support me. I wasn't dizzy or disoriented in any way, just very relaxed physically. I was quite intrigued. I had several more sessions during that weekend and became increasingly more relaxed with each one.

About a month later Ellen and I went to Georgia so she could experience it. She, like Frank, had an out-of-body experience. Given Ellen's medical history this was not unexpected. Ellen has a mild case of narcolepsy, a sleep disorder.

Narcoleptics experience sleep attacks during which it is hard to maintain wakefulness, episodes of cataplexy were they can lose muscle tone in one or more areas of their body with strong emotion, hypnogogic hallucinations which means that they can enter dream sleep at the onset of sleep, and sleep paralysis. This is how medicine defines the condition of Narcolepsy.

I have a good friend Michael, an authority on Narcolepsy, who lives in Cincinnati. He owns and operates a number of sleep labs. He has written more than a hundred publications in the medical literature. He is often asked to speak at medical centers and conferences on the subject. When an expert speaks at a medical center they are often taken into a clinical setting as part of their visit. There they are presented with a patient to discuss. During one such visit Michael found himself in an awkward situation.

The medical student was presenting a classic case of narcolepsy. He had done an excellent job describing the patient's symptoms, which included the four cardinal manifestations; sleep attacks, cataplexy, hypnogogic hallucinations and sleep paralysis. Normally the expert is supposed to comment on something that the medical student had missed. In this case, the only thing that the medical student didn't mention was something that is never discussed in medical settings, out-of-body experiences. Michael was left with two choices. Either add nothing to the conversation and look stupid or tread into an area that is considered taboo.

Typically the professor adds new content into the discussion by addressing the patient directly. Michael did not want to look stupid so he looked at the patient and asked, "Can you tell us about your out-of-body experiences?"

The patient was delighted to talk about her experiences. In truth there should be five, not four cardinal manifestations of narcolepsy as narcoleptics with sleep paralysis regularly have out-of-body experiences.

Sleep paralysis occurs when the narcoleptic awakens in the morning after just having had a dream. During dream sleep there is a collection of nerves in the brainstem that is activated. These nerves inhibit motor activity in the muscles of our arms and legs in addition to some other muscles. In this way we do not act out the movements that are occurring in our dreams. In narcolepsy these nerves remain active for several minutes after the dream.

When some narcoleptics awaken right after their dream they are essentially paralyzed for a few minutes, hence the term sleep paralysis. When these individuals in this state attempt to get out of bed, they find that their energetic or spiritual selves are not only out of their beds, but out of their bodies too.

The medical community does not like to talk about out-of-body experiences. In fact, they do not acknowledge the phenomenon as being real. This is why narcoleptics rarely discuss these experiences with their physicians.

In the late 90's I attended the national sleep conference as I needed my continuing medical education credits. I ran into my old chief of neurology at HCMC, who had since retired. We had purchased one of Paul's devices and were doing sessions with lots of folks to see the effects. Very few subjects actually had out-of-body experiences. Frank and Ellen were exceptions rather than the rule. I hadn't realized that my old chief ran the narcolepsy support group when he was at HCMC and had been exposed to patients with out-of-body experiences.

"I used to stand outside the room before we got started. They didn't know I was there. I would listen to them talk about their out-of-body experiences." he said. He also had a lady friend who experienced them.

Somewhat surprised I said, "So you believe in them?" He did. "Why didn't we ever discuss this phenomenon while you were chief?" I asked.

He responded by telling me that he had his reputation to maintain. At this time in his life, now retired, he felt more comfortable discussing the phenomenon.

The party line in the medical sciences is that the mind and its associated awareness or consciousness results somehow from the collective activity of the neurons in the brain. They view the functions of mind and awareness as a local phenomenon restricted to the head. If they considered narcoleptic patients' accounts as true it would contradict the prevailing theory. Therefore, the vast majority of medical people live in denial of this phenomenon, similar to near death experiences. Group-think can be a powerful motivator when one's job and reputation are at stake; so much for intellectual honesty and curiosity. What suffers is progress.

The unit we had purchased cost us about $50,000 with all of the trappings. We installed it in an office building. Although we planned to run it at safe sound levels, under 80 decibels, we decided to enclose the unit in a sound-proofed room. We had a room built inside a room with sound insulation in between.

Bruce, the Breathe Right inventor came to me and asked if he could help us with the expenses. We formed

114

a company, Round River Research Corporation to study the effects of sound and vibration on states of relaxation and meditation. Several years later when Bruce was no longer committing any time to the venture he decided to bow out and relinquish his ownership. He claimed that he could no longer justify a deduction from the ongoing losses as he wasn't spending any time on the project.

I think his contribution from the outset was his way of paying us back for our faith in him. We had helped him achieve his dream and he wanted to do the same for us. He has always been very open-hearted and generous.

At that time in my life, about the age of forty-four, my heart remained generally closed. As before, love was something I experienced more as a sentiment or thought with only a small degree of physical sensation in my chest. We rarely ask one another how our various emotional states register in our bodies. As for me, I remained mainly head-centric. My experience of life was mainly through my thoughts. If my body wasn't in pain I judged the situation to be good. Therefore not feeling anything was just fine. When anyone would ask me how I was feeling, my response was almost always, "I'm fine."

My relationships were similarly, just fine. They were calm. I disliked turbulence. I had generally been more of a fixer like my mother. I wanted everyone around me to be just fine too. And essentially my family was just fine in that way. Ellen and I never fought and rarely had any meaningful disagreements. Our four children were rarely if ever disciplined harshly. Punishments were mainly confinement to their room. I had constructed an atmosphere very reminiscent of my childhood. It was what I had been accustomed to and what I was comfortable with.

Ellen's childhood was only slightly more turbulent. With three siblings there was more activity, more emotions as well. I'm sure she would have wanted more emotional engagement from me. She rarely if ever complained. I think she realized that it was simply not in my nature. More accurately stated, she probably recognized my deficiency and didn't know how to coax it out of me or change me.

It probably would not have been forthcoming anyway as I would have been resistant. I'm sure in hindsight, she realized all of this. She never brought up couples therapy. I have absolutely no doubt that I would have bristled at the suggestion and I definitely would not have participated. I think she managed the situation as best as was possible given my limitations.

My career path supported this way of being. Medical school, internship and residency are not experiences that nurture one's emotional self. Emotional expressiveness was rare and rarely welcomed. Situations which discourage overt emotional expressiveness also tend to inhibit feeling one's emotions. As physicians in training we were always evaluated on what we thought academically. Therefore it was a thinking rather than a feeling world. Since these tend to be binary states of being, our feeling nature became further inhibited and we as people often became more distant as a result.

The world of business was no different. Rarely did anyone consider how a person felt about anything. It was always, "What do you think about ....?" Some managers recognize the benefit of discord. They will hire someone that is a bit contrary just to shake things up. That usually stirs up greater feeling.

These managers may or may not recognize what they are doing at a conscious level, but it pays to get at everyone's underlying feelings even if it generates a little conflict. Many times we are unable to cognitively understand and articulate an issue that will have a significant bearing on a project or task, yet we can often feel if something is not right. Those feelings usually convey more truth than cognition will allow.

Later in my business career I learned to ask not only what people thought, but also how they felt about an issue. In a way it's very surprising that our society in general functions in such a restricted manner. Obviously we do so because we choose to avoid feeling what we consider to be negative emotions. However, most of us recognize that when we make a decision that goes against our gut feel, it usually turns out badly. Since we generally know this, why don't we honor our feelings more when it comes to the decisions we make?

Our resistance typically occurs for one of several reasons. Either we don't trust our feelings or we are fearful of the actions that we are required to take or the potential outcomes if we follow our feelings. It sometimes takes a great deal of courage to follow our feelings when the seemingly practical reality of such a decision engenders fear. This discord between our true feelings at a deep level and our cognitive brain processes, which are heavily influenced by our egoic fear-based conditioning, often keeps us stuck. We remain in the same unhappy relationships and situations because it's the devil we know and have tolerated.

Even though I was trained as a physician specializing in the brain with additional training in psychology and psychiatry I was never taught much about feelings. As I approached this new endeavor I had absolutely no awareness that it was going to lead me down a path that required and encouraged me to feel so much more deeply.

I didn't have a clue as to how important our feeling nature really was. If I had I may not have ventured down this path unless I received another vision like my Breathe Right vision, but this time I needed to move down this path with less assurance. This path required a leap of faith and ultimately a desire to fully feel more.

On a conscious level, Ellen and I decided to move down this path because we both wanted to become better meditators. Ellen had tried repeatedly and felt as though she was failing. It simply wasn't working for her. I had much more success. I had been doing it on and off for many years and was able to achieve a state of no-thought and equanimity. I had peace during my sessions, although I had a fair amount of peace during my normal activities most of the time anyway. Although my sessions were peaceful, they were uneventful. After a while it became very boring. My meditation sessions were like eating cardboard. It was purely a mental experience.

I had read so many books about many different spiritual experiences and I was anxious to explore these types of experiences and the various states of being that had been reported. In truth, what I was really looking for was more from life. The irony at that time was that I was trying to find it in the world of non-living, spiritual entities, as opposed to truly living more spiritually in the world I was in. It took a while to learn the difference.

Chapter 21: Early Sessions and a Key Experiment

By the fall of 1997 Frank and I began to do sessions together. Ellen soon joined us. For about two and half years we met at 7am and 5pm Mondays through Fridays and 8am Saturdays and Sundays. To say that we were a bit fanatical about this was an understatement, but we were having great fun.

After those two and half years we continued to do sessions daily for months or even a year or two interspersed with lapses lasting as long as a couple of years. We were also experimenting with electromagnetism in addition to the sound and vibration; however we didn't perfect that until late in 2011. That kicked the project into high gear again and caused us to meet and do sessions every weekday in the morning as a group until the present.

We never intended this to become a business venture. Nor did we do it for health reasons. We all had a desire to explore. My deepest desire was to experience and really know without any doubt what we as human beings truly are. I was fed up with platitudes about we are spiritual beings in a physical vehicle or affirmations like, I am God. All of this was head stuff and it was getting me nowhere. I wanted to take all of the self-help books I had read and start a bonfire. I was desperate to have real experiences so that I would know the truth of these things for myself. I wanted to break through the barrier between my conscious awareness and all that I couldn't consciously perceive. Show me the truth!!!

I didn't know what I was getting myself into. We really do receive what we ask for, but we often don't like owning it. This point deserves some dissection. That part of us that wants to return the gifts we receive is our ego, which is our beliefs and conditioning. It wants what it wants and what it wants is rarely the truth. Asking to be shown the truth creates a path for the ego that equates to jumping from the frying pan into the fire. Fortunately, the payoff is worth it if one can remain on that path.

Our early days of exploration were generally a lot of fun and usually educational as we did a lot of experimenting. What follows is one of my favorite experiments.

I had read about an episode that Robert Monroe had reported in one of his books that intrigued me. He visited, while out-of-body, a woman during her sleep. He communicated with her during his visit. His attention was focused at a point above her head during their communication. In one of our earliest sessions together I asked Frank to move out-of-body and communicate with me in the same way. I positioned myself in a conventional chair facing away from Frank. I was going to simply sit there during the session and stare at the wall in the dark.

That session ran for an hour. I was bored to tears and by the end of the session I was also a bit angry. As far as I could perceive the session was a bust, nothing happened. I thought I had wasted an hour. I stood up, turned on the lights and with controlled anger I asked, "So didn't you leave your body?"

Surprised he exclaimed, "I was talking to you the whole time."

Annoyed I inappropriately remarked, "You didn't see my lips move did you?"

"I did exactly what you told me to do. I went above your head and asked what I saw, 'Are you Dan's soul?'"

I started to calm down, as he had done exactly what I had asked him to do. Now he had my undivided attention. "What did it say?" I asked.

"It said no, I'm Dan."

I could feel my anger rising again. This was really confusing. I'm Dan, so how could that be Dan. It had to be my soul or spiritual self or higher self, but not me. As it turned out Frank asked repeatedly and continued to get

120

the same response. The rest of Frank's assignment was to ask to see one of my past lives. I had made the assumption that he was going to be addressing my soul at the level of my 8th chakra, which is regarded as an access point for past life retrieval. Frank was able to successfully negotiate with my energetic counterpart after some debate and was shown a recent past life of mine in the 1800's.

I had to admit that as Frank told me about his dealings with myself so to speak; it did remind me a lot of me. However, I had absolutely no awareness of this communication. How could I have no awareness of a conversation that just happened in my presence between Frank and something that claimed to be me? I was both intrigued and thoroughly frustrated. But deep down I knew that there was a fundamental truth buried in this riddle.

After several years of contemplation and after I allowed myself to consider it from a different perspective, the riddle became clearer. Of course this thing that claims to be Dan is me, but when I think of it from the perspective of my beliefs and conditioning, this other me is a concept that I term Dan's soul. Frank was talking to the unfiltered me. What I consider my in-life self to be is actually the unfiltered me that is filtered through the lens of my ego. So the in-life me, that which I am consciously aware of in this plane of existence, is the filtered me.

The filtered me was entirely bound to our material dimension and did not consciously perceive the spiritual dimension. That is why the filtered me had no awareness of the conversation. The conversation was filtered out by the lens of my ego before reaching my limited conscious awareness. The lens of my ego is essentially the limiting beliefs I hold about myself and the world around me. Our beliefs are filters that limit our perception. This is how we maintain our sense of reality or put another way, our personal illusion of reality. In order to change our sense

121

of reality we must either change our limiting beliefs or release them.

The unfiltered me, my spiritual self, can however communicate with the filtered me because it is really one and the same. Even at that time I was aware of an internal or inner dialogue that occurred from time to time. Our internal dialogue is the conversation we have with ourselves, usually in silence. When I first started to become aware of my inner dialogue it was subtle. I didn't recognize it as it was happening, but only as it was fading away. Then I could remember the last few exchanges. As I became more aware, especially after using our technology, the inner dialogue became much more perceivable.

One of the interesting aspects of our inner dialogue is identifying who is who. Typically for most people the voice that they consider to be themselves is the voice of their ego or filtered self, while the other voice tends to be more instructive and usually exists without assignment. Often this is depicted in cartoons as a demon whispering in our left ear and an angel in our right. This concept in part demonstrates how those of us on a spiritual path often demonize rather than accept our egos.

In medicine we tend not to discuss the concept of inner dialogue, except as regards to certain conditions, most notably schizophrenia. The literal definition of schizophrenia is split-minded. In my opinion, using that definition and the concept of an inner dialogue, we are all schizophrenic. The longer I work with people the more clear it is that all of us can be taught to recognize our inner dialogue. With a greater level of awareness our inner dialogue becomes more apparent as we better perceive the workings of our mind.

Many people today teach and practice mindfulness. This can be practiced at many levels, but its aim is always to expand our conscious awareness and presence. People often begin by learning to be more present during simple everyday actions. This is often no more complicated than just observing our actions while eating a meal, brushing our teeth or taking a walk

In a more advanced form, mindfulness can be used as a practice to understand our subconscious beliefs. This typically involves becoming mindful of our emotional feelings and behaviors. It is then helpful to track back, deeper into our psyche. By doing so we can determine the underlying beliefs that have been triggered by life events and which cause the associated emotional feelings that motivate our behaviors.

As we become much more adept at the practice of mindfulness, we begin to live our lives observing how our authentic self is filtered through our egoic conditioning. After living in this manner for a while an inescapable truth begins to emerge. I am the observer of this life and I can participate in this life, but I am not my ego.

The response that Frank received to the question, "Are you Dan's soul?" was what he and I needed or were willing to hear and contemplate at that time. It's not that it wasn't true, but the response "I am Dan", can be interpreted in a number of different ways. This issue continued to play out for many years to come.

Part II - Considerations

The following chapters are written using the format of inner dialogue. The inner dialogue is between that aspect of me that utilizes my egoic filters and, to the best of my abilities, me as my authentic or unfiltered self, referred to as ego and higher self respectively.

These specific considerations and those that are covered in Part IV tend to be approached quite differently from the vantage point of ego versus higher self. As a result it is often helpful to discern the two voices more clearly in the form of dialogue. This writing style can be helpful in understanding how we truly stand on certain issues.

Chapter 22: Beliefs, Control and Perception

Ego: I really do want to know the truth of things.

Higher Self: Why?

Ego: I don't like being lied to.

Higher Self: Is that how you feel?

Ego: As a matter of fact, that's exactly how I feel. I think the truth is right in front of my eyes and I can't see it.

Higher Self: You have shielded yourself from the truth.

Ego: That's ridiculous. Why would I do that?

Higher Self: You do it in an attempt to maintain control.

Ego: Control of what?

Higher Self: Control of this life.

Ego: Why shouldn't I be in control of this life as you put it? It's my life and so I should be in control of it.

Higher Self: Yes, that is your belief.

Ego: That's not just my belief. That's the truth.

Higher Self: Is it?

Ego: Now I think you're lying to me.

Higher Self: I have no reason to lie.

Ego: Why not? Everyone I know has some reason to lie about something.

Higher Self: I exist in a state of being, not believing. I have no need in preserving anything.

Ego: What does that have to do with lying?

Higher Self: You lie to preserve your version of the truth or in this case your beliefs about this life. You wish to preserve the illusion of control. That is your nature.

Ego: I can take any action I choose and so I am in control.

Higher Self: Do actions dictate outcomes?

Ego: What do you mean?

Higher Self: After you sent the Breathe Right nasal strips to the NFL trainers you had very serious doubts that your plan would work. For a time you did not feel that your actions were sufficient to cause the plan to work. You doubted the outcome.

Ego: That's right, but it did work and it turned out great.

Higher Self: Did your actions cause the desired outcome?

Ego: They led to the desired outcome.

Higher Self: If Otho Davis had not kept stumbling over the carton of strips your plan may not have worked. If Herschel Walker had not scored a touchdown, or the reporter had not done a follow-up story, or the trainer of the 49's had not posted the reprint of that story or Jerry Rice had not worn the strip on Monday night football, your plan may not have worked.

Ego: But all of those things happened.

Higher Self: And how did you cause all of those things to happen?

Ego: Well I didn't, but I sent out the strips. If I hadn't done that then Otho wouldn't have stumbled over them and the rest of the events wouldn't have unfolded.

Higher Self: Yes, your action was necessary, but not sufficient.

Ego: I see what you're saying and I can't argue that point. However, if I was smarter and did a deal with the players and their agents I could have paid them to wear the strips and then the plan would have worked.

Higher Self: Why did you decide not to pursue that path? You are smart enough to have thought about doing it.

Ego: I wanted the players to see the value of wearing it so that they would wear it because they derived a benefit versus being paid to wear it.

Higher Self: Why?

Ego: That would make it more likely that they would continue using it.

Higher Self: And?

Ego: Then I wouldn't have to pay them.

Higher Self: What else?

Ego: When the reporters would ask them why they are wearing the strips they would give a better answer.

Higher Self: Better for them or for you?

Ego: It makes them look better too.

Higher Self: You could have gone to the players and only done deals with those that found the strip helpful.

Ego: That would have taken a long time and what if they thought it was a stupid idea and told the other players that they thought it was dumb idea to wear it.

Higher Self: Is that why you approached the trainers first.

Ego: Yes, I thought they would be more likely to see the benefits. The benefits are real! They are in a position of authority and so if they recommended it to some players it would have more credibility.

Higher Self: You regretted that decision and fled to Reno to get away.

Ego: Yes that's true, but then I got lucky and it all worked out.

Higher Self: Luck, really? Was it luck that showed you the vision you had during your first visit with Bruce?

Ego: Luck is just what I call it when things work out and I wasn't in control. I sure was lucky to have that vision otherwise I wouldn't have had the courage to pursue that plan.

Higher Self: That is why you were given that vision.

Ego: By you?

Higher Self: Would you rather believe that it was luck that provided the vision?

Ego: I guess I would rather know the truth.

Higher Self: The answer is yes.

Ego: So you were counting on me to follow that vision, weren't you?

Higher Self: That was but one path. Others would have availed themselves if necessary.

Ego: Are you saying that Breathe Right was destined to be successful?

Higher Self: It was a critical juncture in your life path that was planned to occur, but outcomes can change.

Ego: So to a degree I do have control.

Higher Self: You have control over your actions, but not the final outcome.

Ego: But I should have control, this is my life.

Higher Self: Why do you believe that?

Ego: Believe that I should have control or believe that this is my life?

Higher Self: Why do you believe that this is your life?

Ego: I am the one that is in charge of this body. I am the one that initiates actions. I'm the player in this life. I may not be in control of outcomes, but I can do whatever I want and so this is my life.

Higher Self: You are the doer, but you experience only a fraction of what can be experienced in this life.

Ego: Yes, but I experience the results of my actions. I make a difference.

Higher Self: You do make a difference, but your beliefs limit what you can perceive. As a result you generally only allow yourself to experience that which is consistent with your beliefs. You limit your conscious awareness in this way to maintain the illusion of control. That is the reality you choose to accept. When you recognize that something has happened outside of your control, you ascribe it to good luck or bad luck. You choose not to examine the situation more closely as that may dispel your notion of reality.

Ego: I like my reality the way it is.

Higher Self: You began this dialogue by stating that you really do want to know the truth of things. Have you changed your mind?

Ego: No, I really do want to know the truth.

Higher Self: Why?

Ego: I don't think I'm seeing the whole picture.

Higher Self: You are not.

Ego: Why not?

Higher Self: You cannot.

Ego: Why?

Higher Self: Your awareness by your very nature is limited, as it is tied to your brain's processes and a little bit of information you glean from your body. You are the sum of knowledge and experience that you have been able to perceive during this life. Based upon these things you have formulated beliefs and created mental processes to deal as effectively as you can with life's events.

Ego: So I am living this life?

Higher Self: I am living this life. You believe you are living this life because a part of me lives through you and it identifies with what you think you are. You and I are actually one and the same, but you perceive yourself to be different and separate because you are unable to perceive all that I am or from your perspective all that you truly are.

Ego: How do my beliefs limit me?

Higher Self: You like to use the phrase, "You don't know what you don't know." That is your answer.

Ego: That's a dumb answer. Of course I don't know what I don't know, but how does that limit me?

Higher Self: You assume that you only know what you are able to think about or process through your brain, which in your way of thinking is how you come to know things. You create a very limited finite world.

Ego: No I don't limit myself that way. I can also perceive through my senses. If something I don't know comes into my field of vision I can perceive it.

Higher Self: That is true, but your eyes can only perceive a small bandwidth of frequencies. The same is true of all of your physical senses. They, like your beliefs, are also filters that only pass small slices of information to your brain for processing. I can perceive frequencies which are outside of those frequency ranges and I am not limited by how the brain processes information.

Ego: Wait a minute. Something happened yesterday that seemed very strange to me.

Higher Self: Now we are getting somewhere.

Ego: What do you mean?

Higher Self: You noticed what happened when the car next to you ran the red light.

Ego: It happened so fast.

Higher Self: What do you remember?

Ego: I was approaching the light, which turned yellow, but I was too far away to go through it even though I was travelling at about 50 mph. The car next to me went through it. It's a bad stoplight because there's another one right after it and too many drivers look at the next one instead, which yesterday happened to be green.

Higher Self: Do you remember anything else?

Ego: I was going to honk my horn because the drivers on the cross street were beginning to drive into the street and it didn't appear that they saw him.

Higher Self: You did not use your horn. Do you remember why?

Ego: All of a sudden I felt very calm and I didn't do anything.

Higher Self: Why not? You thought there was going to be an accident.

Ego: I'm not sure.

Higher Self: It was lucky that you did nothing.

Ego: What do you mean luck?

Higher Self: I am just having a little fun with you. It had nothing to do with luck, but it was good that you did not use your horn.

Ego: Why?

Higher Self: You may have caused the driver who ran the red light to slow down. If he slowed down then another driver entering the cross street would have hit him.

Ego: That's probably true, but I wasn't sure of that.

Higher Self: I was. I am not encumbered by the slow processing speed of your brain.

Ego: So you intervened?

Higher Self: Yes, I provided a level of calm, which caused you to feel that it would be all right. That caused you to relax and not use your horn.

Ego: I was so surprised by how calm I felt during the whole process. Normally that would have got my adrenalin going a bit, but this time I just drove on as though nothing happened. It all happened in the blink of an eye.

Higher Self: Just like your Breathe Right vision.

Ego: But wait a minute. I was able to perceive these things and you're saying these events were happening outside of my brain and too fast for my brain to process. I knew you were lying to me.

Higher Self: I would never lie to you. I would be lying to myself. I have no reason to do that.

Ego: But I could perceive these things using my brain.

Higher Self: In both of those instances I assisted you in perceiving more information than you typically can process. I temporarily suspended your self-imposed limitations and for a brief instant you perceived without your normal filters. However in both of those instances you quickly re-imposed your filters and as a result only partially perceived all the information that was available to you.

Ego: If you are really me or I am you, however this works, why don't you just open this perception thing all of the time. That would help me out.

Higher Self: How so?

Ego: It seems like I would be clued into the truth a lot more. That's what I'm looking for.

Higher Self: You would likely resist.

Ego: Why would I resist having these kinds of capabilities? That was really neat; feeling so calm and relaxed in the midst of what could have been a messy accident. And that Breathe Right vision changed my life. Who wouldn't want to live this way all of the time?

Higher Self: You.

Ego: Why not?

Higher Self: You would perceive it as giving up control.

Ego: I didn't give up control when these things happened in the past.

Higher Self: I suspended your filters.

Ego: What do you mean?

Higher Self: There are filters in place between me and my perceptions and your biology. Your awareness results from your biology, mostly from your brain's processes and some from your bodily senses. Your brain and body are capable of receiving much more information in a slightly different manner, but as long as these filters are in place that information does not register in your biology.

Ego: If you are really me I would think you would want to help me.

Higher Self: I am and I do, which is why we are having this dialogue.

Ego: Why don't you just remove these filters?

Higher Self: The filters will be removed when you are ready and the time is right.

Ego: But you've already removed them temporarily. Why not do it some more?

Higher Self: There may be reasons to temporarily suspend those filters, but there are changes required in your way of being first and then the time must be right in order for the filters to be removed permanently.

Ego: Why must I change?

Higher Self: In part the gulf between your vision of reality and what is truly reality is very wide. Exposing you to the truth in light of your current vision is more than you can accept. Your understanding must be further along in order for you to not reject what you would experience. Furthermore, that reality conflicts with your fundamental beliefs about yourself. The very act of dissolving these filters requires an acceptance of me in a way that may seem to diminish you. It requires that you consider yourself to be me in order to accept me in that way. That tends to diminish your sense of control.

Ego: Really, I'm just looking to know the truth of things. I'm not looking for an identity make-over.

Higher Self: You cannot have one without the other. That is why most people do not consider such issues, because deep within they realize it requires a significant change. How serious are you about wanting to know the truth?

Ego: I'm not sure. It seemed a lot simpler before we had this discussion.

Higher Self: Well, let me know when you are ready.

Ego: That's it? You're not going to try to convince me that I should move forward?

Higher Self: No.

Ego: That's all you have to say?

Higher Self: It seems as though you want to be convinced to proceed. Is that so?

Ego: Isn't that your job?

Higher Self: How am I doing?

Ego: You're trying to trick me into proceeding. You're making a game of this.

Higher Self: It is really not much of a game. I am you, remember? I already know your thoughts. However, you

135

are unaware of mine because you cannot perceive much of me in your current state of being.

Ego: So am I going to decide to proceed?

Higher Self: Why would you want to?

Ego: I'll have to think about it.

Considerations

Beliefs are rarely truths, but that fact is lost on most of us when we are triggered during life's events. We tend to defend our beliefs, often far too vigorously and sometimes with dire consequences. We use our beliefs to maintain a stable sense of reality in an effort to feel safe and secure in a changing world. Rarely do we inspect or change them in the light of our current knowledge.

Those beliefs that tend to be the most private to each of us are those that we hold about ourselves. These beliefs are rarely discussed. We hide them away in the recesses of our psyche. These are the beliefs that most drastically limit our awareness. They are the most difficult to change because we rarely choose to evaluate them.

As you live and hopefully write your story try as best you can to move deeper into your psyche and explore your beliefs, particularly the ones you hold about yourself that are of a limiting or damaging nature. These beliefs are the lies you have told yourself countless times and continue to reinforce, unless they have already been excavated, recognized as lies and discarded, which is uncommon.

Ask yourself:

1. Why do you wish to proceed down a path, which will likely cause you to re-experience pain in an effort to learn the truth? What are the payoffs or

benefits that you believe you will derive from such a journey? Why do you feel it will be worth it?

2. Are you your beliefs? Is this how you self-identify? If you are not your beliefs, what are you? Do you believe that your beliefs and your conditioning represent your ego and not what you truly are?

3. Which beliefs that you hold about yourself do you consider to be limiting or damaging? Why do you believe them? Who in your life taught you to believe them? Are you willing to change them or let them go?

4. How threatened are you regarding letting your beliefs go? Do you feel as if you would be giving up a part of yourself? Do you feel you can do that?

5. What beliefs do you refuse to give up at all cost? Do you feel that these beliefs are truths? Does everyone else agree that these beliefs are truths? What if they are not truths? Are you willing to consider that they may not be truths?

6. Do you consider yourself to be a controlling individual? Do other people consider you to be controlling? Do people that have a controlling nature hold onto their beliefs more tightly?

7. What issues do you feel you must control? What would happen if you exerted less control in regards to these issues? Do you believe you have absolute control over these issues?

8. Do you wish to know the truth of things? Are you willing to let go of many of your beliefs and exert less control in your life in order to know the truth?

Chapter 23: Feeling, Thinking and Knowing

Higher Self: How are you feeling?

Ego: Fairly relaxed physically, but I have a small undercurrent of agitation.

Higher Self: That is better than fine.

Ego: Well I still feel a little agitation.

Higher Self: I meant that in the past when you said, "fine," you were really not feeling anything and now you are. In the past you were shut down most of the time.

Ego: That's true. I feel much more now.

Higher Self: Why are you feeling agitation?

Ego: I have a lot on my plate right now. I'm probably putting a bit too much pressure on myself to get everything done in too fast a timeframe.

Higher Self: You generally create too tight a schedule for yourself. You do not provide enough breathing space.

Ego: You used to tell me that I should spend more time being and feeling versus thinking and doing.

Higher Self: That is correct.

Ego: So why aren't you reminding me of that now?

Higher Self: Obviously you do not need reminding. You have remembered that all by yourself.

Ego: I must need reminding because I'm stuck in my same old pattern.

Higher Self: Not exactly. You are much further along than you were.

Ego: Because I remember that I am better off spending more time in a state of being and feeling.

Higher Self: That and the fact that you do spend much more time in states of being rather than doing and you spend time feeling rather than thinking. Even when you are thinking and doing you frequently check in on your body and see how you are feeling and you remain much more receptive than you were.

Ego: That's very nice of you to say, however I feel that you're about to drop the other shoe.

Higher Self: You feel that I am about to say, but now that you have gotten this far you should….

Ego: Exactly.

Higher Self: You are the perceptive one today.

Ego: Okay so what is it?

Higher Self: You want to feel more from your heart. You do not believe you feel love strongly enough.

Ego: Yes, that's true.

Higher Self: Why do you believe that?

Ego: I just do. Obviously I can't prove it because it's just how I feel, but since I feel other emotions more completely throughout my body I must be able to feel love more completely too. Am I wrong?

Higher Self: You are correct.

Ego: So why can't I feel love as strongly as the other emotions? Is there something wrong with my ability to feel?

Higher Self: If there was something wrong with your ability to feel, you would not be able to feel the other emotions so completely. There is nothing wrong with your ability to feel.

Ego: Then what is it?

Higher Self: What do you think it is?

Ego: Well, since I can feel it somewhat I must not be allowing myself to feel it more.

Higher Self: Why would you inhibit the feeling of love?

Ego: That makes no sense.

Higher Self: Then why do you do it?

Ego: So you're saying I actually do that?

Higher Self: Yes, you do block the feeling of love. Before that feeling emerges you feel something different. You are not willing to allow love to fully express itself. Why?

Ego: I must inhibit that feeling because I don't want to reveal that feeling.

Higher Self: To whom?

Ego: To the other person.

Higher Self: Then why do you tell other people that you love them, which you do, if you are trying to hide that from them?

Ego: Yes, that wouldn't make much sense would it?

Higher Self: None at all. So who are you hiding that feeling from?

Ego: There's no one left, but me.

Higher Self: That is correct. You do not fully experience the feeling of love because it triggers some of your deeper fears.

Ego: I want to be able to feel love completely throughout all of me.

Higher Self: Yes I know you do, but you block yourself from having those feelings.

Ego: What are you referring to?

Higher Self: Dig a little deeper.

Ego: Why would I not want to feel love?

Higher Self: You have adopted an attitude in which you prefer to stand alone and apart in order to protect yourself.

Ego: I do have that tendency.

Higher Self: Why?

Ego: Because I don't want to depend on anyone else.

Higher Self: When you are unwilling to be dependent on anyone else you block the feeling of love.

Ego: Why?

Higher Self: Love makes you feel vulnerable. It puts you at risk.

Ego: Risk of what?

Higher Self: What do you think?

Ego: I'm not sure.

Higher Self: Allow yourself to feel.

Ego: Loss.

Higher Self: Loss of what?

Ego: I would be vulnerable to losing whatever it is that I love.

Higher Self: You have spent much of your life guarding against loss. What did you feel when your mother passed?

Ego: I didn't feel that much.

Higher Self: How do you feel about that?

Ego: It makes me feel different. Most people are very sad when they lose a parent, especially their primary caregiver. They usually grieve over their loss. I didn't shed a tear when she died.

Higher Self: You did tear up at the funeral when you delivered her eulogy.

Ego: That's true, but it wasn't about my loss. It was related to the feelings she had in the story I related.

Higher Self: That story simply precipitated tears of grief from within you. They were your tears.

Ego: But when I think of her being gone I don't feel any sense of loss.

Higher Self: What do you feel?

Ego: I don't feel anything, but it's been nine years since she died.

Higher Self: Do you remember what you were feeling when you sat with her during her time in hospice?

Ego: Most of the time my wife Jen and I were just sitting there while she was in a drug-induced stupor, although Jen was busy watching. I had never realized what really happens to a person while they're waiting to pass. I was fascinated by what Jen perceived. My mother was in dialogue with her higher self, reevaluating what she might have done differently in certain of her life's situations and how she would have felt if she had made those other

143

choices. She lingered in that state for almost two weeks. While we were present Jen was able to tell me what situations my mother and her higher self were reviewing.

Higher Self: So what did you feel?

Ego: I really don't remember feeling anything.

Higher Self: Your mother became lucid before she died and you had a chance to say goodbye. You told her you loved her. Do you remember?

Ego: Yes.

Higher Self: What were you feeling then?

Ego: I felt sad.

Higher Self: Why?

Ego: She was leaving.

Higher Self: What else did you feel?

Ego: I felt somewhat alone.

Higher Self: Your feelings trigger a deeper sense of knowing. Do you understand what your feelings are telling you?

Ego: In my work on myself I recognize that I have feelings of abandonment.

Higher Self: Yet you do not really understand its genesis.

Ego: Not really. I don't recall any event in my life that should have caused such an issue.

Higher Self: You have blocked out much around the time of your brother's birth. What do you remember?

Ego: I don't remember much, which is strange as I was seven years old.

Higher Self: It was a few weeks after your seventh birthday during the summer. You were in day camp during that time, but the issue began even earlier while your mother was pregnant. Your unborn brother was already interfering with your favorite evening seat. Remember how you used to sit up against your mother's abdomen while you and your parents watched TV?

Ego: Oh that's right. I could no longer sit that way. I lost the only physical contact I would normally receive.

Higher Self: That is correct and then after his birth you were never able to sit that way again. That physical connection meant more to you than you realize.

Ego: But I had my freedom.

Higher Self: Yes you did, but did you really want your freedom back then?

Ego: What do you mean, my mother was a nag.

Higher Self: She was not that much of a nag that early in your life. You recall more about that from later years. You were still very much attached to your mother when you were seven. Your brother's arrival changed that significantly. You had been an only child for seven years and you had her undivided attention. The new baby changed that abruptly. Your mother tended to focus on one thing at a time and Cary became her principle focus as soon as he entered the scene.

Ego: Are you saying that my inability to more fully experience love was caused by this one issue?

Higher Self: This was the most significant causative event in this life, but there were many other smaller events that compounded the problem.

Ego: It's hard for me to believe that this abandonment issue is such a big deal.

Higher Self: That fear, although not severe, drives many of your feelings and behaviors.

Ego: Such as?

Higher Self: It reinforces your already strong-willed nature to be independent of others. You prefer to be self-reliant, to stand alone like an island.

Ego: That's not a bad thing.

Higher Self: This is not about good versus bad or right versus wrong. This is about understanding why you are as you are. You are the one who wishes to feel love more completely.

Ego: I don't see why I can't continue to be self-reliant and independently minded and still feel love more completely.

Higher Self: Why is it that you wish to feel love more completely?

Ego: I think that is holding me back.

Higher Self: Holding you back in what way?

Ego: I want to know what I truly am.

Higher Self: Your thought process is quite correct.

Ego: I knew it, but I don't know how to correct it.

Higher Self: On the contrary, you do.

Ego: What do you mean?

Higher Self: You have already stated that you wish to feel love more completely. That is the path for you.

Ego: But I don't know how to do that.

Higher Self: It is not as difficult as it seems. When feelings of love begin to emerge allow them to flow. You are mindful enough to witness how you block the fuller expression of love, are you not?

Ego: Yes, I have noticed how I retreat into feelings of resistance and isolation.

Higher Self: Then what happens?

Ego: I begin to think and not feel.

Higher Self: What thoughts come to mind?

Ego: I think about what I can do to be independent of the situation that has triggered those feelings.

Higher Self: Yes, you defend against any possible future hurt by remaining less dependent upon any deeper engagement with other people.

Ego: Yes, but I do love the people close to me in my life.

Higher Self: Yes you do, but you limit the fuller expression of that love.

Ego: So what are you suggesting?

Higher Self: When those feelings of resistance and isolation appear, acknowledge them and focus on the situation at hand. Allow your feelings of love to expand throughout your body, especially your heart.

Ego: And you're claiming that all of this resulted from the arrival of my brother, which is a commonplace occurrence. This kind of thing happens to many people.

Higher Self: Not everybody has the predisposing factors that strongly influenced you.

Ego: Oh, so there is something deeper.

Higher Self: Yes.

Ego: Well what is it?

Higher Self: You will come to learn of it in time.

Ego: Why can't you tell me?

Higher Self: I can tell you, but it will do you more good when you discover it yourself.

Ego: Why?

Higher Self: If I tell you, you will receive the information at only a mental level. You will not feel it very much.

Ego: So.

Higher Self: It will have much less of an effect on you.

Ego: Why?

Higher Self: Why do you think?

Ego: I don't know.

Higher Self: That is my point.

Ego: You're making no sense.

Higher Self: It is perfectly clear to me.

Ego: Of course it is, but your job is to teach me and that's not helping.

Higher Self: I asked you to think and you responded that you don't know.

Ego: So what does that mean?

Higher Self: You want to know what you are. Do you believe that you can know that by thinking?

Ego: Of course, why not?

Higher Self: Knowing what you are is not a fact that you can prove, such as two plus two equals four. Knowing what you are is something that you experience with your senses. The knowing of facts and your sense of knowing are quite different. The knowing of facts can be gained through your mental faculty, but that alone cannot produce a sense of knowing.

Ego: Why not?

Higher Self: The knowing of fact is just a mental concept. That is not something that can be felt and experienced, like love for instance.

Ego: So why don't you just tell me what the deeper issue is and I'll try to re-experience it.

Higher Self: The origination of that issue is not something you will be able to re-experience in that way. When you are ready, the re-experience will be made available to you. In the meantime, allow yourself to feel more and the rest will come.

Ego: What about my desire to know what I am?

Higher Self: What about it?

Ego: Are you saying that I won't be able to get to that knowledge without a more complete understanding about my abandonment issues?

Higher Self: You have enough of an understanding to know why you block greater expression of love. As long as you open yourself to those feelings you will be able to reach your goal.

Ego: I still only have a vague notion about how my ability to feel love more completely is linked to knowing what I truly am.

149

Higher Self: You seek an understanding that can only be gained through experience. That experience requires an openness to love. Providing more information to you at this time may create expectations or assumptions on your part that would likely limit your experience. I do not wish to serve you in that way.

Considerations

There is no better way to know ourselves than through our feelings. Feelings never lie. When we take the time to understand the thoughts and beliefs which underlie those feelings the truth of what we are in that moment emerges. Most of us are ego-identified much of the time. As a result, many of the feelings we experience are considered to be negative and unwanted. For this reason we tend to avoid our feelings and prefer to think rather than feel.

Thinking and feeling tend to be binary states. We tend to either be in a feeling or thinking state. However that is a choice we make. At any time we can focus our attention on our body and feel what it is experiencing. Only by experiencing our feelings can we know why we feel as we do. Most of us avoid knowing.

That's the problem. If we wish to know what we truly are we must become more cognizant of our feelings. Only by allowing ourselves to experience what we consider to be negative emotional feelings, can we experience the positive love-based emotions too. We must experience all of our feelings as completely as possible in order to experience what we truly are. When we know what we truly are we will no longer consider any of our feelings to be negative or unwanted as we will have transcended the ego-based beliefs which underlie them.

Ask yourself:

1. Do you prefer to think or feel? Do you consider yourself to be head-centric or body-centric?

2. Do you actively seek your feelings or do they typically only become apparent to you when they emerge into your awareness? How often do you check in with your body to see how you are feeling?

3. How uncomfortable do you feel when you experience anger, shame, guilt, sadness, grief and anxiety?

4. How good do you feel when you experience love, joy, happiness, awe, contentment and peace?

5. When you experience the emotions listed in question 3 do you question yourself to uncover the underlying belief?

6. When you experience the emotions listed in question 3, what do you tend to do in order to distract yourself? Do you eat, get on the internet, watch TV or use drugs or alcohol?

7. When you experience the emotions listed in question 4, do they typically result from an event that just happened in your life or do they arise spontaneously and unrelated to any event?

8. How would you define your mood? Do you have lots of ups and downs? Are you even-keeled without a lot of emotional shifts? When you do experience emotions are they typically experienced in a mild or strong manner?

Chapter 24: Mindfulness and Coping Strategies

Mindfulness using the 9-Box Flow Chart

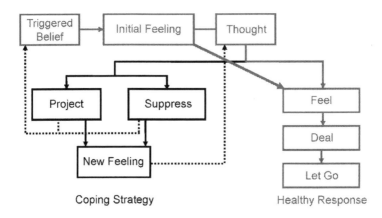

This flow chart is used as an aid to practice a more advanced form of mindfulness with the goal of understanding our subconscious beliefs and their associated feelings and behaviors. At first glance this chart may seem somewhat cumbersome and overwhelming. However with a little practice it becomes quite easy to incorporate into an extremely rewarding mindfulness practice that can yield dramatic personal understanding and growth.

It is easiest to break the chart up into three sections of three boxes each. To begin understanding the process let's begin with the top line of three boxes related to the beliefs we create and maintain about ourselves.

Triggered Belief: A belief, typically subconscious and false, that we have created about our self at a young age and which is usually of a limiting or negative nature. These beliefs are regularly triggered by life's events.

Initial Feeling: The feeling, usually considered to be a negative emotion, which is associated with the belief and is experienced when the belief is triggered. This unwanted feeling motivates us to rid ourselves of it.

Thought: A fleeting thought comes about as a result of the feeling experienced. The thought is typically situationally dependent and precipitates a choice. The choice is to remain conscious and continue to experience the feeling (healthy response) or to slip into one's subconscious, reactive patterned behavior (coping strategy or defense mechanism).

Example: A typical flawed belief may be that I'm stupid and I always make mistakes. An associated feeling may be frustration after making a mistake. The thought may be, "I've done it again, I'm so stupid," thus reinforcing the belief.

The domain of the three boxes that comprise the coping strategy is entered if the person's choice is one of revisiting their often used, old patterned behavior (old tapes) that they learned as a child. The response usually takes one of two forms, either projection or suppression. Either form may result in the formation of a new feeling leading to a new thought or precipitate another triggered belief. Our coping strategies, which we have developed and modified over time, may be convoluted or nested as demonstrated by the looping arrows.

Project: This is an attempt by the person to shift or displace the issue or fault onto another person. It often takes the form of blame or judgment.

Suppress: The person assigns blame or fault to themselves and in the process they swallow or bury the emotion, thereby suppressing it.

153

New Feeling: A new emotion is often generated as a result of the psychological act of projection or suppression, which then leads to another thought.

Example continued: If they have chosen the path of playing out their coping strategy and they exhibit projection they may blame someone for being the cause of the mistake. If they exhibit suppression they may quietly sulk. The new emotion may be frustration elevated to anger or rage or frustration suppressed leading to sadness.

The alternative to replaying one's coping strategy is to travel down the feel, deal and let go path that represents a healthy response.

Feel: Continue to experience the negative emotional feeling and allow it to expand throughout your entire body. Allow yourself to feel it as fully and intensely as possible. The emotional feeling is just a feeling.

Deal: Ask yourself when as a child did you feel this way. Close your eyes and allow an image to form in your mind's eye. Allow yourself to understand what the underlying belief is that is causing this feeling. Ask yourself why you believe it. Determine if the belief is reasonable. If it is not, then allow yourself to release it.

Let Go: Allow the negative emotional feeling(s) to fade away and be replaced by a state of relaxation.

Example continued: Allow the frustration to build into anger and allow it to spread throughout your body. Envision a childhood event that created or fortified the underlying belief. Understand its genesis and let yourself release it. Allow your current state to return to balance and relax.

With practice one learns to change one's attitude towards the negative emotions that accompany triggered beliefs. They become welcomed opportunities to discover our underlying subconscious beliefs that are usually no longer valid or helpful. In fact, they are almost always falsehoods and limitations. After shifting one's attitude in this manner it becomes easier to hold onto the initial feeling as soon as it's experienced, remain consciously accepting and travel down the feel, deal and let go path.

This mindfulness practice is an excellent way to understand the functioning of one's ego. With practice and greater spiritual embodiment this process becomes less necessary as one is typically triggered less often and has typically released some of their false beliefs.

Ego: You never told me why I can't continue to be self-reliant and independently-minded and still feel love more completely.

Higher Self: You already know. You have been through this type of process many times.

Ego: I realize you're going to tell me that it's because I'm playing out a coping strategy.

Higher Self: That is correct. You create an attitude of self-reliance and independence as a form of projection. It is born of fear and fear and love do not mix. It arises out of your fear of abandonment. It is your way of pushing the other person away or at least holding them at bay before they can leave you. It is a defensive posture, which is why coping strategies are also called defense mechanisms.

Ego: Yes, I really do understand that, but I think I can be self-reliant and independently minded without it being a coping strategy and still experience love more fully.

Higher Self: You would like to think so, but you are simply readying yourself to move into a fuller manifestation of your coping strategy. Love is not a defensive posture and so you cannot fully express love while being defensive. Love is a form of acceptance, which is contrary to the control you exhibit as a result of employing a coping strategy. Do you realize how counterproductive this coping strategy is when it comes to your goal of perceiving the truth or experiencing what you truly are?

Ego: What do you mean?

Higher Self: You cannot see what truly is if you are not prepared to accept it. Your idea of self-reliance and independence relies on your ability to hold on tight to these beliefs, which foster separateness and isolation.

Ego: I never looked at it that way. I've been trying to see myself as part of a bigger picture, but you're right, these attitudes keep me apart, alone and separate.

Higher Self: It would be difficult to picture yourself as a drop of water in the ocean if you exist as an island set apart. Any attitude that you hold about anyone or group of relationships generalizes to all of your relationships. This attitude of separateness plays out much more pervasively in your life. For your life to change in this regard you must change.

Ego: This has become so fundamental to my way of being. I don't know how to go about this type of change.

Higher Self: Yes you do. It is what you are already working on. Keep allowing yourself to feel love more completely. Open your heart and let down your guard. Let the walls of defensiveness fall down around you.

Ego: That advice applies to all of my coping strategies, doesn't it?

Higher Self: Absolutely all of them. All coping strategies exist in the absence of unconditional love. They exist to maintain false egoic beliefs. A coping strategy is nothing more than a reflexive process to deflect one's attention away from a false belief, because the ego works to keep that belief intact. It is the mechanism responsible for egoic self-preservation.

Ego: That is why the emotions that are part of the coping strategies don't feel good.

Higher Self: Yes, that is correct. Because those emotions are perceived to be negative and uncomfortable the individual typically chooses to get rid of them as quickly as possible. They tend to be either suppressed or projected. The person becomes so busy getting rid of the negatively perceived emotion that they rarely perceive the underlying belief. It is also important for you to recognize that all addictions are coping strategies. They too, deflect attention away from the underlying belief and they cover over the negatively perceived emotions. It is a form of suppression.

Ego: I don't suffer from any addictions.

Higher Self: Yes you do.

Ego: No I don't. I don't gamble or use drugs or alcohol or have an addiction to sex. Maybe I have a little addiction to sugar, but that's it.

Higher Self: Your primary addiction, not your addiction to sweets, is deeper and so insidious that it is not even recognized as an addiction.

Ego: Then it really doesn't exist, does it?

Higher Self: It exists and you manifest it in a major way.

Ego: Come on, you're joking.

Higher Self: Not when it comes to this.

Ego: Okay, so tell me what I'm addicted to.

157

Higher Self: You are addicted to your beliefs and perceptions regarding yourself. You are addicted to your ego.

Ego: Because I'm a doctor and have been successful in business.

Higher Self: No, it has nothing to do with those achievements, although those achievements in part have been fueled by your addiction.

Ego: Don't turn this into a riddle. I hate when you do that.

Higher Self: You want a simple fix.

Ego: Cut it out. Just tell me what you are talking about.

Higher Self: Your mistaken self-identification with the beliefs and conditioning associated with this life has created a full-fledged, self-sustaining addiction.

Ego: You've been telling me that I am you.

Higher Self: You are the part of me that is assigned to directly participate and experience this life. However, you have become so mired in it that you no longer recognize what you truly are. Fortunately you have retained a yearning to know what you are.

Ego: This is silly. How can I be addicted to myself?

Higher Self: You are addicted to the image you have created for yourself.

Ego: I get the fact that you think I self-identify with the person I am, but that is not an addiction. And right now that is who I am.

Higher Self: That is only who you think you are when you are ego-identified. As such, you are an addict and compulsively engaged in this life, a stream of stimuli which on occasion provides some fleeting rewards. However the adverse consequence of your way of believing is that you have forgotten what you truly are. As a result, you spend much of your time in the dark, striving for ways to feel better about yourself. That persona can never feel better about itself on a sustained basis due to its flawed belief of not being good enough. This state of being that you call the person living this life fits precisely with what your society would define as an addict.

Ego: There are people with serious addictions and you're making light of their problem.

Higher Self: You think I am joking with you.

Ego: I do.

Higher Self: I am not.

Ego: You're really serious about this?

Higher Self: Completely.

Ego: I find this concept somewhat absurd.

Higher Self: That is the nature of addiction. Until you come to grips with it you live in denial.

Ego: Really, you're going to continue this ridiculous line of thought?

Higher Self: Call it what you wish, but it is the root cause of all of your problems. I believe that should be considered serious and not ridiculous.

Ego: Why do you think it is the root cause of all my problems?

Higher Self: Not just your problems, but everyone's problems. Almost all human beings suffer from this addiction.

Ego: That makes it normal.

Higher Self: Yes it does, but that does not justify it or make it beneficial.

Ego: It does not require justification.

Higher Self: You often justify your lies. This is no different.

Ego: How can you say that?

Higher Self: As long as you are addicted to your ego and as such, identified with your ego, you are living a lie, because that is not what you are.

Ego: How can I identify any differently when that is all I know? You say that you and I are the same, but from my perspective I don't perceive that.

Higher Self: You cannot perceive what you truly are through the lens of your ego.

Ego: But that's what I am.

Higher Self: No, you are not. You are a part of me however you perceive yourself and the world around you through the filters of your beliefs, fears and conditioning. These things filter your perceptions in such a way that you have actually self-defined or self-identified with them. As a result you often think that you are your beliefs. You hold them as close as the alcoholic holds his drink. Do you deny that you are addicted to your beliefs?

Ego: I can change my beliefs.

Higher Self: Tell me the last time you changed one of your beliefs about yourself.

Ego: It's hard to remember, but I'm sure I've done so.

Higher Self: You have not changed a fundamental belief about yourself in some time. In fact, you rarely inspect your beliefs.

Ego: Well I know I can do it.

Higher Self: Yes you can and you have. You have gone through several periods in your life when you have actively changed and even released a number of your beliefs. However you have remained fixed for a period of time recently and that is why you have not reached your goal.

Ego: Of perceiving what I truly am?

Higher Self: Yes.

Ego: I keep thinking I'm further along than I am.

Higher Self: You have made considerable progress, but what you seek requires even more house cleaning. This is why you resist admitting to your addiction.

Ego: I still don't believe I'm an addict.

Higher Self: It is so fundamental to your way of being that you cannot perceive how addicted you are. Just take a look at your behaviors.

Ego: What behaviors?

Higher Self: The most obvious is your need to achieve. You work long hours, day after day.

Ego: I love what I do.

Higher Self: You really do enjoy what you do, but why do you do it?

Ego: I enjoy it.

Higher Self: Why else?

Ego: I like to get things done.

Higher Self: Why?

Ego: I like tangible results.

Higher Self: Why?

Ego: Because I like to see something come of what I do. I also think that what I do can help other people.

Higher Self: Do you take pride in what you do?

Ego: Yes I do. What's wrong with that? I don't boast about it.

Higher Self: Your father takes pride in what you do. Would your mother take pride as well if she were alive?

Ego: I'm sure she would.

Higher Self: How much of the pride that you feel comes from how they feel or would feel about you?

Ego: They always wanted me to achieve.

Higher Self: And you have achieved much and you strive to achieve more.

Ego: Where are you going with this?

Higher Self: I am simply attempting to open your eyes to the truth.

Ego: Look, I admit that to some degree I have a need to achieve, but I also do what I do because I enjoy it and it helps other people.

Higher Self: Your parents would certainly have approved of helping other people. As far as enjoying what you do, you also enjoy achieving. You spend much time working to serve that master.

Ego: So are you saying that this is a bad way to be?

Higher Self: Not at all. I am not saying it is bad or wrong. I am simply trying to help you better appreciate the motives underlying your actions. I would like you to see the truth of things.

Ego: That's exactly what I've been saying. I want to see the truth and I want to know what I truly am.

Higher Self: Why?

Ego: I really do believe that I'm living a lie to an extent. I understand that my beliefs are not truths. I want to know the truth of things.

Higher Self: Even with this spiritual quest you have strong egoic motivations.

Ego: Wanting to know the truth? How can that be ego driven?

Higher Self: Are you unable to perceive that this too is another achievement?

Ego: I recognize, that my achievements are in part motivated by attempting to feel better about myself. But I'm trying to break through all of that stuff.

Higher Self: Why?

Ego: Like you said, I've done a lot of work on myself. I have cycled through the mindfulness process many, many times. I know that when I peel the onion of my beliefs and look deeper into my triggered beliefs I always uncover the same underlying belief.

Higher Self: Which is?

Ego: That I'm not good enough or worthy of love. I understand that some of the reason I work to achieve is to prove that I am good enough.

163

Higher Self: Does it work?

Ego: Only for a little while and then I need to achieve some more.

Higher Self: Another fix?

Ego: Yes, okay, I'm starting to get it. It is like an addiction.

Higher Self: Why is your desire to know what you truly are any different?

Ego: I'm not entirely sure.

Higher Self: Why do you think?

Ego: If I don't see myself the same way then maybe I won't need to prove anything to myself.

Higher Self: How are you going to see yourself differently?

Ego: If I could perceive what I truly am, then I would see myself differently.

Higher Self: How can you perceive yourself any differently if you still perceive through the filters of your current beliefs?

Ego: I don't know.

Higher Self: It is no different than your attempt to perceive me directly using your lens of perceptual awareness.

Ego: My hope was to experience more spiritually so that my beliefs would shift, allowing me to perceive more.

Higher Self: You would still be operating using beliefs.

Ego: But those beliefs would be more consistent with the truth.

Higher Self: Nonetheless, beliefs are tied to egoic thought processes, which is a very different state of being as compared to a spiritual state of being.

Ego: Then how can I appreciate what I truly am?

Higher Self: I exist in a state of being, not believing. You must do the same in order to perceive what you truly are, since you and I are one.

Ego: How do I do that?

Higher Self: You must learn to suspend your beliefs and egoic conditioning. When you exist in that state of being, you will not be subject to those filters.

Ego: Easy to say, but how do you do it?

Higher Self: It is time to move your mindfulness practice to another level.

Ego: I have been mindful of experiencing negative emotions, judgments and lies. Isn't that enough?

Higher Self: What have you been doing when you realize you are experiencing an emotion that you consider negative?

Ego: As soon as I realize that I am experiencing that feeling I allow it to spread throughout my body as best I can. I really do try to intensify it.

Higher Self: Does that bother you?

Ego: As I've been working with these feelings I realize they aren't bad and I no longer view them negatively. I just allow myself to fully experience them.

Higher Self: Then what?

Ego: When I am feeling it as completely as I think I can I ask myself, "When as a child did I feel this way?"

Higher Self: And?

Ego: I close my eyes and usually I see a scene of myself as a child in a situation that precipitated that feeling. At that point it is very easy to understand the belief that I am holding that is causing me to feel the emotion.

Higher Self: Do you stop there?

Ego: No. I ask myself, "Why do I believe that?" Usually there is a deeper belief underlying the first one. I continue to query myself in that way. As I spend more time doing that and feeling what the deeper beliefs caused me to feel, I can get to the bottom of it.

Higher Self: What sits at the bottom?

Ego: No matter what my initial belief is that triggered a negative emotional feeling, it always spirals down to the same old belief.

Higher Self: Which is?

Ego: I'm not good enough.

Higher Self: Do you believe that?

Ego: A big part of me does.

Higher Self: So part of you does not believe that.

Ego: I guess so or maybe I just hope so.

Higher Self: Did you ever stop to realize that I am that part of you that believes that you are good enough to receive love?

Ego: In the course of our dialogues I have suspected that, but it is difficult for me to truly think of you as part of me.

Higher Self: And yet, as long as you do not, you will never be able to truly believe that you are good enough. When you peel the onion of your beliefs as you described and you get down to the core egoic flawed belief of I'm not good enough, there is nowhere else to proceed unless you change what "I" represents. Only then can you perceive yourself and the world around you from that reference point and authentically believe that you are good enough. At that point you will feel different and you will know that you are not addicted to your ego.

Considerations

Coping strategies, also referred to as defense mechanisms, old patterns, replaying old tapes, are just that; ways of coping. They were developed in childhood to help meet our needs. We tend to retain them into adulthood and generally throughout life. Unfortunately, when we use them, we move into a subconscious, reactive way of being. We are living life, subconsciously, in auto-pilot as if we are still a small child. Learning to remain consciously aware so that we can be mindful of the process requires that we hold onto our feelings and uncover the underlying beliefs.

In the light of our present day knowledge we are better equipped to understand and more effectively deal and let go of the issues that have remained buried in our subconscious. This process is covered more thoroughly in the book, *Claim Your Basic Rights*, book one.

As long as we employ our coping strategies we remain ego-identified, as it is our ego which has created and utilizes these processes. Since all of our coping strategies result from false beliefs, whenever we utilize them we are being untruthful. Practicing mindfulness allows us to perceive the workings of our egoic mind. The next chapter will provide more insight into this practice.

Chapter 25: Judging and Acceptance

Ego: How do I move my mindfulness practice to another level?

Higher Self: First you must understand what happens during the act of being mindful.

Ego: It's pretty straight forward. I just pay attention to what I'm doing.

Higher Self: Are you observing yourself?

Ego: Yes, that's exactly what I'm doing.

Higher Self: Do you do it all of the time?

Ego: Actually no. I'm only aware of it some of the time.

Higher Self: That is interesting that you refer to it as "it."

Ego: What are you talking about?

Higher Self: You just said, "I'm only aware of it some of the time", it being your ego.

Ego: What I meant was that I'm only aware of being mindful some of the time.

Higher Self: What is it that you are being mindful of?

Ego: How I feel and what I do as a result of my feelings.

Higher Self: Why are you only mindful some of the time?

Ego: I don't know.

Higher Self: Could it be that the rest of the time you are so preoccupied with portraying the role of your ego that you lose that elevated awareness?

Ego: Are you suggesting that when I'm mindful I am observing my ego?

169

Higher Self: Actually, when you are mindful you are observing yourself as you are influenced by the filters of your ego.

Ego: Okay, now I understand this process a little better, thank you. You're saying I'm really observing myself as opposed to my ego.

Higher Self: Yes, your ego isn't a real person. It just seems like a real person when you bring it to life by operating through its filters. It is actually nothing more than beliefs and conditioning stored in your brain and body.

Ego: Then what am I?

Higher Self: You are me, remember?

Ego: It just doesn't seem like that's true.

Higher Self: Why not?

Ego: Because we are in dialogue. You seem like someone else.

Higher Self: That is because it is difficult for you, even though you are part of me, to fully detach from your egoic filters. It only seems as though we are different. However, when you are being mindful you have detached enough from those filters so that you can observe that aspect of yourself that is more attached to those filters.

Ego: And so if I was fully detached would I be able to perceive you?

Higher Self: You would realize the scope of what you are. Your point of reference would shift from being a drop of water in the ocean to the entire ocean itself.

Ego: So that is why you are suggesting that I move my mindfulness practice to the next level.

Higher Self: Yes, as that will allow you to better perceive the truth of things and what you truly are.

Ego: Okay, I get it. How do I do that?

Higher Self: For starters remain mindful all of the time.

Ego: Wow, that's a big job. It's actually a full-time job. How am I going to do that and get anything else done?

Higher Self: Do everything you would normally do, but observe yourself in the process. Remain mindful.

Ego: That's a lot different than what I was doing. Before I was just trying to be mindful when I experienced a negative emotion or became judgmental or untruthful. Those were my cues.

Higher Self: Yes this represents a significant change. That is why it is the next level of mindfulness.

Ego: Yes, but you said to do this for starters. What else is part of this next level so to speak?

Higher Self: Be accepting in the process.

Ego: You mean accept this challenge and do it.

Higher Self: That is not what I meant. I mean for you to be accepting of all of yourself in the process.

Ego: But in the past when I observed myself I stayed with my feelings as best I could and tried to avoid moving into a coping strategy.

Higher Self: You were not accepting of yourself in the process.

Ego: No, I tried to change what I was doing. I was critical of myself.

Higher Self: And in being critical of yourself you did what you thought you should do based upon your beliefs. In the process you pulled yourself out of being mindful as you became more attached to your beliefs about how you should be.

Ego: Yes, but as part of that process I was learning about the triggered beliefs I was holding onto that fueled my coping strategy.

Higher Self: Yes and that was very helpful in understanding that at the core of those triggered beliefs you will find the same belief time and time again. Now I would like you to accept your ego for what it is, a collection of beliefs and conditioning.

Ego: So let me get this straight. You don't want me to dig deeper and get down to the bottom of my triggered beliefs. Instead you just want me to stay mindful and observe what I feel and do.

Higher Self: Yes and in the process, while you are observing, I would like you to be accepting of what you are doing as you operate through your egoic beliefs. If you should choose to change what you are doing in the process, that is fine as well, but remain mindful.

Ego: What is the point of all of this?

Higher Self: When you can maintain mindfulness during this whole process you will much more clearly perceive that you are not your ego. You will come to know with great certainty that you, as your authentic self, simply work through filters composed of beliefs and conditioning in the material realm. As such, you will have greater ease in detaching from these filters in order to perceive what you truly are.

Ego: I see the logic of it, but it still seems like a stretch.

Higher Self: It is a bigger stretch attempting to detach from your egoic filters without knowing for sure that you are not that. This level of mindfulness will provide you with the knowledge and motivation to release yourself, what you truly are, from the bondage of your egoic beliefs and conditioning. You will self-define differently as a result.

Ego: I don't know that I'm ready for this.

Higher Self: It is not really that much different from what you have been doing. Think back to a relatively commonplace example when you or someone close to you was judgmental.

Ego: You want me to remember an example of when I thought that someone was wrong or bad.

Higher Self: It does not have to be you. In fact, your mother was often very judgmental. Do you remember when she was critical of your daughter Whitney for not doing the dishes right after eating?

Ego: Yes, we used to call Whitney dump and run when she was in her early teens. That used to drive my mother nuts.

Higher Self: Why?

Ego: My mother had a rule about doing the dishes right away. She wanted everything to be in its place, nice and tidy.

Higher Self: Describe the process more completely.

Ego: Her triggered belief, in this example, took the form of a rule; the dishes should be washed and put away right after a meal. When this rule was not followed that belief would be triggered, which would cause an initial feeling of anger. The associated thought was that it was wrong to not wash and put away the dishes right away.

My mother would then project a judgment which had befallen her and judge Whitney as bad or wrong.

Higher Self: It did not end there did it?

Ego: That would create a new feeling, typically resentment, which was associated with a new thought; they don't respect me. That would cycle back down into the coping strategy, but this time my mother would suppress her feeling of resentment so that she wouldn't act on it. In this way she would stop complaining so that Whitney would still love her.

Higher Self: In her mind the process would continue further still.

Ego: Yes, I'm sure she cycled through feeling unloved and finally depressed. She always thought of herself as a door mat. At the root of it all was a belief that she had to perform for love. By following the rules she would be praised, otherwise she would be criticized. As a result in her mind, everyone else should also follow the rules.

Higher Self: That is correct. In her mind she was replaying the tapes from when she was five years old. She would look at Whitney and subconsciously say to herself, "Why doesn't she have to follow the rules? I have to otherwise I won't be loved."

Ego: That's about right. I'm sure those thoughts were rattling around in her head, irrespective of whether or not she was consciously aware of them.

Higher Self: Moving forward, it would be helpful if you could remain consciously aware of the thoughts and feelings that you experience.

Ego: When I am judgmental?

Higher Self: Then too and particularly when you are judgmental, be accepting of your thoughts and feelings.

Ego: Why then in particular?

Higher Self: The egoic mind is a judgment machine and that is not a bad thing. It is simply doing its job in an effort to keep you safe and alive. People make judgments all of the time for that purpose. When you are walking on a trail and you see some mushrooms, you often think about how you like to eat mushrooms, but almost immediately a judgment about the safety of those mushrooms comes into play and you realize that they are probably not safe to eat. We often tend to overuse this judgment machine and apply it by judging others based upon what we had to do as children in order to receive praise or avoid criticism. Whether we use our egoic machinery to stay safe or to judge others, it is still just machinery. It is not what we fundamentally are. By witnessing and being accepting of the entire process, you will be able to very clearly observe that you are not the egoic machinery of your lower or egoic mind. When you realize what you are not, you will more readily self-define differently.

Considerations

Therapists and coaches often prescribe mindfulness practices for their clients as a way of gaining insight into their triggered beliefs, feelings and coping strategies. This process can be very helpful in bringing into our conscious awareness beliefs that we have formed as children and not reevaluated since. Oftentimes, these practices are used to guide clients through cognitive and behavioral alternatives that may be healthier or at least more acceptable for the client and others.

By taking the mindfulness practice to the next level and observing the entire process with an attitude of complete acceptance, one can become mindful of the mindfulness process itself. At this level of observation, the witness has elevated their conscious awareness to the point where they have a better view of their lower mind. In other words, they can perceive a greater separation between their lower and higher minds. From this vantage point it becomes much easier to allow for sweeping changes in how we operate as we no longer think of ourselves in the same way. We have undergone a more fundamental transformation.

Mindfulness using the 9-Box Flow Chart

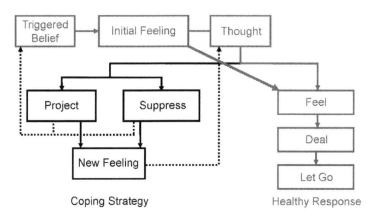

Ask yourself:

1. Remember the last time you felt angry or frustrated. What happened to cause that feeling? What action did you take? Did you blame another person (projection)? Did you stuff the feeling (suppression)? Did that process generate any secondary feelings? What did you do with them? Can you identify the underlying triggered beliefs?

2. Remember the last time you felt sad or depressed. What happened to cause that feeling? What action did you take? Did you blame another person

(projection)? Did you stuff the feeling (suppression)? Did that process generate any secondary feelings? What did you do with them? Can you identify the underlying triggered beliefs?

3. Remember the last time you felt fearful, anxious or worried. What happened to cause that feeling? What action did you take? Did you blame another person (projection)? Did you stuff the feeling (suppression)? Did that process generate any secondary feelings? What did you do with them? Can you identify the underlying triggered beliefs?

4. Remember the last time you were judgmental. What happened to cause that? What did you feel? What action did you take? Did that process generate any secondary feelings? What did you do with them? Can you identify the underlying triggered beliefs?

5. Do you wish to develop a mindfulness practice or if you do so already do you wish to deepen it? Commit the 9-box flow chart to memory and use it in life. Identify as you are being mindful which box you are functioning in (in the moment if you can). Try to stay in the feeling box. If you can maintain an awareness of how you feel more of the time it will be easier to identify in which box you are operating from. Try to be accepting of what your lower mind is doing without being critical of yourself. Make this a game, not hard work. Reward yourself in the process.

Chapter 26: Trust, Faith and Hope

Higher Self: Do you trust me?

Ego: I guess I do.

Higher Self: Do you have faith in me?

Ego: Since I trust you I guess I have faith in you.

Higher Self: Why?

Ego: Your advice seems pretty reasonable. I believe you are trying to help me.

Higher Self: You still do not perceive yourself to be me, do you?

Ego: Not yet, but I'm open to the possibility.

Higher Self: How much do you trust yourself or have faith in yourself?

Ego: I was going to say that I trust myself completely, but when you ask if I have faith in myself I'm no longer so confident.

Higher Self: Why is that?

Ego: I don't know. It's a bit unsettling now that I think about it more.

Higher Self: How does it make you feel?

Ego: Like I'm on shaky ground, a little anxious.

Higher Self: What are you afraid of?

Ego: I'm fearful that I may not have what it takes to deal with everything that life can throw at me.

Higher Self: You certainly seem a little unsettled.

Ego: Yes, that's how I feel. If you are me, are you feeling that way too?

Higher Self: I can sense what you are feeling, but I do not feel as you do.

Ego: How are you feeling?

Higher Self: I feel quite excellent.

Ego: Why don't I feel that way?

Higher Self: You do not have faith that everything will work out just fine.

Ego: I guess I don't.

Higher Self: Why not?

Ego: Everything hasn't always worked out for me. Why should I trust that it will in the future?

Higher Self: What are you referring to?

Ego: My project hasn't worked out and I continue to bleed cash. At this rate I'll be broke in a year.

Higher Self: Maybe that is the plan.

Ego: That doesn't sound very encouraging, nor do I like that plan. Why should I feel trusting about my future if that is the outcome?

Higher Self: People file bankruptcy every day. Maybe that would help you in achieving your goal.

Ego: My goal has never been to file bankruptcy or not be able to support myself and my family. If I run out of money then I can't finish the project I'm working on and I always thought that was part of my plan.

Higher Self: I thought your highest goal was to know what is true and to experience what you truly are. Is that not so?

Ego: Yes that is true, but do I have to be poor in the process?

Higher Self: There is a famous passage in the Bible that addresses that point. It is easier for a camel to go through the eye of a needle, than for a rich man to enter into the kingdom of God.

Ego: I don't know much about the Bible, but I've heard that saying. I thought it has more to do with going to heaven after a person dies.

Higher Self: Your goal of knowing what you truly are is experiencing yourself as a spiritual being. Entering the kingdom of God is simply experiencing one's self as a spiritual being. There is no difference in experiencing that in life or after life as a spiritual being never truly dies.

Ego: So are you saying that in order for me to experience what I truly am I must be broke?

Higher Self: Not at all.

Ego: But you're saying that I would have as much of a chance of experiencing what I truly am as a camel passing through the eye of a needle.

Higher Self: You are no longer rich.

Ego: Oh, that's right.

Higher Self: But you may become rich again.

Ego: So maybe I will experience what I truly am in this window of time before I become rich again.

Higher Self: Maybe the saying really has less to do with being rich and more to do with becoming preoccupied with and trusting in riches.

Ego: As opposed to what?

Higher Self: As opposed to being focused on the goals you espouse. Do you believe that people who are spiritual, charitable and giving of themselves, who also happen to be wealthy, but are not focused on that wealth would be excluded from the kingdom of God?

Ego: That doesn't make much sense.

Higher Self: You need not worry.

Ego: Because I'm not rich?

Higher Self: Because that is not your focus.

Ego: But I am concerned.

Higher Self: Despite your concerns you have continued on your path. Your actions have demonstrated your intentions.

Ego: Yes, but I have doubts. My trust is waning.

Higher Self: Just as it did right before the football players began wearing Breathe Right strips, although you are less anxious at this time.

Ego: I'm still hoping that everything will work out.

Higher Self: Hope is a limited version of trust. It will not alleviate your uncertainty.

Ego: I wish I could experience trust more rather than just hope. How is it that you can trust, while I can only hope? Do you know the future?

Higher Self: Your future is not set in stone. I trust because I have no fear and I have faith that everything will work out as it needs to.

Ego: You don't have fear because you don't have to pay any bills. You're not worried about putting food on the table or a roof over your head.

Higher Self: Those difficulties have never happened to you in this life.

Ego: But it could. It happens to many people so it could happen to me.

Higher Self: Yes, it could. However opportunities have been presented to you in the past and will again in the future.

Ego: I just want to be able to pursue my path without having to worry about money.

Higher Self: You are pursuing your path.

Ego: But I am concerned about money.

Higher Self: You learned that from your mother.

Ego: Don't I know it! She was always preoccupied with money. She was a child during the great depression and she saw what it meant to be without.

Higher Self: She exposed you to those fears and you allowed them to become your fears. Despite those fears you have persisted in your efforts.

Ego: Still, it would be nice to have the level of trust that you seem to have.

Higher Self: When you are in your sessions you have no fear.

Ego: Yes, that's true. I have absolutely no fear and much less fear or none throughout the day after a session.

Higher Self: You also appear to have greater trust.

Ego: More than I have at this moment, but not as much as you seem to have.

Higher Self: I am sure you understand why you do not experience trust as I do.

Ego: I assume it's because I don't experience myself as you.

Higher Self: That plus the egoic fears you have adopted in life create doubt.

Ego: Still, I would feel better if I trusted more.

Higher Self: Well then…

Ego: Well then what?

Higher Self: Keep pursuing your goals.

Ego: Can't I develop more trust in advance of experiencing what I truly am?

Higher Self: The more you can experience what I am, the more trust you will have. The more you identify with your egoic beliefs and conditioning the less trust you will have. That is why when you are ego-identified you work so hard and focus on achieving material success. You are attempting to overcome your fears through the accumulation of riches. When you are ego-identified in that way and have enough wealth to lessen your fears, you are no longer motivated to seek greater trust.

Ego: So I can deal with my fears by either developing greater trust like you or generating wealth, like I typically do.

Higher Self: Or both. There is no reason that those with trust cannot have wealth, however those with greater trust do not feel the need for wealth.

Ego: And those with wealth do not feel the need for trust.

Higher Self: That is typically correct in regards to material wealth, but they may have other reasons to cultivate trust.

Ego: People don't know how to cultivate trust very well.

Higher Self: Trust is usually gained through life's experiences. People typically learn to trust. There are many people who seek assistance in this matter in a different manner.

Ego: How so?

Higher Self: They practice faith. They appeal to a higher power.

Ego: Does it work?

Higher Self: It works for those that are more comfortable developing strong faith.

Ego: How?

Higher Self: They have faith that a higher power will see to it that everything will work out as it needs to.

Ego: That sounds a lot like trust.

Higher Self: Faith is more of a felt sense at a deeper level. That is where I reside. Trust is a by-product of faith.

Ego: I feel more comfortable with trust.

Higher Self: You have already admitted that you do not trust all that much. Maybe you should consider manifesting greater faith.

Ego: To me faith feels like religion. I never liked Hebrew school. I don't want to have to follow a bunch of dogmatic beliefs.

Higher Self: You can choose to believe what you wish or not be observant of any religious practices other than faith in a higher power. You do believe in a higher power, right?

Ego: Yes I do.

Higher Self: Then you have a means of cultivating greater trust without the need to believe in other rules or observances.

Ego: I'm not sure about all of this. I feel as if you're somehow tricking me.

Higher Self: You can choose to think and believe as you wish. It is you that has a desire to experience greater trust. Alternatively, you can stick with hope.

Ego: I already have hope, but that doesn't do that much for me.

Higher Self: You still worry and suffer. Hope is not the antidote for suffering.

Ego: And trust is?

Higher Self: Yes, particularly when it is derived from faith.

Ego: I agree that it would likely be helpful to do something along these lines, but exactly what I'm not sure.

Higher Self: It will come to you.

Ego: I hope so.

Considerations

Hardship reveals our level of trust and faith. Many people feel that when hardships arise, their level of trust and faith is being tested. A simpler approach is to just ask yourself, "How much do you trust or have faith that everything will work out just fine?" How do you measure your response?

Ask yourself:

1. How much do you trust or have faith that everything will work out just fine? Are you searching in your mind for an answer or are you trying to feel a response in your body? What does your mind say? What are you feeling in your body?

2. Consider your last hardship. How trusting were you when it arose? Did your level of trust and faith help you through the event? Do you believe that your level of trust and faith played a role in the outcome?

3. Do you believe that your level of trust and faith are being tested during periods of hardship? Why do or don't you believe this?

4. How much do you trust yourself? How much do you have faith in yourself?

5. Do you have faith in a higher power? How do you exercise that faith?

6. What can you do to have more trust in yourself?

Part III – My Story Continued

Chapter 27: Early Exploration

Working with Frank during those first two and half years was one of the most fascinating periods of my life. He was able to move out-of-body at will when using our technology and for the most part had willful control while out-of-body to move about as he desired. Of course the genie that he operated had its own set of rules so Frank didn't have absolute control.

I'm sure some of my scientific colleagues would have preferred if Frank had been subjected to a series of experiments to prove that he actually was doing what he claimed, but I didn't feel the need. By then I had already come in contact with a number of people who had similar capabilities and there are many books that contain similar stories. I didn't feel that any proof was necessary, as I was not trying to convince anyone of anything. We were simply exploring and trying to understand the phenomenology and meaning of what we were encountering.

For some time we explored the phenomenon of past lives. However in a domain where time doesn't exist, referring to these presumed other lives as having occurred in the past only reinforced our lack of understanding. Nonetheless it was entertaining to have Frank witness these lives and report back. He tended to visit lives in which all or most of us present in session were alive. He would tell us who we were and how we were related to one another. From Frank's reports it certainly seems as though we return in groups adding a small measure of support to the concept of soul groups.

For the most part, past life investigation for us was entertainment. Our egos were always hoping that we were someone of significance and praying that we had not committed some egregious crime with a big karmic debt to repay, assuming such a system is actually in play. During those days we didn't come across anything of a practical nature that could help us in the here and now.

However later, I experienced that certain past life events can have an impact in our current life and explain some of our otherwise unexplainable psychological tendencies and possibly more.

In an out-of-body state Frank could perceive what has been termed soul color. Michael Newton, Ph.D. has written two books describing what happens to us upon death and what we do in between lives. His books were derived from many case studies during which he was able to induce a hypnotic trance sufficiently deep and stable such that the client was able to recall such information. The consistency across cases was reported to be quite good. In the process of synthesizing his information he also developed a chart of soul colors corresponding to a soul's level of evolution or advancement.

Again, we found that our interest in soul color was ego-based and not particularly helpful in this life. However Dr. Newton's books *Journey of Souls* and *Destiny of Souls* are must reads if you enjoy reading about this topic. Or if you have a significant fear of death or a fear of the hereafter and reading can soothe your fears then these books may be of great benefit to you. Alternatively there are a growing number of psychologists who can actually assist you in experiencing these phenomena during a hypnotic past life regression session.

Frank also had the ability to perceive our energy systems. At the time I had only some rudimentary understanding of chakras and auric bodies. Frank could see the size, shape and color of our chakras and how fast they were spinning. As our technology matured and our energy systems transformed these and other observations became increasingly more informative. Later we were able to see the effects of our technology on how our energy system manifested or expressed itself and correlate those changes with how we were experiencing life.

189

Early in our work together I desperately wanted to be able to experience what Frank could do. Nothing I tried worked. I was glued to my body with the gravity of a black hole. That little light of mine was never going to escape as best I could tell. At one point Frank asked my energetic self why that was. The response was that he and I represented opposite ends of the spectrum.

He was able to move his conscious awareness outside of himself by taking much of his energetic self with him and explore. At some point in the future I would be able to perceive everything by expanding my conscious awareness from within, but stay put. I didn't understand what that really meant, but at least I felt better about my failed attempts to be like Frank and I stopped trying.

We didn't call what we were doing meditation. Meditation conjured up past memories of a head-centered practice trying not to think, sitting in a lotus position with a straight posture and repeating a mantra in silence. Our technique was considerably different and focused on the body as a whole. It was an exercise in feeling and not thinking. We were lying down and positioned very comfortably. We played music at normal sound levels. Over time we learned to create layered music such that multiple melodies were playing simultaneously. Furthermore, we could feel the vibrations from the music. One acquaintance called our process, lazy man's meditation. It certainly was easier and got people into the state very quickly with very little effort.

There are many different forms of meditation with different goals. As we learned more our goal became very simple. If we are indeed spiritual beings occupying a physical body, why can't we experience our spiritual nature more directly? When we started experimenting I was forty-four years old. I didn't want to go to Tibet and sit in a cave for the rest of my life to answer this question. With all of our scientific and medical developments related to our understanding of brain function there had

190

to be some clues as to how to proceed with greater efficiency and reliability. Ultimately we uncovered and used them.

I chose to explore sound and vibration because Frank and Ellen experienced an out-of-body state and I got very relaxed so there was something to this form of stimulation. But my goal was to experience my spiritual nature directly. It took me a little while to figure out how sound and vibration were beneficial and how to use those stimuli more effectively. I also thought I knew what I needed to add to it, in order to achieve my goal.

During the first several months I became increasingly more physically relaxed. Our physical bodies are in their most relaxed state during sleep. Robert Monroe had used the phrase, mind awake body asleep, to describe the state he achieved before moving out-of-body. I wanted to achieve the mind awake body asleep state too. With that intention I learned to fall asleep and then wake up mentally, yet leave my body asleep or nearly so.

As it turned out, the music and vibration produced by our technology could be used quite nicely to facilitate the development of this state through their effects on the nervous system. Embedded in the seating structure is an amplifier and transducers. Layered music from a CD or mp3 player is amplified and played through the transducers to produce the sound and vibration. We later learned how to produce a synchronized magnetic field, which further assists in this process and confers another key benefit.

Our brain is designed to detect change, as its most important function is to keep us alive and safe. Using our brain we are always, consciously and subconsciously surveying our environment for potential danger. This is how we manifest our survival instinct. We use mainly our senses of sight, hearing and touch to perform this function.

Depending upon our level of fear regarding our safety we operate at various levels of vigilance. For instance, someone who has always felt safe and secure and has a more laid-back personality has a low level of vigilance. Someone with Post Traumatic Stress Disorder, PTSD, has a very high level of vigilance.

Regardless of a person's level of vigilance, pleasant music and gentle vibrations cause areas of the brain related to hearing and touch to become habituated. These areas are in effect lulled to sleep. When areas of the brain become habituated with repetitive stimulation those areas are no longer useful at detecting change. As a result, other areas of the brain inhibit these more primary receptive areas. In addition during a session, the room is darkened and the user is instructed to close their eyes and so they receive no alerting visual stimulation either.

The user is positioned on a comfortable seating structure, covered with a blanket and instructed to fall asleep. Due to the intention to fall asleep and the habituating effects of sound and vibration with no visual stimuli, a state of sleep is greatly facilitated and easily achieved.

Neurologically however, the best way to wake someone up is by stimulating their senses of touch and hearing. Therefore we periodically change the intensity of the music and associated vibrations. After just a few sessions the user learns to be drowsy or awake with a nearly asleep body. If one becomes very proficient using this technique they are able to be consciously aware and observe their sleeping body.

Why bother? What's the point of learning to be this way? Well as it turns out, we human beings are very good at recreating states of being that we can feel as part of the experience. It's no different than a golfer or tennis player who learns the feel of a new swing. As I learned what my deeply relaxed body felt like, I was able to recreate that level of relaxation whenever I wanted by simply recalling what it felt like. When I began this work my blood pressure typically ranged between 120/80 to 130/85. I didn't like the fact that at times my blood pressure was creeping higher than I liked.

It was clear to me that my blood pressure reflected my level of stress. I was learning to control how much stress I experienced by inducing greater levels of relaxation. In the late 90's I remember going for my routine physical exam. I decided to induce a deep level of relaxation when the nurse was taking my blood pressure. It registered 106/70. I never wanted to become obsessive about such things so I have made it a point to not monitor myself, other than my own practice of mindfulness.

Chapter 28: Beyond Relaxation

Reducing my level of stress was a nice side benefit, but my goal was to experience my spiritual nature directly. Was I making any progress on that front? Not really. Something was missing. I had learned to fall asleep and then wake up with a sleeping or nearly asleep body. I was able to feel my level of deep relaxation. I also could observe that there was a difference between how I experienced myself in session and how I experienced myself in life.

In life, although I was generally calm, I always had a lot of thoughts running through my mind. I had previously learned during meditation to quiet my mind, but the state I was now in seemed different. There was a deeper stillness and peace and a profound level of relaxation. We tended to run sessions that lasted about 75 minutes, but they seemed to pass very quickly even though I was seemingly awake and alert.

During the next year, 1998, and for the next two years, I would occasionally experience loss of consciousness during my entire session. It would happen every session for about one week. During these sessions it was curious how my conscious awareness would reappear just before the last song began to play. It was as if a switch had been thrown. One second I was gone and the next I was completely alert. The experience was nothing like awakening from sleep. After these weeks, which tended to occur about every three or four months my sessions seemed different. I had the feeling that I was gradually being transformed.

As pleasant as my sessions were, they did not measure up to my expectations. I wanted to have spiritual experiences that were real to me. I wanted to see, hear or feel something that registered with me in a way that signified it was real. I had been tinkering with wire coils and signal generators in my attempt to integrate magnetic fields into the mix. My reasoning led me to believe that using magnetic stimulation would allow me to directly stimulate my energy system, which I equated with my spiritual self.

My rationale seemed relatively straightforward. Our brain is an electro-chemical organ. Chemical changes create synaptic potentials. These synaptic potentials are electrical in nature and account for what we see in an electroencephalogram, EEG. If we choose we can make the same measurement using a magneto-encephalograph. The only difference is that magnetic and electric fields are ninety degrees out of phase with each other. Otherwise they convey the same information. In truth the brain generates an electromagnetic field because you can't have one without the other, which is why this form of energy is referred to as electromagnetism.

Is it a two-way street? Can the brain with its electromagnetic field also receive information, directly or indirectly, via electromagnetic interaction or some form of energy that can interact with electromagnetism or directly with the brain? In my way of thinking the answer was yes. I felt that our inner dialogue results from this interaction between our spiritual self as an energy field and our physical brain.

Also people that experience out-of-body phenomenon realize that their consciousness or awareness is located where their energy resides and not where their brain is. Their sense of self and mind is tied to their energy field and not to their brain. Frank realized he was up at the ceiling, not lying on the platform. If this scenario is true then clearly our energy field does interact with the matter of our brain, either directly or with the electromagnetic field that the brain creates.

During my sessions I was now experiencing this aspect of mind. Although I remained local to my body, my sense of mind and self was expanded beyond the confines of my body. Experiencing this level of mind was different than the mind I was used to. My waking mind was filtered through my ego. Since the ego primarily results from my beliefs and conditioning it is really nothing more than a function of the brain. I had learned to be mind-awake, body-asleep and so in effect since the ego is a function of the brain, in this state of being it had been put to sleep. As a result I was experiencing my higher mind during my sessions and it was bigger than my body.

Some people refer to the egoic mind as our lower mind. The brain it appears is where the interaction between higher and lower mind takes place. This could account for our inner dialogue. It also could explain the thought transmission from our higher self to our filtered self, as occurred with my Breathe Right vision for example. With this as my hypothesis, it made sense that magnetic stimulation should be able to directly stimulate our higher mind or whatever we choose to call it. The higher mind is referred to as higher self, spiritual self, soul and has other names as well.

My tinkering in the realm of magnetic stimulation of our higher self in the late 90's was amateurish at best. I didn't know where to apply the stimulation or what intensity to use. I didn't know if it made sense to use discrete frequencies or specific ranges. After a while I realized my efforts were fruitless and futile. I looked up and asked for help. I soon learned that help can take many forms.

Chapter 29: Help Arrives

It was Monday, April 5, 1999. Frank called and asked, "Can you come earlier this afternoon? I have some people I would like you to meet. We can all do a session at 3pm."

I arrived about 2:45pm to set up the equipment. About five minutes before they came, while standing in the middle of our sound-proofed room I heard a voice to my left. It simply said, "Hello." It was so clear and audible that I was startled. I turned knowing full well that no one was with me in the room. I then heard, "You're about to meet your next wife."

This was nothing like my internal dialogue or any experience that I could remember. The voice registered in my mind as though it was spoken by an actual person. I was not only startled by the event, but also by the implications. I was married with four children. I wasn't in the market for a second wife. All I could do was sit down and replay what had just happened. Before I could make any sense of the occurrence I was about to have another new experience.

The two sets of doors connecting the outer room with our inner sound-proofed room opened. Frank introduced me to Jennifer. All I could see were her green eyes. Every other detail of her face and the rest of the room faded from view. I was completely spellbound for what seemed like minutes, although I'm sure it lasted only a second or two. I recognized her immediately, but I had never met her.

Receiving that message and connecting with another person in such a surreal manner left me speechless. So was she. She had received the same message before entering the room. We tried to make small talk, but didn't have anything meaningful to say to one another, but we both knew we would.

This episode rocked my world much more than even the Breathe Right vision. With every cell in my body

I knew without question that it was necessary to act on the information I had just received. I knew Jennifer was going to become my next wife.

It has always been my belief that spiritual forces are regularly attempting to communicate with us. We either receive thoughts that may or may not register in our conscious awareness or signs appear in the form of happenstances that we may not recognize or wish to acknowledge. We also often receive messages in the form of dreams.

This episode, like the Breathe Right vision was not one of those subtle signs or communications, nor was it a dream. It was even more impactful than the Breathe Right vision in regards to its effects on me. It was as if a higher power was telling me in the clearest possible way that this is my path and I had better follow it. The lightning bolt sensation that electrified me from head to toe when I saw Jennifer punctuated the importance of this message. The message was not to be taken lightly.

But what it was asking of me was in another sense horrific. I felt sick to my stomach and was distraught about the effects it would have on Ellen and our kids. Why did it have to be this way? The message was so clear, short and to the point that it wasn't a matter of it being misinterpreted. I heard it as clearly as if it were a bomb going off next to my ear, which it was.

Nobody but Jennifer would understand. My actions up until this point in my life had always been explainable even when unconventional. I decided that using this message to explain my actions was not the way to proceed. It was insanity. I wasn't a prophet. However in this instance I had complete faith in the message's intent and meaning.

For the next fifty days, before Ellen and I decided to separate, I experienced terrible angst. I had been raised by my mother to never hurt another person. Ready or not it was time for my heart to begin its opening process and for me to feel the kind of pain I would have wished to avoid at all costs. I could not avoid this situation because I could not disobey the message. Yet I did not wish to experience this level of pain and guilt. I would only allow myself to feel it in brief waves and then I would shut it down and retreat into my head.

During these early days I was only beginning to understand why my path was taking such an abrupt turn. I had always been on the lookout for psychically gifted individuals. I had been exposed to some of these individuals during my adolescence. My earlier experiences left me with mixed feelings. Clearly these folks or at least the ones with real capabilities were tapping into something special and seemingly otherworldly. However, their lives seemed to be rather chaotic, complicated by health or personal issues. My sample size was very small and so I realized that I shouldn't draw any firm conclusions, but it did leave me with a less than clear sense about these folks.

Jennifer was psychically gifted from birth. She was able to see, hear and feel aspects of our energy system that I had never read about or even heard of. The spirit realm was as easy for her to perceive as it was for me to see the living. In fact her entire sense of reality was 180 degrees out of synch with mine and most people's sense of reality.

Yet, just like everyone else she had to learn how to navigate in the material world. This was confusing for her as a child. She could readily perceive and communicate with a person's filtered persona and unfiltered self simultaneously. She quickly learned that almost everyone is outwardly lying much of the time. The unfiltered or authentic person would communicate one thing to her, while the filtered persona would very often communicate or act in a contradictory, less genuine manner. She learned that she couldn't completely trust the filtered persona, which is all that most of us have to deal with.

She perceived the unfiltered self as a transparency superimposed on the material, filtered individual. I only believed that everyone was split-minded. She had known and experienced it since early childhood. During her whole life she had been able to witness and study how the higher and lower minds actually operate. If only our psychiatrists, psychologists and counsellors could operate in this manner. If only all of us could perceive ourselves and each other in this manner. The world would clearly be different.

Growing up her mother was intolerant of talk about spiritual entities. The only adult in her childhood that could offer confirmation of this realm was her maternal grandmother, Myrtle. When Jennifer was about four or five years old Myrtle confided in her that she saw them too. By the time she was attending grade school, teasing from the other children and her siblings caused her to remain quiet about such things. Those wounds produced lasting effects that still linger.

At different times in her childhood and adolescence she shut down, becoming less receptive to the spiritual realm. However, from the time she was a young adult until the time I met her when she was forty-three years old, she had spent many years meditating and refining her gifts. As part of her own survival or adaptive skill set she also became a student of how and why people operate as they do as well as becoming very adept at her own mindfulness practices. Spiritual beings of great experience were almost always available to her for consultation, even as a child. They provided reassurance and were a vital source of knowledge. She could trust these entities completely, more than other living humans.

For more than two decades beginning in 1980 she engaged in various healing practices and psychic consultations with clients. She preferred to help people understand their current health and psychological issues, but grew tired of the work over time.

When we met she was separated from her husband, although they were living in the same house with their two daughters. She was definitely not looking to enter into another relationship. Even if she was, it would certainly not have been with a doctor. She viewed doctors as being too head-centered, analytic and closed-minded. After our meeting she felt some internal resistance, but a big hand on her back kept pushing her forward. She quickly reached the point when she knew there was no path other than to move forward, together.

Chapter 30: Changing Relationships

Ninety days after we met Jen and I and her youngest daughter moved into a small townhome that we rented. It was about a mile away from Ellen and my kids. My two youngest, Michael and Whitney who were sixteen and fourteen at the time helped us move, as did Jen's daughters. They all wanted to be a part of the process. Although their help was welcome, the pain of their participation for me was substantial. Ever since childhood I had been very well practiced at hiding and stuffing my emotions. By this time in my life I was no longer able to stuff them as easily, but I could still mask them.

For a number of years I went to Ellen's home three times during the week to visit the kids and exercise using the equipment we had purchased. Whitney and I had lunch dates most Saturdays. David was in college and Jason, the eldest was out and about. We also had Sunday night dinner together for years. Most people considered our ongoing relationship to be quite strange, however when they took a little time to consider it, many of them thought it was a nice way to proceed. Ellen and I continued to work together as partners in Round River Research and did our morning group sessions together.

The process of moving apart, while maintaining a close family and working relationship was awkward and uncomfortable some of the time. We all did the best we could and we continue to do the best we can. Even after fifteen years our work in this regard is not finished, but every day it gets better and the discomfort of the past usually remains in the past. For most couples and families, separation and divorce creates a definitive split and the parties go their separate ways. That's how the game of life is typically played from the perspective of one's ego, but in truth we really never separate from one another. Why should we pretend to?

Early in my new relationship with Jennifer it was clear that this wasn't going to be a typical boy meets girl relationship. Obviously we weren't kids anymore, but as Jen said soon after we met, "This relationship was going to unfold at the soul level."

I was clearly at a disadvantage. My experiment with Frank had already demonstrated that. I felt as if I was the third party in a relationship built for two. She had no difficulty communicating with my higher self, while I was left in the dark. This was weird. Fortunately she had a lifetime of experience in this matter, but I had none. It was her job to manage this situation since I was so ill equipped.

I had learned in business what it's like to be a good manager. A really good manager works with people in a way to bolster their confidence in themselves so that they can achieve goals they never thought possible. In the process they become more successful, accountable and happy. This is all very achievable provided the person being managed is not too willful.

Managing a person that is willful, meaning they have a strong ego, makes the manager's job much harder. There's less of a need to bolster the person's confidence. Instead the manager needs to give them free reign and be there for them to provide advice and support when needed and most importantly, allow them to fail. Given my strength of ego, Jen needed to stand by and let me fail.

She also needed to correct a number of misconceptions I had. I had always thought that a person's higher or spiritual self was gentle, compassionate and loving. Clearly I had bought into the demon versus angel scenario, which apparently is far from the truth. Jennifer would look at me when I would voice these types of misconceptions as if I was a visitor from Pluto.

Most people have a fundamental flaw in their perceptions of others. Jen was no exception. When they have a strong innate capability they often assume that other people are similarly endowed. I would remind Jen that she was the different one and teasingly say, "Yes everyone I know also sees and converses with all the dead people around us." After fifteen years she is starting to get it. Everyone's ego causes this kind of issue because deep down we don't realize or refuse to acknowledge that each one of us is special in some different way.

As it turns out, a person's higher self has what most of us would refer to as personality. It isn't all airy fairy and blissful. According to Jen, my higher self has a more willful nature. As I became more successful in the material world my ego or lower mind became more self-assured and willful too. I couldn't easily discern the difference between the two except during my sessions, but Jen had absolutely no difficulty. She learned pretty quickly how to manage me and I learned how it felt to be managed.

To an outside observer Jen tended to appear fairly passive, but in reality she was incredibly discerning and decisive. She intervened and offered advice only when necessary and usually in the form of gentle suggestions. However, on rare occasions she would be more forceful.

Up until 2006 we were mainly dabbling at Round River Research. We were still experimenting in sessions using mainly commercial equipment. CNS was in the process of being sold. We didn't yet have the funds to heavily invest in the research and development that would be required to test our hypothesis concerning the ability to directly stimulate the human energy system.

Several years earlier when it was clear that a sale of CNS would result in having sufficient funds, I flippantly remarked, "I'm not sure I want to seriously pursue this idea."

Jen and I had both been standing during this conversation. She immediately positioned herself directly in front of me, looked me square in the eyes and firmly stated with a resolve I was unaccustomed to, "You may want to rethink that decision." We had been together for seven years by that time. She wasn't at all asking me to rethink that decision. This was her way of informing me what she wasn't allowed to tell me directly; that I had better pursue this project. It was important.

Although Jen has access to information that I would love to know, she is also told what she can and cannot share with me. There have been many, many times when in response to an inquiry; I've heard her tell me, "They told me not to tell you." It has a lot to do with how we walk our path in life. It is rarely a straight line.

We tend to meander quite a bit, picking up different information and skills along the road of life that will be needed at some future date. If our ego knew the intended destination, it would likely plot a straight line causing us to miss the experiences that we will need or cause us to arrive at a key decision point at an inopportune time. Although our egos don't like to hear this, based upon my experiences, I believe we are all being managed by spiritual forces in one form or another. Apparently I needed more help than most and so Jennifer was sent to assist.

It became apparent soon after Jen and I got together, that I had an awful lot to learn. Between the two of us, I far outdistanced her regarding degrees, certifications and material successes. I wasn't boastful, but I was proud of my accomplishments. I was my mother's son and I worked hard to achieve these things that society considers important. Yet I would have traded them in a heartbeat for what she had.

As newborns we are fully open and receptive to the spiritual realm. As such, little babies are essentially enlightened beings. Over time, they integrate with their physical body and lower mind, form beliefs, develop fears and coping strategies and learn to exert control to obtain what they want. The ego develops, grows, morphs somewhat and remains with us throughout life. The ego isn't a bad construct. It is the workings of the brain and its function is to assist us in being safe and secure so that we can survive in physical form. Our ego is a judgment machine designed to make choices that keep us alive. It has its purpose and there is no reason to demean it.

Children transition from enlightened babyhood to early childhood during which they may retain an openness or receptivity to the spiritual realm until later childhood when they typically become less receptive. As their ego grows and they conform or don't conform to familial and societal norms, their spiritual awareness becomes progressively masked. They have grown away from enlightenment and have forgotten what they are. They begin to self-identify with their egoic beliefs, but as they do they may create some unusual transitions.

When my son Michael was about three years old he had an imaginary friend by the name of Max Lee. As Michael was dealing with power issues during that year Max Lee morphed into Max Cleo. Max Cleo was ninety-four years old, so in Michael's eyes he was senior to me. If I did something that Michael disagreed with he would inform me that Max Cleo was going to punch me in the stomach. As Michael resolved his issues Max Cleo transitioned to Poly Eagle who was a more reasonable soul. Soon thereafter Poly Eagle took flight, never to return.

As a baby I was the consummate daydreamer. I don't remember those days, but my mother would tell me stories about how I would simply sit and look around in the playpen. She became so disturbed by my immobility and seeming lack of interest in the world around me that she removed some of the playpen's bars in the hope that I would take notice and escape. I simply sat and smiled. I can only imagine what I perceived. I remained in that state for some time and only began to walk at the age of seventeen months. I was probably reluctant to join the so called real world.

Imagine what we would be like if we never lost our awareness of that spiritual connection or state of being. What would we be like if we could grow up and become adults and still retain our spiritual awareness? Welcome to Jennifer's world. That was the world I wanted to become reacquainted with. That had been my goal. Jennifer's appearance in my life wasn't a response to my plea for help in regards to the parameters of magnetic field stimulation. My needs were much more pervasive. Also to a lesser degree in my opinion, I was of some assistance in fulfilling some of her needs. Relationships after all, are two-way streets.

Chapter 31: Claim Your Basic Rights

Although I continued to tinker with our technology between 1999 and 2006, I spent even more time learning some of what Jennifer had to teach. The knowledge she had gleaned from 40 years of simultaneously observing the filtered persona and unfiltered self was very impressive. My knowledge gained from my limited study of psychology and psychiatry and all of my medical and neurologic studies and extracurricular reading paled in comparison.

She had developed a system that linked a person's Basic Rights as defined psychologically and spiritually with aspects of the human energy system. Jennifer recognized my limitations and as a result she had a tendency to simplify the human energy system for me. We worked with the ten chakra system and she avoided many of the additional energetic structures at that time.

Each Basic Right was correlated to a specific chakra. This was very helpful for me and others like me who couldn't perceive the human energy system. Her Basic Right system had sufficient depth to allow a person to perform a very complete psychological and spiritual inventory for themselves without the need to have her perceptual gifts.

For instance the first Basic Right associated with the root chakra at the base of the spine is defined as the right to exist as a human being in the physical world. Each right is further detailed by its elements. There are six elements for the first Basic Right. They are: 1) accept and respect yourself, 2) be grounded in the physical, 3) feel safe and secure, 4) meet your material needs in a reasonable manner, 5) operate with healthy boundaries and 6) feel vital, participate in physical activities and nurture yourself.

The ten Basic Rights are hierarchical just like the chakras. More fundamental rights are the building blocks for higher rights. Deficiencies in claiming and maintaining our early rights create issues that make it difficult to fully manifest our higher rights. The first three Basic Rights pertain mainly to our egoic functioning. Basic Rights four through seven pertain to our higher self and Rights eight through ten are transpersonal in nature. The ten Basic Rights are:

1. The right to exist as a human being in the physical world.
2. The right to experience physical sensations and to feel and express emotional and intuitive feelings.
3. The right to think, choose, and create beliefs about yourself and the world around you.
4. The right to bring love into the world, to accept it for yourself, and to give it to others.
5. The right to have personal truths and to test those truths for Truth.
6. The right to envision the purpose of your love in the world.
7. The right to know and manifest your soul's wisdom.
8. The right to accept yourself beyond space and time.
9. The right to accept yourself as part of an evolving greater whole.
10. The right to spiritualize matter and manifest the higher purpose of humanity.

After developing and teaching course work around these rights with mindfulness practices, the 9-box flow chart and exercises we authored two books covering the first seven Basic Rights. They both are entitled, *Claim Your Basic Rights.*

Before meeting Jennifer I had read about chakras and how several authors interpreted them, but I was not well versed in other aspects of the human energy system. All of our chakras emanate from the central spirit line or Hara line that runs vertically through the body in front of the spine and extends infinitely above and below. This structure represents our Source of life and bridges the spiritual and physical.

Meaningful spiritual practices aim to unmask this energy allowing for its fuller expression in the material realm. Authentic spiritual awakening results from a much fuller expression and integration of this deeper energetic structure in conjunction with a personal realization of what we truly are.

Jennifer offered to instruct me in ways to develop more of my perceptive skills psychically, but I declined. It seemed like too steep a hill for me to climb. I wasn't prepared to learn more esoteric information about auric bodies and their portals to different dimensions, additional energy vortices and other energetic structures that relate to our physical existence. It was not that I didn't believe in their existence. It was more about my desire to experience at least the basics before moving on to further frontiers.

I figured that if I simply progressed spiritually, whatever psychic skills I needed would develop in due course. In truth, although I would have loved to have developed greater abilities along these lines I wasn't prepared to do the extra work. What she offered to teach me was in fact more spiritually based rather than just enhancing my perceptive skills, but I was already overwhelmed.

It was as if she was offering a course in advanced theoretical mathematics and I needed a course in remedial algebra. Very often it was difficult for us to communicate. Her level of know-how was so sophisticated and natural to her that she was often unable to realize my knowledge and perceptual gaps. It became abundantly clear why she needed to be my wife. We loved one another and lived life as man and wife in all respects. However, at the same time, I felt like a student 24/7. There was a lot to learn and much of my learning was provided by example, through life's experience and Jennifer's guidance.

It also became clear that it was my job to distill the information she knew down to a usable form. Although we were developing technology to facilitate spiritual transformation, the information and know-how that she had was an invaluable accompaniment to accelerate the process. During these years it became painfully obvious that one of my biggest hurdles in my own development process was the need to enhance my feeling nature. I needed to work on Basic Rights two, four and six.

Chapter 32: Detour

Our path in life rarely proceeds in a straight line and mine was no exception. By the end of 2006 I wasn't sure what direction I was heading. CNS was sold. The technology we were working on at Round River remained in a relatively unrefined state, although we had an idea as to how to take it to the next level. The big question was; if we could take it to the next level, what exactly would we do with it?

From the beginning this project was a hobby. It was for our own development. We didn't consider this to be the start of a new business venture. If we committed significant funds to the project at this time, that would change. Our indecision arose from several disparate lines of thought.

On the one hand we saw some medical results that were compelling. We had an excellent tool for inducing profound states of relaxation. This meant that it was an easy to use therapeutic modality to counteract stress. We had also seen some people have improvement in their medical conditions that seemed unrelated to stress, which was frankly both puzzling and intriguing. What else could this technology do, especially if we were able to refine it further?

Despite our successes, I wasn't convinced that the technology we had at that time was sufficiently potent to be a breakthrough therapeutic tool. That was one reason I wanted to develop it further.

The other big issue with exploring this as a medical device was that it would cost a significant amount of money to do all of the clinical tests necessary to gain claims from the FDA. That would likely require more money than we had.

We started this venture with the idea of enhancing our meditative practice and also to facilitate direct spiritual experience. If we were able to improve the technology and accomplish these goals, was there a market for a device with these meditative or spiritual benefits? I didn't think so, however I wanted to move the technology forward for our own development, but at what cost?

In essence I wanted to take the technology to another level, but there wasn't a clear enough business case to justify millions of dollars of investment. The brief interchange that I had with Jennifer years earlier, when she said, "You may want to rethink that decision," in response to my statement about not moving forward with the project, was the difference maker. Deep within I knew that was the path to take, but I was at a total loss as to the path's destination.

What I didn't know was how long and troubling a path it was going to be. Having gone through long years of schooling and training and CNS, a business venture that lasted twenty-four years, I was accustomed to delayed gratification. But with age and fewer career years ahead of me than behind me, delayed gratification was less appealing and for that matter, less practically doable. If my ego understood the pain associated with this path, I don't know for sure that I would have opted for it, despite Jennifer's encouragement. I guess that's why she frequently said, "They told me not to tell you."

"Thanks a lot," said my ego, while my higher self was smiling and nodding in the affirmative.

I had been happy during the past seven years working on the *Claim Your Basic Rights* books one and two and related course work. We had taught courses using our material and people enjoyed and benefited from their participation. Working on this material and using it to assist others was helping me in my own development.

I was unearthing lots of subconscious beliefs that I considered excess baggage. During my sessions I occasionally experienced releases that I assumed were the energetic equivalents of these old and useless thought-forms. I was learning how to feel much more as well in the process. I was also learning a lot more about the human energy system from Jennifer, but not necessarily putting it into full practice.

The other reason that created some resistance to moving forward with the project was that I tended to operate in a very binary manner. It was easy for me to pursue my own spiritual development when I didn't have any business concerns to occupy my mind. I knew that if I had to flip back into a business mode I would move straight into my head-centric way of being, which would stall my development. It doesn't need to be this way, but I had a strong tendency to operate in this manner and to focus on just one thing at a time.

By early 2007 we were deep into our project and I was back in my head. We were working with two engineering firms and a separate mechanical engineer with an in-house support staff. Our goal was to develop a very sophisticated computerized amplifier, which would give us great sound capability and flexibility, but also allow for us to develop a number of different algorithms to manipulate the sound signals for research purposes. We were also designing our own sound transducers, which would provide for synchronized sound, vibration and magnetic fields.

To complicate the project even more, we decided to embark on developing our own seating platform to house the technology. We had learned that trying to retrofit existing furniture with our technology dramatically diminished the effects, so it was necessary to design the furniture around the technology. Years earlier I had stated that we would never design our own furniture. I've since learned to avoid the word, never.

I've always enjoyed technical challenges. As it turned out this was the project of ten thousand decisions. I gave it everything I had and by the end of 2008 we had a product ready for shipment. That was when the US economy tanked.

We had developed a very high end product. Since we recognized that we would ultimately need lots of dollars for clinical research and regulatory affairs we had decided to make a multi-use product, with a major emphasis for entertainment. It provided for a significant enhancement for home theaters as high-end customers were already paying a lot for home theater seating.

Our seating was ultra-comfortable, but it had the added advantage of personal surround sound with a vibratory component. Users felt as if they were transported into the movie experience. We thought that we could build a business in this market and use the profits to fund medical research. Unfortunately the home theater business stalled after the market crash of 2008 and we couldn't gain a foothold in that market.

My binary way of being seemed to be my undoing. I had thrown myself into this project with the full force of my personal will. My ego was completely engaged. I was so focused on achieving success in this arena that I stopped using our technology for daily sessions.

In hindsight I find it hard to believe how thick my blinders must have been to not allow me to see what I was doing to myself. It also didn't help that the entertainment application was entirely unrelated to why we created the technology in the first place. I was using the technology more for watching movies than for my own spiritual development.

After selling CNS in late 2006 I had set a personal limit to the financial investment that I would commit to this project in order to retain a certain level of funds. After the market crash of 2008 and the losses I incurred, I had abruptly reached that level. But I couldn't stop. My egoic beliefs told me to persist and that I would find a way to make it successful. I also had a tremendous fear of failure.

The weather in Minnesota around Thanksgiving is usually not conducive to taking a leisurely walk in the woods. Fifty percent of the time there is snow on the ground and the rest of the time it is usually fairly cold. Thanksgiving 2008 was an exception. We typically celebrated Thanksgiving dinner twice. The first was at our house with Jen's family around noon. We would go to Ellen's house at about 6pm.

I rarely if ever go for walks alone. I also had never abandoned dinner guests. After cleaning the dishes at our house I excused myself and went for a solitary walk in the woods. It may have helped to walk off the first of two dinners, but the walk didn't help alleviate my anxiety. I could see the sadness in Jennifer's eyes when I left and again when I returned from the walk. It was a sad look filled with compassion. She understood exactly what I was feeling.

She knew what was happening as well as what was in store. This was just the beginning. Fortunately, I remained in the dark. I really don't know how Jen could do what she did. Actually, I really do know how she did it, but it's sometimes very difficult to believe what others can do when you realize you can't possibly do the same. She understood how I felt without me having to tell her. Furthermore, she knew that it was going to get worse and yet she also knew that it was something I needed to go through.

As a result she patiently, but nervously, stood by and intervened only slightly when she thought it may be of some benefit in terms of my understanding. She sat by with full knowledge and allowed me to dig a deeper hole, psychologically and financially, understanding it was necessary.

If I were she, I would have jumped in and tried to fix the situation, which would have been a mistake. She understood the grip that my ego had on me and the only way to manage the situation was to allow me to fail and find the right path on my own, with a little guidance from her. She was managing me very well, but neither of us liked it.

216

Chapter 33: Go Home or Stay for Prom

Depression affects people differently, especially in terms of our own idiosyncratic behaviors. Little things provide meaningful clues. I used to floss my teeth at least once a day. So what did it mean when I began to skip some days? I used to avoid high fat potato chips and only have a can of Coke once a week. I used to use our technology for sessions almost every day and now I was doing it maybe once a week at most. I wouldn't have diagnosed myself as being clinically depressed from late 2008 through most of 2010, but in hindsight I was.

I don't think anyone but Jennifer would have diagnosed me as being depressed, unless I had gone to a therapist and complained of such. I just kept trying to turn the situation around. Some people define insanity as continuing to do the same thing while expecting different results. Although I kept trying different things I was experiencing the same results and I was beginning to feel the insanity of my situation.

The universe was clearly telling me that I was on the wrong path, but I wouldn't listen. My ego only knew how to keep trying and it wouldn't stop. I was totally addicted. There was absolutely no difference between me and the alcoholic who couldn't stop drinking. And just like the alcoholic, I couldn't see it.

About five years earlier I could see a similar form of depression in a fellow board member of a company on which I also served. He and I were on the compensation committee together. We had a committee meeting one afternoon at a local restaurant with the CEO of the company. This person's depressed state had a fair bit of agitation associated with it, which caused him to be more excitable than usual. Normally he was quite a lively individual with a sharp wit and a good sense of humor, but during this meeting his behavior was over the top in my opinion.

What I didn't know was that his new business venture was failing. He hadn't told anyone that his business had been financially distressed for months. My relationship with him was nonexistent other than serving on that Board of Directors together. After the meeting I phoned the CEO to see what he thought of Walt's behavior. The CEO thought that Walt was himself, but I voiced my concerns.

He agreed to call Walt's wife. I also called Walt directly. He assured me that there was nothing wrong. The pressure that Walter must have been experiencing was more than he could take. He drove out of town a week later and killed himself in his car alone on the road. He was survived by his wife and two young children.

By 2010 I had tried everything I could possibly think of to make our business successful. With every failure there was another idea. I could deem one attempt a failure on Tuesday and by Wednesday morning wake up with another idea. Implementing these ideas typically took a month or two and then we would see if they worked. When you fail time after time it becomes easy to forget that you've ever been successful. With every failure my monetary reserves diminished and I kept adjusting the level at which I would cease investing.

It was about that time that I took notice of how I was feeling physically. Something was wrong. I thought about visiting my physician, but I had stopped seeing him a few years earlier. He had given me some advice that I thought was incorrect, so I decided to not bother with him anymore. There was no shortage of other physicians in the Twin Cities, but I decided I wasn't ready to seek medical attention for any purpose other than my routine colonoscopy. I thought about Walter.

Some people have such a strong fear of death that they simply can't think about it. Since adolescence I had a strong belief in an afterlife. Furthermore I had friends who believed similarly, a close friend who could go out-of-body at will and a wife that could perceive and communicate with spirits. I didn't believe that death was anything more than a transition. From my vantage point at that time, death seemed like a nice release.

Even for those people who won't consider discussing the topic of death, the prevalence of suicide in our society is so high and so regularly in the news that it's hard not to think about it periodically. From my clinical experience I knew that there are different levels of concern about suicidal intentions. For instance a person that has figured out how they would commit suicide is more at risk than a person who only has occasional thoughts of suicide.

I hadn't thought about how I would commit suicide. In fact I never thought about killing myself. I held a belief that my life wasn't mine to take in that way. On the other hand, I had to ask myself whether not seeking medical attention for a condition that may be fatal and treatable was a form of suicide. Was not seeking help, the same as pulling the trigger?

I wasn't certain that I was ill. I just felt, mostly at an intuitive level that I was. A month of contemplation on the matter wasn't too much to ask for so I decided to ponder my situation. My first consideration was whether or not I wanted to live anymore. I had always considered this to be a question one asks oneself very late in life. Maybe this was a question I should save for thirty or forty years, but then again I could entertain the question at a future date as well. What did I want now, at the age of fifty-seven?

People die at every age, but fifty-seven seemed young to me. Jennifer had taught me several years earlier what seemed like a strange notion about dying. She said that there are several points in life when we can decide to exit, but when it is our time it is no longer our choice. Deciding to exit did not mean suicide. Although we are given a choice, the choice to exit means not to desire life anymore so that we can leave and go home as opposed to taking one's own life. It appeared to me that I had reached my first decision point.

If I decided to stay, what would be my plan? Would I go for a routine physical exam and a bunch of tests? If they found something would I choose traditional therapy? I wanted to figure out all of the steps before deciding if I wanted to live. I wanted the whole plan to make sense to me, in order to feel it was the right plan. There were also other considerations. Was I prepared to leave Jennifer behind? What about my children? Had I achieved my purpose in life? Was I simply being a coward?

Obviously a decision of this magnitude affects many people, yet this is ultimately a personal decision. I wasn't looking for input. I didn't discuss my thoughts with anyone. I didn't even discuss the matter with Jennifer until it was completely resolved. Silly me, she knew the whole time. Why was I surprised? I must have been more depressed than I realized to not have picked up on that.

In the early spring of 2010 she coaxed me into taking a walk in a nearby park. It must have been a mild winter because there was no snow on the ground and there were green leaves on the shrubs. It was a nice day with a slight breeze and lots of sun. It felt good to be out in the woods. We came upon a fork in the path. Jen asked me to choose which path to follow. I selected the one on the left. After a short while we came upon rose petals in the middle of the path, arranged on the ground in a small semi-circle. There was enough space to stand within the semi-circle. From that vantage point one could see red letters composed of rose petals at eye level pinned to the trunks of five trees surrounding the path. The letters read PROM? Some romantic young person had created a very nice prop to pose the question. It was a nice gimmick. They probably received the answer they were looking for. Maybe the question was one that I needed to answer as well.

I chose the path that presented that message. Signs are best deciphered by each individual who perceives them. I've always asked for signs that are easy to interpret. What did this mean to me? What else could it mean? Was I going to graduate and stay for the celebration?

Chapter 34: Live another Day

I could always leave tomorrow. What's the hurry? I decided to live. Some would think it was a moot decision since I didn't even know if I was sick, let alone dying. However, this is a consideration that we may want to ask ourselves regularly. Do I want to live? The answer may be a surprise. If the answer is affirmative, then the follow-on question is, why? What do I want to do or be with the rest of my life? The answer to that question may be even more revealing.

I was still convinced that I was ill. It was still just a feeling, but it was very real to me. If I had something like cancer, which is what I suspected, I didn't want chemotherapy. My mother and her three brothers died of colon cancer. That is why I continue to visit the gastroenterologist every five years. I had a benign polyp removed earlier so between that and my family history my testing regimen has been accelerated to every five rather than ten years.

It isn't necessarily rational to want to live and yet avoid chemotherapy for colon cancer. The survival rates these days are very good. If I was acting as a physician advising other people with colon cancer I would most likely advise that they go through with the chemotherapy. Since I didn't know I had colon cancer I didn't feel the need to follow what would have been my own advice. To avoid considering that advice I decided not to see a physician or have any tests performed. I didn't want to become medicalized, to think of myself as being ill.

I began eating healthier and most importantly I significantly re-energized my spiritual practice. I began doing sessions again, every day and my intention was to live and heal. I prayed and asked for help. I felt I was improving.

It wasn't long thereafter that I got a call from my gastroenterologist's office. It was time for my routine colonoscopy. I don't like the effects of anesthesia and the procedure is fairly benign so I remain fully alert and Rick talks me through the procedure as I watch the screen with him. "What the hell happened there?" he exclaimed. He was looking at a very large scar on the wall of the colon. He asked, "Were you in an accident or did you have abdominal surgery that you didn't tell me about?"

There was nothing to biopsy as whatever had been there was gone. I told him that I hadn't had surgery or any abdominal trauma. He moved on and finished the procedure without incident. The scar citing never made it into his final report. With a smile and a sense of wonder I left the room whispering, "Thanks." It is important to realize that I never knew if I was truly ill or what that scar really represented. For all I know, I could've swallowed a paper clip.

A few months later a friend of mine scheduled a lunch meeting. He confided in me that he had a terminal condition. He was on a drug that kept the condition stable, but the side effects were so severe that his dosage of the medication had to be reduced. He was concerned that due to the reduced dosage his condition would worsen. He wanted to know if our technology could possibly be of benefit.

I couldn't make any promises, but since our technology didn't appear to have any negative side effects and we never charged anyone for its use, he decided to give it a try. He came in for hour-long sessions three times a week during his lunch hour. We were hoping that it would have an effect on his underlying condition or at least allow him to relax to a greater extent. We were very surprised to find that it had an almost immediate effect in terms of dramatically reducing the side effects of his medication.

Five months later when he had his routine testing to determine the status of his underlying condition we were all delighted to find that he was better. Since his condition had been deemed terminal and since he had had it for five years, everyone involved was a reluctant to discontinue the medication, especially since he was no longer having side effects. Finally, three months later at my friend's insistence the medication was discontinued. He claimed that he wasn't willing to continue the treatment as he no longer felt he had the disease.

This incident and several others were very helpful to me. It proved to me that our technology had become more potent. Albert Schweitzer once said, "We are at our best when we allow the doctor that resides in us to work." What is that doctor that resides in us?

I was reminded of my first day in pathology in medical school. The professor stood in front of the class and said, "You are all training to become physicians. That's great, but understand this, physicians don't cure illness. Patients get better under their own power. Physicians treat them and give them the time they often need to rally from within." Obviously that professor was a fan of Albert Schweitzer.

I often complain about aspects of our medical system, but I doubt I would be alive without it. When I was thirteen and was hospitalized with bronchitis, my situation was getting pretty grave. I had lost twenty-five pounds. I was mostly skin and bones, vomiting what looked like yellow galaxies of mucous in bile stained fluid three times a day. Our family doctor was slow to take action and I had been sick in bed for three weeks. Once hospitalized, the staff cultured the mucous and placed me on intravenous fluids and the correct antibiotic. Within a few days I was getting better.

It's clear that in the US and some other countries we've over-prescribed antibiotics and have created some bacteria that are drug-resistant. But how many tens of millions of lives have been saved by them.

I complain about physicians immediately prescribing drugs to treat high blood pressure, when in many cases non-drug therapy would work. However it is important to remember that before there were drugs to treat hypertension, about twenty-five percent of hospital beds were occupied with patients with severe hypertension. Those cases often worsen, turning into what is called malignant hypertension which proves fatal. Furthermore we live in a society in which many people would rather take a pill rather than have to commit time and effort to a non-pharmacologic treatment.

We may be at our best when we allow the doctor within us to work, but putting that doctor to work requires effort and commitment. We now live in a society that considers healthcare to be a right, not a privilege. In reality, healthcare has always been a right, but don't we have a big part to play in that process?

Presently in the US we spend over seventeen percent of our gross domestic product, GDP, on healthcare. It may not be too many years before that number reaches twenty percent, which is an outrageous percentage of our GDP when considering what other developed nations spend on healthcare. Many people believe that our healthcare spending is unsustainable and that at some point our economy will not be able to support it.

More and more people are adopting self-care techniques to wean themselves from our high cost medical system. It's not rocket science to realize that preventing illness in the first place is far preferable to treating illness. Most people are smart enough to realize that they are going to die sometime, but until that time wouldn't it be great to avoid the discomfort, inconvenience and incapacity of disease?

My version of self-care is like a three-legged stool; a deep spiritual practice, healthy diet and moderate exercise. I've never been fond of what I call half-measures. Many physicians recommend meditation for their patients, but they prescribe short sessions of fifteen or twenty minutes. In my way of thinking that was like prescribing a half-strength anti-hypertensive drug. Sure, it may lower one's blood pressure a little, but not enough to derive the full benefit.

Meditation, just like drugs, is dose dependent. I'm not suggesting that everyone go to Tibet and spend the rest of their lives sitting in meditation, but an hour of meditation a day is a full measure. We've found that people claim they don't have an hour to commit to that type of practice. However we've also discovered that doing an hour session using our technology doesn't cost us any time whatsoever. Once a certain level of proficiency is gained, we've found that we need less sleep, so why not do it for an hour and reap all the benefits.

By 2011 I was beginning to move back into my right mind and doing daily sessions again. Our technology had progressed to a level of greater effect. It was time to reconsider what we had and what we were going to do with it.

Chapter 35: Stop

My renewed sense of purpose during 2011 resulted in several potential product redesigns. It was clear that we had developed a new technology that had real value. We were ready to identify the absolutely necessary componentry and figure out the best way to cost reduce the final product. Our experiential research continued as we fine-tuned certain parameters, but overall we had a very good sense of exactly what technology the product needed to have in it.

Our biggest challenge at that point was how to cost reduce the delivery platform, the seating structure itself. Fortunately we had enough experience designing and manufacturing furniture that we could create several designs and then cost them out to see if they could be manufactured at a reasonable cost.

By the fall of 2011 we had finalized all of our technology considerations and tested the technology to our liking. We had also settled on a design for the seating structure. Unfortunately in order to manufacture the seating structure several large molds were required. Patterns for the molds needed to be constructed first. We gave the approval and the process began.

We had done enough market testing to realize that there were consumers who would purchase such a device at a reasonable price point. However the claims we could make about the technology were limited and the actual target market was still fuzzy. We had made considerable progress in terms of understanding the technology and how it worked for inducing profound relaxation and to facilitate spiritual development.

We really hadn't made any significant progress however with the other business considerations pertaining to market definition, product positioning and selling channels. In those regards we weren't much further along than we had been in 2007.

One morning in early December, 2011 I woke up and realized that I didn't have a clue as to how we were going to proceed. I had done it all over again. I had proceeded on blind faith supported by the successful responses in a few interesting medical cases, which was meaningless from a practical standpoint. We couldn't afford to go down the medical route and do all of the required clinical testing. And now we were spending all of this additional money to make patterns and molds for a product we didn't know how we were going to position or sell.

That morning as I was driving to work I came to a stop at a red light. All of these thoughts were invading my brain like electro-shock therapy. I didn't have anyone to yell at other than myself, but I had berated myself enough and it didn't work. There were no other cars in sight and so I looked up and screamed out loud, "God what do you want from me?"

Immediately the answer came, "You're done."

By that time my internal dialogue was very well developed. Getting an internal response was of little surprise, but the feeling that came over me was incredibly different. In one second I had gone from a thoroughly frustrated inventor/entrepreneur who was completely invested in the outcome of this project to someone who was completely unattached. In some other-worldly manner it was as if someone had just sprinkled me with fairy dust that totally eliminated my attachment to the outcome.

All of my concerns had magically vanished. I hadn't noticed at the time that I had been stopped at a red light while travelling on Pioneer Trail. The cross street was Flying Cloud Drive. One moment I was the entrepreneur, often depicted as a pioneer lying dead on the trail with arrows in his back and now I felt as if I was floating on cloud nine.

Ten minutes later I was at work discussing the matter with Ellen. She was in total agreement. We had a

229

handful of contract employees. That day we reluctantly informed them that we were going to stop the project.

I had thought I would have experienced a sense of disappointment and feelings associated with failure. Instead I experienced relief and a sense of freedom. I also had this sense of wonder about what had happened. The message must have somehow resonated with me in such a way that it was transformative. I really didn't even understand what the message meant and so its power to transform clearly wasn't due to some newfound cognitive understanding.

I felt great, but I didn't understand. I did feel as if the technology we had developed was done, but the product was incomplete as we halted production of the molds. The project was obviously far from done as we couldn't introduce an uncompleted product to an undefined market.

Maybe this was just one of those very expensive hobbies that should have never progressed any further. We still had our chairs and we were able to make all of the refinements we needed to update our technology, which we had already done. We continued to meet as a small group and continued to explore.

Use of our improved technology began to be reflected in our own advancement. As soon as we turned on the new chair we could feel a strong activation of our root chakra followed by greater flow in the rest of our energy system. We had progressed to the point that each of us could feel our energy systems fairly well.

Frank had noticed that when new people tried the technology it tended to balance their chakras very quickly. They all became of normal size, shape and color and would spin uniformly. By that time my chakras during sessions turned white associated with an expanded Hara line. They also exhibited a faster spin rate. In addition I was experiencing more energetic releases, which I assumed were the result of releasing energetic blocks associated with greater spiritual energy flow.

I was also experiencing expanded conscious awareness during my sessions. I began to perceive spiritual beings on occasion. During one session I asked Frank to meet me in the middle of the room. I did not go out-of-body as Frank did, but I could place my awareness outside of my body. It was interesting to perceive Frank in that way. He showed up as a considerably younger man with a robust build, blond wavy hair and a ruddy complexion. We shook hands. He had a strong grip, which seemed very odd for a non-corporeal being.

Although it was nice to have spiritual experiences such as these, I already had strong beliefs in such occurrences. As a result it had little effect on me. After that I didn't feel the need to do any similar types of exploration. I was more intrigued with my changing energy system. What did that represent and what was to follow? My interest began to shift. Could our sessions be used to significantly shift our energy systems in a way that we could derive significant spiritual benefits outside of our sessions?

Time would tell and that's what I now had a lot more of, time.

Chapter 36: Resurrection

Dr. B. was a friend of mine who had a genuine interest in our project. He founded and organized the local chapter of the Minnesota Holistic Medicine group. I owed him a phone call to let him know that we had shelved the project. He was quick to respond by saying, "You can't do that. Let's get together."

At that time his group of holistic practitioners numbered just over 400. They had regular gatherings with speakers. He wanted to set up a meeting and have me speak to his group. I was happy to comply, but since their calendar was booked, the conference I was to speak at would have to wait until January, 2013.

In the meantime Dr. B. wanted me to meet with Dr. S, a holistic Psychiatrist and fortunately not because he thought I was completely nuts. The three of us met for breakfast in the summer of 2012. After apprising Dr. S. on the particulars of our project, Dr. B. asked, "What prompted you to start this project in the first place?"

"We did it for our own spiritual development," I replied.

"Then why don't you produce the product for that application. People are ready for a product like this," he said.

That was the first time I ever heard anyone tell me that people were actually ready for a product that facilitates spiritual development. I thought he was joking, but he wasn't. Still, I didn't believe it. I sarcastically responded by saying, "I'm from Missouri, show me."

He wanted to prove his point. He asked Dr. S. and me to plan the conference, the format of which had always been purely informational. I suggested that at the end we throw down the gauntlet and let the audience know that if indeed they wished to see such a product manufactured, thirty of them would have to order it and pre-pay. That wouldn't come close to covering our expenses, but it would demonstrate that Dr. B. was correct and that a market actually did exist for spiritual technology. The size of that market would still remain an open issue.

Since our technology provides for an experience I offered that anyone interested in trying it from his group could visit us and do a session. During the fall of 2012 leading up to the conference about sixty members of the group gave it a try. After the conference another forty or so tried it as well. By the spring of 2013 fifty people had signed up to purchase a unit. Dr. B. had proven his point. By the end of 2013 we were able to make good on the delivery of their units.

The units consist of an amplifier and transducers built into a comfortable delivery platform, which uses layered music to induce synchronized sounds, vibrations and electromagnetic fields, producing physical, emotional, mental and spiritual effects.

Of the fifty people that first ordered, forty of them wanted to learn more about using the technology as part of a more comprehensive program for spiritual development. We met weekly in groups of four, using the four old style chairs I had. Those meetings began in April, 2013 and lasted until August. After the delivery of their chairs we formalized a ten-week course to further the experience.

I thoroughly enjoyed working with forty holistic practitioners. The group consisted of physicians, nurses, psychologists, energy healers, dentists, coaches and chiropractors. They had varied backgrounds and they had tried many different approaches in their quest for greater spiritual expression. Since our meetings consisted of doing sessions and having discussions it was necessary to formulate a common language. I took the lead and defined a number of terms based upon many prior discussions with Jennifer and our earlier coursework.

Chapter 37: Spiritual Progression Chart

To provide a more global framework I crafted a spiritual progression chart from a number of the various terms we used in the course.

The chart shows some energetic and psychological parameters categorized by four states of being; Ego Identified, Soul Embodied, Source Awakened and Source Manifest. We defined these states of being as follows:

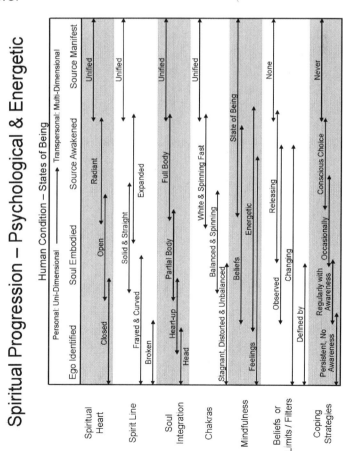

Ego Identified: a person who is primarily self-identified with their beliefs – they believe they are their beliefs. They often respond in a manner consistent with their conditioning and regularly employ their subconscious, reactive coping strategies without being aware that they are doing so. They may believe they have a soul, but they don't believe they are that soul. Their life is a never ending series of ups and downs (drama) based upon life's events. They often seek to exert control when they can or they passively follow group-think and norms. They tend to live in a reactive manner, but may overcompensate by being willfully purposeful much of the time. They are generally not receptive to spiritual influences and rarely consider their spiritual path.

Soul Embodied: In the fully embodied form, this individual is regularly present throughout their body as their soul. They self-identify as their soul / spiritual being. They rarely experience fear-based emotions and do not regularly employ their coping strategies, although when they do, they are consciously aware in the process. They recognize that their beliefs are not truths and that they represent limitations, which filter their perceptions and experiences. They tend to be actively working on releasing their beliefs. They recognize that they are not in control of outcomes and are generally less attached to them. They tend to be accepting and non-judgmental and recognize some of the spiritual underpinnings to life. They are aware of their energetic self.

Source Awakened: this individual realizes they are Source. They are abidingly consciously aware. They are without an egoic sense of self, but maintain a sense of being in the material world. They realize in a profound and absolute way that they and their reality are not what they previously thought. They can live and act in the material world, but their sense of self and reality transcends the material world.

Source Manifest: these living masters are extremely rare. They are the unknown and radiate pure Spirit.

The concept of a soul almost always generates interesting discussions. Many people feel that the word soul has a religious connotation. I cannot speak to religious matters as I am so uninformed on that topic, so I won't attempt to do so. I use the word soul because I think that it is generally believed to be our non-physical, immortal essence. In addition I also believe that the word soul is often considered to be different from spirit, which tends to be thought of as more transcendent and less identified with the personal.

Both of these descriptive frameworks fit nicely with the energetic structures, soul and spirit line, as we define them. Energetically we define the spirit or Hara line as a small white column of energy that passes vertically through the physical body just in front of or within the spine. It extends infinitely above and below us.

The soul is defined energetically as an outgrowth of the spirit line. It assumes a level of integration or approximation with the physical body that is dictated to a large extent by our egoic beliefs and fears. The soul is an outgrowth of spirit and has a more personal function. We also use the word soul interchangeably with higher self and spiritual self.

Some teachers make no distinction between soul and spirit. Soul is simply considered to be an outgrowth of spirit and therefore they have the same origin. These folks tend to think along lines of wholeness and unity, which is considered true at a metaphysical or spiritual level. Extending that thought, one would also lump in our physical nature as that too is energy, just vibrating more slowly. Admittedly, this is a preferable way of considering ourselves when in session or meditation as well as in life.

237

This way of believing facilitates our self-identification with Source, which is the end-goal or the truth of things, as some would consider.

However, in our discussions, we have elected to differentiate between the two terms as they have different energetic expressions and seem to confer different levels of functionality. It also allows for the characterization of a Soul Embodied state of being, which seems very appropriate as the spiritual state of Soul Embodied is clearly different from that of Source Awakened. Having this middle or transitional state of being also allows us to focus on some of the important transitional aspects, particularly our mindfulness practices, beliefs and coping strategies.

Another nice feature of the Soul Embodied state is that it can be facilitated by the interaction of egoic thought and the soul's urgings. This helps build cohesion and partnership between ego and our spiritual self and ultimately, Source. This state of being also has its own rewards and can be a very nice stepping stone on our spiritual path.

Chapter 38: Approaching My Goal

My goal of wanting to know what we truly are, as human beings, had morphed somewhat. Or at least it had taken on a new definition with the development of the spiritual progression chart. In order to understand and know the truth of things and our relationship to Spirit it was necessary for me to experience the Source Awakened state of being. Without that experience, my understanding would be limited to hearsay or imagination. I wanted first-hand knowledge that can only be gained through experience.

With the enhancements we had made to our technology I was undergoing more rapid development. By the fall of 2012 I had become quite adept at achieving the Soul Embodied state of being. I tended to view the soul as an energetic shape-shifter that could occupy any space and form any shape.

As a child I had developed a belief about my soul as an unintended consequence of my childhood prayer – "Now I lay me down to sleep, I pray the Lord my soul to keep, if I should die before I wake, I pray the Lord my soul to take." The belief I had formed was that my soul was independent of me and was not with me when I slept.

In the fall of 2012 I was waking up at about 3am with anxiety. Was I going to have enough money to support my family and continue to work on this project? After my morning session and during the remainder of the day I rarely experienced any negative emotions or had any fears. During my session I could feel a dramatic upsurge of spiritual energy flow. I decided to experiment with these middle of the night episodes of anxiety.

When I awoke with anxiety I would literally add fuel to the fire. I would purposefully think of the future in a negative way. The anxiety would worsen and then transform into deep feelings of shame. After those feelings became intense I would call in the cavalry. I would call in my soul. I immediately felt an inrush of spiritual energy. I would feel it as if it was entering at the location of my crown chakra and it would spread throughout my entire body. All of the negative emotional feelings were immediately replaced by feelings of peace and tranquility.

My ego enjoys developing a sense of mastery. It was fascinating to experience such a rapid disappearance of my severe negative emotions. I no longer had any fear associated with negative emotions since I could disarm them so completely and quickly. After about two months of playing this game I decided it was time to end it.

To do so all I had to do was change my belief about my soul. I asked that it would be with me always and my 3am episodes abruptly ended. This process was in my opinion greatly aided by regular sessions with our technology, as during those sessions I learned how to recreate that state of being. Recreating and then learning to maintain the Soul Embodied state of being during wakefulness became second nature.

By that time during my sessions I also experienced a greater radiance from my heart area and just above it. Frank was witnessing a change in my spirit line. It had widened quite a bit to encompass my physical body. As the white became brighter he lost the ability to perceive my physical body, which I'm sure was still present in the chair.

During an eighteen month period from the late 2012 through the spring of 2014 Frank watched as the white light continued to expand until it filled the room and later appeared to be infinite in all directions and brighter in intensity. During that transition he witnessed a number of different geometric shapes around my body. The first was a box that was rectangular in shape oriented lengthwise from head to foot. He then saw a pyramid followed by a cube. Each lasted a number of months. At one point he saw an egg form around me and one day it broke and he saw what looked like egg shell fragments beneath me.

None of us understood sacred geometry. We didn't understand the significance of those shapes or their origination. Did they play a role as a part of the transformational process or simply were they communicating information about it? Since I didn't understand their significance I didn't purposefully intend to create those shapes around me.

On April 4, 2014 I had an interesting session. I was presented with two doors representing different spiritual paths. I was asked to select. The first door represented a path that had come to its end, which was my current state of being. The second door represented my path if I was to continue to progress. Before I could choose, the first door closed, leaving me only door number two, in essence I had no choice. The accompanying words were, "This is the path you had chosen."

In this vision I was then transported into my kitchen. A frying pan was on the stovetop. In it were some herbs mixed in olive oil. Potatoes and meat were added. It transformed into a casserole that was placed to my right. On my left was a bowl filled with salad. In front of me was a bowl, but there was a film covering its contents. I was given a plate and a serving spoon. I went for the casserole first, but I was only allowed to take the potatoes.

I then took some salad, but still had a lot of room left on my plate. I looked at the bowl in front of me and the film disappeared. It was filled with steamed broccoli and cauliflower. I normally ate vegetables, but always considered them to be a side dish. I reluctantly added the broccoli and cauliflower to my plate.

The message was clear. To move on spiritually I had to change my diet. On that day I became a vegetarian. It only lasted a month. I added fish to my diet to make it easier for me to get the protein I needed and to feel as if I was eating some meat-like substance. I've remained a pescetarian. Hopefully it's enough of a change.

An intriguing question arises. How much can a spiritual practice change the physical body and how much does diet change the consequences of a spiritual practice? Several medical studies have shown that even short periods of meditation change the physical expression of our genes and appear to increase the content of grey matter in the brain. Presumably deeper levels of meditation could do more.

Other medical studies have shown that the telomeres, which are the terminal DNA–protein complexes that protect chromosomes, are shortened by stress and lengthened by relaxation. When the telomere becomes too short the cell can no longer divide. The length of the telomere is considered to be a candidate biomarker of aging.

My father takes great pride in the many compliments he receives about his youthful appearance given his age of almost 92. He attributes it to our technology, which he has used daily for the past six years. My father is not particularly interested in spiritual development. He likes to relax and eat whatever he chooses to.

I decided to change my diet based upon the session I had in April of 2014 and based upon a belief I had concerning physical matter's ability to conduct spiritual energy. April, 2014 was at about the end of the eighteen months that it took for Frank to see my spirit line first start to expand until the radiation of white light seemed to be infinite. It seemed to me that while that process was happening, my physical body was adapting to the presence of higher spiritual energy. Maybe the need for physical adaptation is why the process took as long as it did.

The reason it seems as if higher spiritual energy is present is most likely related to one's increased vibratory experience. This phenomenon begins very early in the process and continues to advanced levels. Most people that use our technology learn to feel their inner vibrations and many can hear them too. As the process unfolds, one feels finer vibrations and hears higher pitched vibrations. As a result it seems as if we are being exposed to higher spiritual energy. In fact, what is most likely occurring is that we are being exposed to the same spiritual energy. However our physical bodies over time are able to carry and thus perceive higher and higher frequencies of that spiritual energy.

During that time I had many sessions that seemed to stretch me. I could feel what seemed like expansion. In many of those sessions it felt as if all the particles of my body were spread out, only to coalesce at the end of the session. However, after those sessions I felt different. I would feel expanded and light. I would walk up the stairs feeling as if the gravity of the Earth had lessened. The effects would only last a few minutes after each session, but they were quite noticeable.

I also noted an interesting visual effect. At the end of those sessions and for about ten minutes afterwards it seemed as if there was a fine mist in the air. It was as if the air itself had a texture to it that I couldn't see before. This would fade as the gravity of the Earth also returned to normal.

By April of 2014 it was possible that I needed to adjust my diet in order to carry even higher spiritual frequency content. Therefore a diet that was more plant-based and less animal-based was necessary. By the end of 2014 my sessions were changing once more.

Sometimes it is difficult to put words to states of shifting consciousness because we haven't experienced similar phenomena during regular daily life and so have had no need to describe them. Oftentimes the word deeper is used to signify a state further removed from our normal waking awareness. I was experiencing a shift in conscious awareness that I was entirely unfamiliar with. It

243

seemed as though I was rapidly moving back and forth between two different states of consciousness. One was a state more of a spiritual nature and further removed from ego and the other, was what I normally experienced as my conscious awareness during session with some egoic presence.

Frank saw this as alternating infinite white light with periods of total blackness. The total blackness filled the area of the chair. He could not see my physical body, just blackness. That wasn't surprising as with the bright light he couldn't see my physical body either. On the last day of 2014 he saw the black and white beginning to mix. He described it as forming chocolate milk.

I could see the mixing as well in my mind's eye during the session. To me it appeared as black and white paint being mixed. I also heard the words, "It is coming." These words seemed to issue forth from a great depth. It was as if I had heard them in a dream and was repeating them to myself as I was awakening.

Part IV - More Considerations

The following chapters follow the same format as the chapters in Part II. They also represent my story.

Chapter 39: Energy, Grounding and Presence

Higher Self: Over the years the appearance of your energy system has changed much. These energies can be perceived differently amongst different people. Do you remember how you began to experience your energy system?

Ego: Yes I remember the early days when I first began to feel my hands and face tingle and then my hands seemed to get puffy and balloon out.

Higher Self: You were just beginning to perceive your energy system and some of what you perceived was beyond the borders of your physical body.

Ego: I assume I felt it in my hands and face first due to the greater abundance of nerve endings in those areas.

Higher Self: That is correct. Your physical nervous system is designed to perceive your spiritual energies, but they are more subtle than other physical stimuli so most people never perceive them.

Ego: Over time I experienced that sense of mild vibration throughout my entire body and a greater sense of expanded self beyond the borders of my physical body.

Higher Self: The subtle vibratory sense you perceived was the interface between your energetic self and the matter of your body. You also developed an awareness of your energetic self that exists beyond the physical and is larger in size.

Ego: I could hear the vibrations as well.

Higher Self: The subtle sense of vibration is registered in the areas of your brain used to convey both touch and hearing. It is registered in the areas that give you the ability to feel vibration on your skin as well as to hear. Over the years you have been able to carry higher frequency energy throughout your body. You sensed it as a finer vibration, felt throughout your body and you have also heard it as a higher pitch due to the higher frequency content.

Ego: After years of being able to feel those progressively finer vibrations throughout my body I no longer can.

Higher Self: That area of the brain registers only a small bandwidth of frequencies. Your subtle energies are mapped onto that small bandwidth. Due to that limited range and the faster frequencies that you now conduct, you have lost the ability to sense those frequencies as a felt vibratory phenomenon. However you do still sense it in your skin, but differently now, is that not so?

Ego: Yes, it feels like sunburn instead of a fine vibration.

Higher Self: The vibrations you now perceive are more akin to the vibrations of light rather than sound. These vibrations are much higher in frequency. That is why you are feeling it as you do. That sensation of feeling sunburned will pass over time as well.

Ego: That makes sense as that sensation was associated with Frank's observations of the light extending infinitely from me and becoming much brighter.

Higher Self: Your auditory cortex however registers a larger bandwidth of frequencies. You can still hear the vibrations, correct?

Ego: Yes, but the pitch is very high.

Higher Self: In time you will lose that too.

Ego: I would like to perceive more rather than less.

Higher Self: Feeling and hearing those vibratory phenomena have been useful for your mindfulness practice, but you no longer need them. You have learned to perceive much and there is more that you will perceive as you progress.

Ego: I don't perceive all that much.

Higher Self: You perceive much more than you used to. You can perceive much of your energy system. In session you can perceive other spiritual entities. Your dialogue with me and your mindfulness practice is far more advanced than it was.

Ego: Little by little I have learned to perceive more, but I would like to perceive the whole picture, not just small pieces.

Higher Self: Why?

Ego: Other people perceive them, why can't I?

Higher Self: You have spent very little time learning how to develop your own perceptive gifts. You have happily relied on Frank and Jennifer for their perceptions.

Ego: They have been the source of great information. This project would be nowhere without them.

Higher Self: That is one of the reasons you were all brought together.

Ego: What are the other reasons?

Higher Self: There are many reasons. Another of those reasons for you is a need to work in close partnership and learning to enjoy one another in a deep and meaningful way.

Ego: So you're saying that if I had those capabilities I wouldn't have worked in close partnership with Frank and Jennifer.

Higher Self: That is not what I am saying. Even if you had the ability to perceive spiritual energy more completely you still would have had the need to work in close partnership with them.

Ego: Why?

Higher Self: Why do you consult with both Frank and Jennifer?

Ego: They perceive our energy systems differently.

Higher Self: And so will you.

Ego: Why?

Higher Self: You each have different filters. You may perceive the energy system more like Jennifer or Frank, but it will still be different.

Ego: So you're saying I'm going to be able to perceive other people's energy systems.

Higher Self: To a variable extent depending upon how you progress.

Ego: Why?

Higher Self: Because I can and you and I are one. As you filter what comes into your conscious awareness to a lesser degree, you will perceive these energies to a greater extent.

Ego: When will this happen?

Higher Self: To a significant degree it depends upon you and the progress you choose to make.

Ego: What do I need to do?

Higher Self: Continue as you are. In session continue to deepen your state of being as you are and recreate that state intermittently during the day.

Ego: Should I do anything differently with my grounding practice.

Higher Self: I have been meaning to discuss this with you.

Ego: We haven't talked about this for years.

Higher Self: I have been watching as your process has changed.

Ego: Jennifer and I have discussed it from time to time.

Higher Self: Which is why I have not intervened, but there are a few points to bring to your awareness.

Ego: Okay, so what am I doing wrong now?

Higher Self: Why do you so readily assume you are wrong?

Ego: It's in my nature.

Higher Self: Yes it is, but it is time to lose that and some of what we are discussing will assist you in that process.

Ego: What are you talking about?

Higher Self: When you first began to pay attention to the process of grounding you thought of it as connecting to the Earth's energies.

Ego: Yes that's right.

Higher Self: You imagined connecting to those energies by growing roots into the Earth and later by allowing the Earth's energies to pass into your feet and root chakra like light energy.

Ego: And I also allowed energy to enter me from above.

Higher Self: Yes and then you added all sorts of convolutions to those energy patterns. You created loops and toroidal shaped structures that were very complicated. You added energy to your chakras and expanded your auric bodies.

Ego: Yes I went through many phases.

Higher Self: And Frank witnessed that what you intended came to pass in terms of the appearance of those energy structures.

Ego: Yes that all happened.

Higher Self: And then Jennifer suggested that all of those energetic contortions were no longer necessary as you and I were rooted in at your core and heart area and your light radiated from that location outwards.

Ego: Yes that happened as well.

Higher Self: Yet you have continued to set up your energy system in all these ways as you begin your session.

Ego: It happens really fast so I don't spend much time doing so.

Higher Self: What is the point of it all?

Ego: A lot of it is just habit.

Higher Self: Old habits carry and reinforce old beliefs.

Ego: What are you getting at?

Higher Self: You began these different grounding practices many years ago. They carry with them old concepts that slow your progress.

Ego: How so?

Higher Self: When you began these different grounding processes, why were you performing them?

Ego: I was trying to become better connected.

Higher Self: Trying to connect implies that you are separate. Are you?

Ego: I see your point. I realize in my head that I am not separate, but I don't always feel that way.

Higher Self: That realization in your head is only a concept and not an embodiment of wholeness.

Ego: I understand.

Higher Self: When you went through all of those energetic contortions and Frank witnessed them, what did you learn?

Ego: I was learning to feel those energies.

Higher Self: Anything else?

Ego: I learned that how I thought about those energies affected how they appeared.

Higher Self: Why do you still refer to them as "those energies"?

Ego: Old habit.

Higher Self: Old habits consist of old thought patterns.

Ego: I need to keep reminding myself that I am those energies, which is why when I intend them to take a certain form they do, because it is me that is taking those forms.

Higher Self: Yes, that is a manifestation of your free will.

Ego: So what is the point of grounding at all?

Higher Self: You tell me.

Ego: It has allowed me to learn how to feel those energies, or better stated to feel myself in that manner.

Higher Self: Yes that is helpful. However you still do not truly identify with those energies. You consider it to be separate from you even though you can feel its presence.

Ego: That presence has taken many forms over the years. How am I to know what it is?

Higher Self: It is you who have dictated its form.

Ego: Oh that's right. Frank saw what I intended and I experienced it differently as it changed.

Higher Self: It is only recently that you have allowed it to be without manipulation.

Ego: Yes, that's when it turned black.

Higher Self: When it was white light radiating infinitely it was you who dictated that materialization.

Ego: I thought I was just allowing the expanded expression of Source from my Hara line.

Higher Self: You were and it happened every time you allowed it once you were capable of transmitting those energies. Still, allowing it was intending it, because that is what you expected to happen.

Ego: Then why did it turn black?

Higher Self: You allowed it to simply be without manipulation.

Ego: I'm totally confused.

Higher Self: What confuses you?

Ego: Why did it stop expressing itself?

Higher Self: I already told you. You allowed yourself to be.

Ego: I realized when that happened that I had achieved a new level of being.

Higher Self: And energetically that is what you looked like. What you truly are is that.

Ego: That seemed like the absence of everything.

Higher Self: That is exactly what it is from your perspective.

Ego: What do you mean from my perspective?

Higher Self: The level of being that you had achieved at that time was devoid of ego. As such you stopped directing what you are, which is why it was expressed and witnessed in its native form.

Ego: But that form is nothing.

Higher Self: Yet that form can become anything as you have previously demonstrated by causing it to take all manner of forms.

Ego: Why did the black representation start to mix with the white?

Higher Self: What are you experiencing in your daily life that may reflect that change?

Ego: I am beginning to experience states of being during the day that resemble those periods in session when I am devoid of ego. Is that what is happening?

Higher Self: You are beginning to integrate a higher degree of being and receptivity into your way of being while in your normal waking state.

Ego: Okay then, we'll see where that takes me.

Higher Self: Yes you will.

Ego: But I have noticed what I detect as a different sense of presence. I could feel greater presence associated with the state that Frank perceives when there is greater white light radiance.

Higher Self: The new state is still very new to you. You will see how it unfolds as you become more consciously aware in that state. Presently when you experience that state your awareness is still limited. At every level along your spiritual path you have experienced the presence of your spiritual self differently, but it has generally taken a little while for it to fully express itself.

Ego: I have come to rely on that sense of presence as part of my mindfulness practice. It has become very helpful for me to maintain in a higher state of being.

Higher Self: That can be helpful, but it can also cause you to stay stuck at a particular level by recreating the same energy pattern. That is why it is so helpful to experience still higher states of being during session so that you can recreate them during life.

Ego: Yes I recognize that in this new state I am not yet fully aware. I lose conscious awareness when I move into this state in session. I have experienced this in the past when I transitioned to a new state of being.

Higher Self: As your conscious awareness returns in session you will experience a new state of presence.

Ego: What can you tell me about that?

Higher Self: Nothing. I do not wish to create expectations.

Ego: You sound like Jennifer.

Higher Self: She is indeed wise.

Ego: I'm glad the two of you get along so well.

Considerations

If one considers his or her self as a being consisting of spiritual energy and occupying a physical vehicle then it becomes relatively simple to think of being grounded in the physical, spiritually embodied and physically present as equivalent terms. Conceptually, it is sometimes helpful to think of our spiritual and physical self as a Venn diagram and ask; how great is the overlap?

In an ego-identified state of being the overlap may be quite small, while in a soul-embodied state it is very large. The spiritual self we are considering in this state is what we have defined as soul or spiritual or higher self. As the Hara line expands in a Source Awakened state of being, again the Venn diagram shows an increasing overlap. However in this state of being the spiritual energy is now transpersonal Source versus personal higher self.

Our experience of spiritual presence differs dramatically based upon our state of being. With higher levels of soul embodiment come greater calm and equanimity. Negative emotions are experienced far less frequently and coping strategies are employed much less often. Mental clarity and recall are also improved. Energetically, one often experiences a physical sense of full body presence.

Still greater peace and tranquility accompany a Source Awakened state of being. There are associated feelings of deeper connection and compassion. Understanding replaces beliefs and trust often manifests at levels that supplant the need for coping strategies. Energetically, one often experiences a physical sense of radiance from the heart area or full body.

Ask yourself:

1. Are you a being composed of spiritual energy occupying a physical vehicle?

2. Draw a Venn diagram showing the overlap between your spiritual self and your physical body. Where in your physical body are the points of maximal overlap?

3. Do you feel your spiritual self? What does it feel like? How do you perceive it physically in your body?

4. Can you perceive other peoples' spiritual energy? Can you perceive the presence of someone entering the room or nearby if they are out of sight?

5. Can you perceive the spiritual presence of other spiritual entities? Have you experienced the spiritual presence of loved ones that have passed?

6. Have you experienced the presence of loved ones that have passed in your dreams?

Chapter 40: Spirituality and Consciousness

Ego: Some of my friends ask me what the word spirituality means.

Higher Self: What do you tell them?

Ego: I tell them that it has so many meanings to so many people that it has lost its meaning.

Higher Self: Does that satisfy them?

Ego: No.

Higher Self: So what then?

Ego: I ask them what they think it means.

Higher Self: What do you think it means?

Ego: Well you should know. Why are you asking me?

Higher Self: It is just a word. I have watched you struggle with some of your discussions concerning this word. You have as much difficulty with the word consciousness.

Ego: That's for sure, but we have to deal with words. That's how we communicate.

Higher Self: You have been given a wide range of experiences on these topics. You can discuss much.

Ego: I often use words that relate to experiences, but if people haven't had similar experiences it is frequently difficult for them to relate to my experiences.

Higher Self: Then why discuss it? A discussion is a poor substitute for experience. Do you remember some of your early experiences?

Ego: When I began to meditate?

Higher Self: Earlier. Do you remember when your mother's close friend Helen visited with her son, Sam?

Ego: Yes, I remember it well. I was bothered by that visit for years until I learned more in medical school.

Higher Self: What do you remember?

Ego: I couldn't connect with him. He was a lot older than me and we were supposed to play together.

Higher Self: What do you mean that you couldn't connect with him?

Ego: I would look into his eyes and I struggled to make a connection. When I read about the history of schizophrenia in medical school I learned that it used to be called Dementia Praecox a long time ago. Back then, clinicians used the term praecox feeling for the inability to connect with the patient when they looked into the eyes of a schizophrenic. It is like looking into the black eyes of a shark.

Higher Self: What did you take away from the experience with Sam and then later when you cared for patients with schizophrenia?

Ego: It reminded me of the expression, the lights are on, but there's nobody home.

Higher Self: Contrast that with the first time you met Jennifer.

Ego: That experience represented the other end of the spectrum. All I saw were her eyes, but in an otherworldly sense. Everything else faded away and I felt as if I was falling into a deep well.

Higher Self: You said that you recognized her, although you had not met her in this life.

Ego: Yes, it was a deep sense of knowing.

Higher Self: That awareness resulted from the deep connection you made when you looked into her eyes.

Ego: Why are you reminding me of these experiences?

Higher Self: You wanted to discuss spirituality and consciousness. There you have it, no further discussion is required.

Ego: We've had no discussion.

Higher Self: Those examples illustrate those concepts and you had a chance to see them with your own eyes.

Ego: Very funny. I see it as clear as mud.

Higher Self: How did you feel when you were with Sam?

Ego: I told you that I couldn't connect with him.

Higher Self: So how did that make you feel?

Ego: I felt alone. I was groping to make a connection with him.

Higher Self: How did you feel when you first looked into Jennifer's eyes?

Ego: I felt totally connected. In fact I completely lost myself in the experience.

Higher Self: With Sam you experienced isolation and separateness. With Jennifer you experienced union or oneness. That is the spectrum of experiencing spirituality from the ego's perspective. Those different spiritual manifestations conferred different states of consciousness or awareness.

Ego: What do you mean when you say from the ego's perspective?

Higher Self: What I mean is from the perspective of your filters. You can only perceive the effects that your spirituality has on your awareness in a very limited manner when you are ego-identified and tied to your material plane of existence. Spirit is not bound by those constraints. Those two examples illustrated separateness and union. During that separateness you experienced your egoic aloneness and during union you released your egoic constraints and experienced oneness.

Ego: That sense of oneness was wonderful.

Higher Self: Welcome to my world.

Ego: Some of my friends don't believe in that world.

Higher Self: Let them believe what they choose to believe.

Ego: I do, but they challenge my beliefs.

Higher Self: You used to defend your beliefs, but you rarely do that anymore.

Ego: I have no need to defend my views. Some of my other friends are interested in spirituality and like to discuss these matters, but many of them have no point of reference other than their religious beliefs.

Higher Self: Is that a problem?

Ego: My knowledge of religious matters is exceedingly limited. I can only tell them of my thoughts and experiences. They often have difficulty making sense of these phenomena within the rules and beliefs of their religions.

Higher Self: Rules and beliefs are limitations that do not exist in the spiritual realm. You had many discussions with a Rabbi friend of yours while he lived in the Twin Cities.

Ego: Yes we met for lunch several times a month for four years. He tried to turn me into an observant Jew and I tried to convert him into a non-denominational spiritualist. Neither one of us was successful.

Higher Self: You were both successful. You enjoyed each other's company very much.

Ego: I looked forward to those lunches and not just for the tuna fish sandwich. He was very scholarly and we had wonderful discussions.

Higher Self: Did you discuss religion?

Ego: We discussed God.

Higher Self: Did it matter that his perspectives were based upon Judaism and yours from your experiences and spiritual learnings?

Ego: As long as we were discussing God or whatever name anyone chooses, I don't think it would have mattered what religious tradition informed the discussion. Ultimately our discussion centered on our views about God and our relationship to God.

Higher Self: How did those discussions make you feel?

Ego: They were always uplifting. I loved our discussions. I miss them.

Higher Self: Why?

Ego: Our discussions were very passionate. Sometimes other people in the restaurant would stare at us when we got too loud. We learned to seat ourselves in the back corner of the restaurant.

Higher Self: He was committed to his religious path and spent every morning reading and meditating. You were on your spiritual path and spent many hours in meditation and reading. Even though you had some different views you both admired each other's dedication and commitment.

Ego: Yes we did.

Higher Self: You were on the same path, but your enjoyment arose from your differences.

Ego: What are you talking about?

Higher Self: You both loved the discussions and the debates. Without your differing viewpoints you would have had nothing to discuss. You would have not connected and you would have not been uplifted.

Ego: I never realized how beneficial our differences were.

Higher Self: In another religious tradition it is said that, for where two or three are gathered in my name, there am I among them. God is the oneness of your connection, of your union. That is spirituality and the resulting consciousness is uplifting.

Ego: I see what you're getting at. It's no different than being in nature and feeling that connection and expansiveness. It's even the same as the connection I have when I make eye contact with our dogs and the feelings in me that are evoked.

Higher Self: That is correct. It is connection. Spirituality is found in simple everyday life as long as people take a moment to appreciate it. It is not complicated and maybe that is some of the issue.

Ego: Often spiritual discussions are about more sensational metaphysical phenomena, like near death experiences.

Higher Self: They are interesting and informative experiences, but I would not recommend that everyone seek them out.

Ego: These episodes are being reported more commonly.

Higher Self: Many people have become more open to the possibility and so there is less fear around discussing this issue.

Ego: I think near death experiences or NDEs are discussed in regards to spirituality because these types of experiences relate to a spiritual realm that we become a part of when we die.

Higher Self: People's fear of death can be alleviated by a belief in a hereafter. They often perceive that a part of them survives.

Ego: Well doesn't it?

Higher Self: I never die.

Ego: What about me?

Higher Self: As I have said, you and I are one.

Ego: But I do not live on as I am now.

Higher Self: With a body?

Ego: Of course not. I realize that. What I mean is that I don't live on with a sense of individuality.

Higher Self: Not in the way that you consider individuality. The experiences that you and I have had in this life live on through me. Some of the effects of those experiences are incorporated into my being. You survive in me.

Ego: What about my history and all of the details of my life. Do they just fade away?

Higher Self: I integrate what is necessary.

Ego: So, what you deem to be important makes its way into the spiritual realm, is that it?

Higher Self: You have this tendency to separate or divide things into parts, as you do with the concept of a spiritual realm.

Ego: But it is a different realm of existence, isn't it?

Higher Self: As long as you hold this belief that is how you will perceive it.

Ego: That's the issue. It doesn't appear to me at all, except for sometimes in session, but it's not part of my waking daily life. That's the way it is even for those people who can visit it from time to time.

Higher Self: What people are you speaking of?

Ego: People that have NDE's, out-of-body experiences or other expanded states of conscious awareness. Those people visit the spiritual realm and then they come back to this realm that I exist in. It's the same for people who have lucid dreams. They find themselves consciously aware during their dreams, while asleep. Some of them can then direct what happens during those dreams. They are in a different realm, but then they wake up.

Higher Self: Why have you excluded me from "those people"?

Ego: I don't really consider you a person, like me or them.

Higher Self: That is why you do not experience those realms, as you call them, during your typical daytime experience.

Ego: Are you suggesting that just because I don't believe that I am you, I cannot perceive the spiritual realm?

Higher Self: That is a big part of it.

Ego: What's the rest of it?

Higher Self: You do not believe you have the capability to perceive more than you do, which is surprising at this stage in your development.

Ego: Why is it surprising?

Higher Self: Because you can perceive spiritual beings during your sessions. Why do you choose to believe that you cannot perceive them during the rest of the day?

Ego: I just assumed that when I am in session I achieve a state of being that allows me to perceive those things and otherwise I am not in that state of being.

Higher Self: That is another excellent example of how you segregate your experience of life.

Ego: I am in a different state of being during my sessions. That's why I do them.

Higher Self: Why do you do sessions?

Ego: So that I can learn to deepen those states of being. In that way I can learn to replicate that state of being during my waking life.

Higher Self: You already achieve conscious awareness during these states of being that you are not experiencing during your waking life. What are you waiting for?

Ego: I'm not waiting for anything. It just hasn't happened yet.

Higher Self: Why has it not happened?

Ego: I must not be sufficiently in that state while I'm doing my everyday activities.

Higher Self: That is another belief that you hold.

Ego: Are you saying that I can perceive them during the rest of my day?

Higher Self: I certainly can.

Ego: But I am not you.

Higher Self: What do you think is really happening during your sessions?

Ego: That I am being transformed into a more spiritual being.

Higher Self: Really?

Ego: Well yes, really. That's what I think.

Higher Self: I see.

Ego: Isn't that correct? Aren't I being transformed into a more spiritual being?

Higher Self: As I have said repeatedly, you and I are one. Since I am a spiritual being so are you. You already have one foot in what you term, that other realm.

Ego: Then what is happening during my sessions?

Higher Self: You are becoming more consciously aware of me, by sensing what it feels like to be me. In other words you are becoming more familiar with what you already are.

Ego: Then I'm not really being transformed?

Higher Self: Transformation is taking place at several levels, but you are already a spiritual being, so in that sense you are not being transformed into a spiritual being.

Ego: Then how am I being transformed?

Higher Self: The matter of your physical body is becoming more accustomed to carrying higher frequency spiritual energy. It is vibrating at a faster rate. Your sessions are very helpful in that regard. In addition, as you experience your true self to a greater extent you shift your beliefs, so in that way you are transforming yourself.

Ego: My beliefs change very slowly.

Higher Self: Yes they tend to change slowly, however you can shift them much faster if you choose.

Ego: But as long as I hold the same beliefs I will perceive only what I allow myself to perceive.

Higher Self: That is correct. Your beliefs act as filters to maintain your conscious perceptions in alignment with your sense of reality. This is why your reality is a self-fulfilling prophecy.

Ego: So my sessions provide me some experiences which help me shift my beliefs. As my beliefs change so will my sense of reality.

Higher Self: That is typically how it is accomplished.

Ego: But that is a slow process.

Higher Self: Yes, but you feel comfortable taking small steps. Faster progress is often unsettling to the ego, as it feels as if it is giving up a part of itself. Every belief that changes represents an old belief that is discarded and so the ego feels as if it is losing some of itself in the process. That is why it fights to hold onto old beliefs.

Ego: How can I move this process forward at a faster pace?

Higher Self: Experience what you truly are so that you will understand that you are not your ego.

Considerations

Our connectedness is the stuff of spirit. It is what unifies us and makes us one. Spirituality pertains to everything related to that, which in essence is everything. Our consciousness is our living, breathing awareness of our unity or wholeness. Our consciousness informs our sense of reality.

When we operate from the vantage point of our beliefs our consciousness is limited to what we have experienced in the past because our beliefs were formed in the past. Only when we suspend our beliefs can we have new experiences. This occurs when we ask ourselves a question and are open to receive an answer. This happens when we wonder what something may be like.

To wonder allows us to experience what our ego does not know. It removes our filters so that we are open to experience and change.

Ask yourself:

1. How do you define spirituality? How much have you been taught about spirituality? Are your beliefs about spirituality different than your beliefs about religion?

2. How do you experience spirituality? What does being spiritual feel like to you?

3. How do you define consciousness? How do you experience consciousness?

4. How do you experience connectedness? What does it feel like to you? What people or pets in your life have you been or are you deeply connected to? How does that make you feel?

5. How do you experience nature? How does nature make you feel?

6. How open are you to change? Would you like to change what you perceive to be your reality? How would you like it to change?

7. What do you wonder about? What would you like to wonder about?

8. If you were alone in a room with God (or however you define or refer to God) and you could ask three questions, what would they be?

Chapter 41: Self-Identity

Ego: I wonder what it is like to be you.

Higher Self: You and I are one.

Ego: But I don't know what that is like.

Higher Self: You do to an extent.

Ego: How so?

Higher Self: You experience more of me, which is what you truly are, when you are in session.

Ego: What I have experienced has changed a lot over the years.

Higher Self: Yes, you have learned to appreciate more of what I am. How do you experience me now in session?

Ego: Very peaceful and often timeless.

Higher Self: And how does that impact you during the day?

Ego: I remain much more peaceful. Things make more sense to me in my life.

Higher Self: Are you satisfied with your current way of being?

Ego: No.

Higher Self: Why not?

Ego: I really do believe that I am more than I perceive myself to be. Given that belief I would like to perceive the rest of me.

Higher Self: How do you plan to accomplish that?

Ego: I don't have a plan. I've been trying to figure that out.

Higher Self: But you have made progress. Why not continue as you have been doing?

Ego: I'm not sure I can get much further using the same tactics. I think I need a different approach.

Higher Self: Why?

Ego: I think I've gone as far as I can, doing what I've been doing.

Higher Self: What have you been doing?

Ego: I've been doing a lot of things, but as I do all of them I keep watching to see what will happen. Dr. S. keeps joking with me. He tells me that I'm trying to take a video camera into my meeting with God.

Higher Self: Dr. S. is correct.

Ego: It's like trying to fall asleep with one eye open. It's not working.

Higher Self: Yet you have made considerable progress. Do you understand why?

Ego: Some of what I've done must have worked to a degree.

Higher Self: It is less about the doing. In many of your sessions you spend quite a bit of time simply being. During those times you have not been doing anything. You have simply allowed yourself to be. You realize this.

Ego: And I guess that has been helpful although it's hard to know what has accounted for my progress as I have tried many different approaches during my sessions.

Higher Self: By simply being you, you experience the peacefulness I experience and when you are that way understanding can enter. You have become well practiced at simply being and that way of being has transferred to a significant degree into your way of being during life. You have observed the experience of that way of being and you have learned how to replicate it. However, Dr. S. is correct. You still open one eye to look around at times in session.

Ego: It's a bad habit. It's hard to break.

Higher Self: Your training of mindfulness during your sessions was necessary in the past. It was important for you to experience how relaxed your physical body becomes, the status of your energy system and your experiences related to those energetic states. All of these learnings have occurred. It is now time to let that practice go.

Ego: I want to remain consciously aware during this process.

Higher Self: Of course you do.

Ego: Why can't I?

Higher Self: You cannot perceive All That Is through the lens of the ego.

Ego: Why not?

Higher Self: Like perceives like. Your egoic self can perceive your egoic nature and other egos, but it cannot perceive All That Is.

Ego: Why not?

Higher Self: Because it does not know All That Is. It only has limited beliefs about that and so that is all it can perceive. All That Is has not been experienced by your ego and as a result your ego does not have a meaningful reference.

Ego: Wait a minute. Why are we discussing All That Is? I was interested in perceiving what it is like to be you.

Higher Self: I do not differentiate between myself and All That Is or Source. They are one and the same.

Ego: I thought you and I are one and the same.

Higher Self: We are.

Ego: That would mean that I am All That Is too.

Higher Self: That is correct.

Ego: Whoa, that's way outside of my comfort zone.

Higher Self: Why?

Ego: All this time I've been trying to better understand you and how you and I are one. I was not considering that there is more to this equation.

Higher Self: That is what happens when you attempt to consider what I am through the lens of the ego. You have personified me as being something like yourself. You have done so because that is what you are familiar with. That is all you know. You tend to think of me as an other-worldly ego.

Ego: Well it's hard to think of you differently.

Higher Self: Yes I understand your difficulty however you have experienced more.

Ego: What are you referring to?

Higher Self: In your sessions you have experienced what it feels like to be infinite, bright white light.

Ego: That is what Frank sees. I just experience peacefulness and a high vibratory state.

Higher Self: And how was that different from the experiences associated with Frank's visualization of you as blackness?

Ego: I did not have my customary sense of self.

Higher Self: Some of your filters were put aside. You were no longer your egoic self and as a result you could perceive more of what you truly are.

Ego: I did not perceive anything. It was nothingness.

Higher Self: You were still in a transitional state, much less ego, but still somewhat filtered. As a result what you mainly perceived was the absence of egoic self as you existed in a state of pure potential.

Ego: When is this pure potential going to turn into something real?

Higher Self: Do you remember the message you received during the session that you perceived the blackness and the infinite white light mixing?

Ego: Yes, I heard the words, "It is coming."

Higher Self: When you heard that message it was not as if it was being delivered through your normal sensory apparatus, correct?

Ego: It was distinctly different. It was as if a completely different aspect of me had heard those words and as I was coming into my normal awareness I found myself repeating them in my mind.

Higher Self: When you received that message your awareness was outside of your normal egoic framework. The message was still present in your awareness when you were returning back to your egoic framework. You had the sense that you were hearing the words as if they were reverberating because your awareness was transitioning between those two states.

Ego: Yes, that's exactly what it was like. I felt as if I was in an echo chamber.

Higher Self: Spiritual and mental, that is correct.

Ego: So when is it going to materialize?

Higher Self: The process has begun.

Ego: What process?

Higher Self: Your spiritual path concerns manifestation and expression in the physical and that is happening.

Ego: I have perceived over the years how my vibratory sense has elevated.

Higher Self: Yes that is part of the process. The matter of your physical body has and is being conditioned to carry spiritual energy of higher frequency.

Ego: To what end?

Higher Self: To express Source energy more directly in this material plane of existence. That is what the human body is designed to do. Humanity is moving toward this state of being and more people are experiencing this transition.

Ego: Sounds like science fiction to me. I saw an episode of Star Trek like that, but it wasn't happening on Earth.

Higher Self: Hollywood has a habit of introducing many concepts, but it is happening on Earth. You have suspected this for many years. That is why you have been working on your technology.

Ego: We've been working on this technology to enhance our spiritual experiences, but we didn't fully appreciate what that meant.

Higher Self: Even this past week you have experimented with a change to the technology that improves this effect.

Ego: Yes, we were surprised by the results.

Higher Self: What did you experience?

Ego: The change produced a greater embodiment of our spiritual energy. I had never experienced my tenth chakra under my feet so expanded. It caused a greater influx of energy through my crown.

Higher Self: This change is helpful in grounding your spiritual energies more completely in the material plane.

Ego: What does that actually mean?

Higher Self: For years you have thought of me as your soul, a personal spiritual self. In part, I do play that role as I am here with you. An extension of me permeates your physical body when you allow it and you have allowed it over recent years. This has brought you much calm and relief from suffering.

Ego: Does that also account for the subtle vibrations that I feel throughout my body and for the vibrations that I hear?

Higher Self: Yes and as your body has been conditioned to carry higher frequencies, what you have felt has become finer and the pitch of what you have heard has become higher.

Ego: This is what we have been calling the soul embodied state of being.

Higher Self: You have split the process of spiritualizing matter into discreet stages, but as you suspect, it is a singular process that gradually emerges.

Ego: I have a habit of splitting things into parts in order to better understand them.

Higher Self: The mind of the ego can often digest the information more easily in that manner.

Ego: I felt as if my spiritual development had stalled. I wasn't experiencing much of a difference day after day.

Higher Self: You were experiencing a subtle shift in your vibration as you could carry higher spiritual energies.

Ego: I guess so. I did experience an intensification of what I was feeling, but it seemed like simply more of the same.

Higher Self: You would prefer fireworks.

Ego: That's about right.

Higher Self: Some people experience more abrupt changes during this process and you may too as it proceeds.

Ego: What exactly happens during this process?

Higher Self: Your physical body has been conditioned to carry higher spiritual energies, but these energies are not well integrated with the functioning of your nervous system. As the process continues this integration unfolds.

Ego: That makes a lot of sense to me. It has always seemed as if my energetic and nervous system functioned independently. How does this integration happen?

Higher Self: The chakra system is the interface between spiritual energies and the physical body. This system metabolizes spiritual energy and readies it for use in the body. It also can provide the nervous system with information. Having access to this information is what you have been seeking. It is that which provides for greater spiritual experience and awareness.

Ego: What prevents me from having that access?

Higher Self: The communication pathways between the base of the chakras, where they connect to the spirit line, and the nervous system are sealed. The dissolving of those seals or filters provides greater access.

Ego: How do I dissolve those seals?

Higher Self: It is best for those seals to be dissolved by me and not you. Forcing that energy to flow into the nervous system before it is ready to accept them is unwise.

Ego: Okay, so please proceed.

Higher Self: I am.

Ego: I don't feel anything.

Higher Self: I am not doing it in a manner that you will feel.

Ego: I thought you were doing it right now.

Higher Self: It has been happening for a while now and it will continue to happen for a while. Do you remember the session you had several weeks ago when Frank reported that he could see your root chakra.

Ego: That was strange. He hasn't been able to see my root chakra for years.

Higher Self: When you questioned him, after speaking to Jennifer, he provided more detail.

Ego: Yes, he said that what he saw was a reddish colored flame in the area of my root chakra.

Higher Self: And, as Jennifer explained to you, that was the beginning of the process that melts the seals. It started several weeks ago.

Ego: What can I do to accelerate the process?

Higher Self: Let it be. Allow it to proceed naturally at its own rate.

Ego: Okay. I feel better now that I have some understanding about this process.

Higher Self: You feel better now because you know that something is happening.

Ego: That too. How will this process change me?

Higher Self: It will provide you with a greater sense of oneness. You will be less likely to consider yourself in parts, as you do now.

Ego: What does that mean?

Higher Self: It will change how you perceive yourself and everything around you.

Ego: Because I will be able to better perceive the spiritual realm.

Higher Self: Your perceptual pathways will be more open. How you determine to use them and your willingness to accept the information provided will still remain a choice. As a result, what you perceive is a decision that only you can make.

Ego: I'm sure I'll decide to see the truth. That is what I've been after all along.

Higher Self: You will see.

Ego: You doubt me?

Higher Self: I am open to all possibilities.

Ego: I am assuming the change that is coming will be significant enough for me to open my eyes so to speak, so that I see more.

Higher Self: It certainly can do that and that can promote a change in a way that shifts your self-identity.

Ego: I'm interested in perceiving more.

Higher Self: As long as your filters are in place you may not perceive that much more. The change that is coming often disrupts those filters. In so doing there is a greater likelihood that you will perceive yourself differently. As that perception about yourself changes, so do your filters.

Ego: This seems like a more fundamental shift than I had in mind. It seems as if I am going to change.

Higher Self: It is actually only a change in your awareness of yourself. You already are that which you are about to perceive. You will realize what you are.

Considerations

Most of us self-identify with our egos. We believe we are that because it is what we are most familiar with. Actually, what we are most familiar with is our beliefs, which is why when we are ego-identified we often think of ourselves from the standpoint of our beliefs. We believe we are the roles we play in life. Self-identifying in this manner traps us into a way of perceiving that maintains our identity as we believe it to be. As such our reality becomes tightly bound to our roles in life and our daily happenstances.

We attempt to play those roles in the way that we deem appropriate. Typically the standards we adhere to are those that we have adopted from our parents, friends, relatives, superiors and society at large. As soon as our performance against these standards slip and we no longer feel we are living up to those standards, our ego kicks into gear reminding us that we are inadequate in some way.

But, when things go well we feel rewarded and our ego is happy. Our addiction has just been satisfied and the wheel keeps spinning. There is no freedom from this addiction as long as we remain ego-identified.

Ask yourself:

1. What is it about your ego that you like?

2. What is it about your ego that you dislike?

3. If your ego is a judgment machine, a tool to keep you alive and safe, how well has it worked for you in the past? Has it ever let you down and if so, why do you think that happened?

4. Do you self-identify as your ego/beliefs?

5. Do you have a soul? Are you that soul? Do you self-identify as a spiritual being?

6. Do you self-identify as All That Is?

7. What do you think you are? What do you think you can be?

Chapter 42: Purpose, Free Will and Destiny

Ego: I would like to know my purpose in life.

Higher Self: Why?

Ego: So that I can get on with it and get it done.

Higher Self: Your purpose is constantly unfolding.

Ego: It's unfolding because I'm doing it.

Higher Self: Do you remember when you sent the boxes of Breathe Right strips to the NFL trainers?

Ego: Yes.

Higher Self: And do you also remember that many other occurrences had to happen in order for the plan to be successful?

Ego: Yes.

Higher Self: And do you remember that those things that had to occur were outside of your control?

Ego: Yes, but I did my part.

Higher Self: That is how purpose unfolds.

Ego: Okay, so we all have to do our parts?

Higher Self: That is one way to think about it.

Ego: You mean to say that is how the ego thinks of it, right?

Higher Self: That is correct.

Ego: So how do you think about it?

Higher Self: It is difficult in your current state of awareness to consider life in your material plane of existence in a manner consistent with a more unified perspective.

Ego: Why?

Higher Self: Your vantage point is as a singular being amongst other individual beings, when in fact you are one being.

Ego: I asked a simple question and you've launched into a metaphysical dissertation. This makes me feel like you're working another agenda. Why can't you simply answer the question about my purpose in life? Is that too difficult? I just want a simple answer.

Higher Self: Just be present and live and enjoy the life you have chosen.

Ego: What kind of ridiculous answer is that?

Higher Self: It is the simple answer you requested.

Ego: That's not a simple answer and furthermore it makes no sense. What do you mean the life I have chosen?

Higher Self: It is the life I chose, but you and I are one. This is in part why you struggle with the answer provided. The reference point from which you experience life is sufficiently limited such that you do not remember what you have done before entering this life.

Ego: This seems like far too much unnecessary information. Why do I need to understand this in order to know what my purpose is?

Higher Self: Your ideas concerning your purpose are very limited. You think of it in terms of what you, as an individual, need to do or accomplish. The purpose of living is to experience life.

Ego: So that's it, just experience the life I have chosen?

Higher Self: You chose this life to live and experience.

Ego: Why did I choose this life?

Higher Self: This life offered you the possibility of experiences that you desired.

Ego: For what purpose?

Higher Self: To feel and understand those experiences more completely.

Ego: Why?

Higher Self: Why did you go to school?

Ego: To learn.

Higher Self: It is for that reason, to learn, grow and experience.

Ego: I always thought I came here to do something.

Higher Self: That is because your reference point has become the life you are experiencing as opposed to what you truly are.

Ego: What you are saying would suggest that the life would live itself and I'm only along for the ride.

Higher Self: The life you have chosen has a trajectory, a path of its own. Allow events to unfold, be present and receptive and take action when called upon.

Ego: This is so contrary to how I've lived. This is a bit too much to take in.

Higher Self: You have always thought of yourself as a doer, someone who is action oriented.

Ego: Exactly, that's how things get done.

Higher Self: Please consider how many things you have done that have resulted in outcomes that you deemed negative. Alternatively, remember how some events have worked out well by your standards when you have simply let things happen.

Ego: You are correct. There have been many things that haven't worked out well that I've worked hard at and some that have worked out very well when I've simply gotten out of the way.

Higher Self: Do you remember the conversation you had with your friend the Rabbi about this topic?

Ego: Yes. It was frustrating.

Higher Self: Why?

Ego: His thoughts about doing left me feeling uncertain.

Higher Self: Uncertain about what?

Ego: About how to proceed.

Higher Self: Explain what you remember?

Ego: He said that in regards to every outcome, I had a part to play and God had a part to play and that ultimately the outcome was entirely in God's hands.

Higher Self: Your friend also said that in his opinion you took too much upon yourself in the process.

Ego: Yes, he said that I regularly crossed the line and did more than my part.

Higher Self: Do you agree?

Ego: In hindsight, yes I agree. I do that most of the time.

Higher Self: Why have you taken that course of action so often?

Ego: I was impatient. The outcome I wanted wasn't forthcoming on my schedule so I kept pushing harder. I can see why you call this an addiction.

Higher Self: How do you view it as an addiction?

Ego: I was striving for an outcome to feel good about myself by accomplishing my perceived purpose. Even if the outcome was deemed to be positive by me, I would have only felt good for a short while. Then I would have been right back at it, trying to do more. All the while I am focusing on the tasks I have assigned myself to the exclusion of much else. It's not a good way to live.

Higher Self: That is quite excellent.

Ego: Are you saying that's the way I should be?

Higher Self: That is not what I am suggesting. Your understanding of this issue is now quite excellent. This experience is an aspect of your purpose.

Ego: What do you mean?

Higher Self: You have lived through much to experience what you have learned in this regard. That is one of life's lessons that you desired to have more experience with.

Ego: Is that it? Is that my purpose?

Higher Self: It is an aspect of the broader experiences you seek, but it is an important piece of the puzzle.

Ego: You speak of this as if it's a game.

Higher Self: And you take this game far too seriously.

Ego: I have a lot of decisions to make. I need to take life seriously.

Higher Self: Why do you believe you have so many decisions to make?

Ego: Who else is going to make them, you?

Higher Self: You once worked with a person named Rob years ago that had a different perspective about making decisions.

Ego: I didn't like his process.

Higher Self: Needless to say, his approach was wrong in your eyes.

Ego: Rob's approach was to put off every decision until he couldn't avoid it any longer. I was exactly the opposite. I made my decisions as fast as I could. Are you suggesting his approach is better than mine?

Higher Self: Those approaches are at opposite ends of the spectrum.

Ego: I suspect that in certain situations one or the other approach may be preferable.

Higher Self: Yes, however your approach remains relatively constant despite differing circumstances.

Ego: I still like my approach? Is there something wrong with it?

Higher Self: Nothing is wrong with it if that is how you consciously choose to operate in regard to each decision. However, acting that swiftly deprives you of knowledge that may be forthcoming and that can sway you in making a different decision. That may result in a different outcome that you may enjoy more.

Ego: If new information presents itself I can always reverse my decision.

Higher Self: Yes you can and that is what you often do. However you expend far more effort than is necessary and it takes away from your enjoyment of life. You have placed doing and accomplishing ahead of experiencing. You would be happier allowing destiny to take its course.

Ego: I prefer free will to destiny.

Higher Self: Of course you do.

Ego: I have free will and I intend to use it.

Higher Self: And you do, often resulting in outcomes that you deem negative because your efforts have not accomplished what you intended. Do you know why you act as you do?

Ego: I take action so that I can get things done.

Higher Self: We have been through that. Why are you not more patient?

Ego: I am the one responsible for making the decisions.

Higher Self: Yet you are not responsible for the outcome.

Ego: But the desired outcome won't materialize unless I do my part.

Higher Self: This is playing out in your life right now in regards to your spiritual technology project.

Ego: Yes I am trying to figure out how best to make people aware of it.

Higher Self: People are becoming aware of it already.

Ego: But I don't know if that will continue or if it will grow and be as beneficial as it should be.

Higher Self: How beneficial should it become?

Ego: I don't know, but I want to give it a chance to become what it can be.

Higher Self: You have already done your part in that regard and you have been informed as such.

Ego: I have? When?

Higher Self: When you received the answer to your question while stopped at that red light several years ago.

Ego: When I heard the message that I was done?

Higher Self: Yes. Do you remember how you felt?

Ego: I felt great. I was completely relieved.

Higher Self: You closed your office and halted the entire project.

Ego: Yes, that's what happened. That was three years ago.

Higher Self: Slowly over the past three years you have begun to shift back to your old way of being.

Ego: What are you referring to?

Higher Self: How did you interpret the message you had received?

Ego: I wasn't entirely sure. On the one hand I had thought the technology was done or at least done enough. It conferred excellent benefits. However the project as a whole was far from done. There was still so much to figure out about how to position, distribute and launch the product.

Higher Self: Yet you took a definitive action and shut the whole project down, despite claiming not to fully understand the message.

Ego: What are you implying?

Higher Self: Your actions were driven by the feeling you had which was so pervasive at that time.

Ego: Are you saying that I made the wrong decision.

Higher Self: You made the decision based upon the feeling you had despite your lack of mental certainty regarding all aspects of the project. Deep within you it was clear that you realized your efforts were no longer required. You had lost all attachment to the outcome, not just related to the product, but related to the entire project.

Ego: It was a wonderful feeling, something I never expected to feel.

Higher Self: That feeling allowed you to have trust that everything would work out fine. You were willing to allow everything to play out on its own.

Ego: I got out of the way.

Higher Self: That is correct. The project has a life, a destiny of its own. Your continued efforts would have only delayed or hampered its progress.

Ego: I can be my own worst enemy sometimes. I kept feeling as if I had to exert my will to make progress. I hadn't been able to trust that things would work out well.

Higher Self: That old abandonment issue resurfaced. You felt isolated and alone and everything was on your shoulders. You had been so locked into a course of action that you were no longer receptive, until finally you asked, "God, what do you want from me?"

Ego: Getting an answer from what I perceived was a higher authority made all the difference. The pressure was off.

Higher Self: And since you have backed off, look at how the project continued to unfold.

Ego: It is beginning to make its way into the hands of practitioners, but more importantly we are beginning to develop a group of trainers that can use all of the materials generated to facilitate classes in stress reduction and spiritual development at many levels.

Higher Self: You had originally thought that the technology was the initial focus.

Ego: I had it backwards. The educational component comes first and then those that wish to accelerate their practice can use the technology. It is a much more natural transition. As a result, the support for the technology is already in place and is ready to teach all of the underlying principles required for best use of the technology.

Higher Self: Do you now believe that your free will was actually at odds with the outcome destined for this project?

Ego: I have come to believe that is true.

Higher Self: How do you know?

Ego: I can feel that this is the correct path. It feels really good. I don't know why I couldn't see it earlier.

Higher Self: It was not the right time. You are often ahead of yourself and this was just another example.

Ego: If I was more like Rob then maybe I would have been better off.

Higher Self: Possibly or possibly not. Rob delays his decisions because he fears being criticized if things do not work out well. That is why Rob tends to be a conformist. You do not fear criticism in that way and as such you have been able to choose a path less traveled. You have been developing yourself along spiritual lines that will soon play a more prominent role in your life.

Considerations

The egoic self seeks control, as it wants to have its perceived needs met in the manner of its choosing. It relishes in the concept of free will and detests the idea of destiny, which it cannot control. Since at this time in humanity's development, most of us spend most of our time ego-identified, free will is believed to be the primary if not the only driver of outcomes.

This scenario makes sense to the egoic self as it strives to achieve what it wants and blames itself or others when it fails. It has come to know and accept this way of life. In fact, it has become addicted to this way of life, fueled by life's positive rewards.

To the ego-identified, destiny seems like an unyielding master that cannot be manipulated. With destiny as part of the equation, life is a game that may not be winnable. We seem more like marionettes with no sense of control and many of us feel this way much of the time.

Obviously free will exists. If one assumes that destiny co-exists with free will, then life's challenge becomes striking a balance between the two. To do so we ask, "How do we know when we are on our path and when do we take what action?" Welcome to the game of life. However you choose to play it, enjoy the ride.

Ask yourself:

1. Do you believe in free will, destiny or both? If you believe in both, which one do you believe plays a bigger role in your life?

2. If you believe mainly in free will, are you a person that likes to be in control? Why do you think that is?

3. If you believe mainly in destiny, are you a person that avoids making decisions? Why do you think that is?

4. Is your sense of purpose related more to doing and accomplishing something or related more to feeling and experiencing or both?

5. Does your egoic self have a different purpose than your spiritual self? If so, what are the differences?

6. Do you believe that your life has a destined path to follow? Are you on that path? How do you know when you are on that path? How do you know when you are off that path?

7. Do we as human beings have a collective purpose? If so, what do you think that is?

Chapter 43: Letting Go and Surrender

Higher Self: During your sessions or when you meditate, you used to practice letting go and now you practice surrender. Why?

Ego: Even though the concepts are roughly the same, those words seem to be quite different. Early on during my sessions it was easier to use letting go. Back then I was uncomfortable with the term surrender.

Higher Self: What were you letting go of?

Ego: I was letting go of all of my cares. I would allow them to drift away.

Higher Self: Is that all you were letting go of?

Ego: Actually, now that I think about it I was letting go of more than that. I was also letting go of my boundaries to an extent. I was allowing you to move throughout and around all of my body.

Higher Self: You had not realized then how you tended to protect your physical space in that way. You prevented my presence throughout all of you.

Ego: I was also letting go of the need to control everything. That was probably the hardest thing to let go of.

Higher Self: How did that impact your sessions?

Ego: It made it easier to simply be. I didn't have to do this or try that all of the time. I could just let things happen. I wasn't like that all of the time or even most of the time, but I did exist in a state of being more often as a result.

Higher Self: Was there anything else you let go of?

Ego: I can't think of anything else. That was probably all.

Higher Self: What about your beliefs?

Ego: Oh yes, I forgot. I would regularly ask for help in letting go of my beliefs.

Higher Self: Why?

Ego: I began to realize how much they impacted me and that their impact wasn't helpful.

Higher Self: It is not easy to release one's beliefs. How did you approach this?

Ego: The beliefs that I really wanted to release were those about me that were limiting and negative in nature. I wanted to get rid of all of the, I can't do this or I shouldn't be that way. I would ask you for help in releasing them.

Higher Self: How did you realize you needed my help?

Ego: I realized how these beliefs defined me. It was almost as if these beliefs were a part of me and so letting go of them was like chopping off my arm. I felt I needed help in getting the job done.

Higher Self: Did it work?

Ego: At first not much happened. I think it took me a while to adjust my attitude, just so that I was willing to release some of my beliefs. Then slowly I began to make some progress.

Higher Self: There was a little more to it. Do you remember what you called the love consideration?

Ego: Yes I do. I realized that my beliefs were like cerebral reflexes. Because I had all of these beliefs I felt that I knew what to do in most situations. I didn't have to think about anything. I could respond reflexively using my beliefs, which were associated with my old subconscious, reactive patterns of behaviors. All of these limiting beliefs would get triggered by life's events. They were the root of my coping strategies.

Higher Self: You were comfortable with those beliefs. They had served you well when you were younger.

Ego: They weren't serving me well anymore. They were very limited patterns of thought and behavior. I didn't need them anymore.

Higher Self: But they informed your actions.

Ego: Relying on those beliefs was the easy way out. They were unproductive lies that I used to protect aspects of myself that no longer required protection.

Higher Self: So what did you do?

Ego: I decided that I would ask myself what love would do in those situations.

Higher Self: Did you actually do that when your subconscious beliefs were triggered?

Ego: Not really.

Higher Self: Why not?

Ego: I never had to. A number of things seemed to happen at the same time. Once I made that decision to consider what love would do something clicked for me. I realized that for the love consideration to work as fast as a reflex I couldn't just stop the world and consider what love would do. I had to be love in a sense and just respond from that vantage point.

Higher Self: How did you do that?

Ego: I had been allowing you to be present throughout all of me. I began to equate you with love. I allowed the love that was you to become more of me. In that way when an

297

old belief was triggered it was easier to respond out of love and not rely on old beliefs.

Higher Self: That also allowed you to feel more.

Ego: Yes, my feeling nature became more enhanced at that time.

Higher Self: It did so because you allowed yourself to be love. Love is a state of unconditional acceptance. You gave yourself permission to feel everything as well as release your old patterned beliefs that were the underpinnings of your coping strategies. Once you did that you allowed much to come to the surface including your feelings. That is when you became soul embodied, as you call that stage.

Ego: I enjoyed having mastery over my negative emotions and coping strategies. I liked calling you in during the middle of the night when I would awaken feeling stressed.

Higher Self: You realized something else soon thereafter.

Ego: I realized I had learned to practice spiritual escapism or as my friend Shelli calls it, spiritual bypassing.

Higher Self: You had developed a powerful capability.

Ego: It is a seductive tool. I was using my spiritual know-how to escape my negative feelings. I was bypassing them and all the while thinking of myself as being very spiritual. It was just another coping strategy.

Higher Self: You did not stay stuck for long.

Ego: It took me a little while to realize what I was doing, but once I did, I corrected the situation.

Higher Self: How so?

Ego: I encouraged myself to allow all of my deep feelings, particularly those that I considered to be negative, to come to the surface.

Higher Self: You did even more than that.

Ego: I allowed the center of my consciousness to shift deeper into my body. I could feel it shift from my head to my chest and abdomen. I wanted to sit in my feelings and not allow them to elude me.

Higher Self: You realized that you had been avoiding them.

Ego: Yes I was, but when I stopped avoiding them I found that there wasn't much to be concerned about. Many of my issues had already been dealt with reasonably well.

Higher Self: You were a little disappointed.

Ego: In fact I was. I was hoping for a reservoir of negative stuff to deal with. I was hoping that by breaking the dam and dealing with the flood I would be elevated to another level. I needed to reevaluate my situation.

Higher Self: What did you learn?

Ego: I was letting go of aspects of myself, but I still retained essentially the same self-identity.

Higher Self: But you felt more soul embodied.

Ego: I realized that was still a personal way of self-identifying. It was more like being a spiritualized ego. Granted I was in a much better state of being and any suffering I experienced was dramatically reduced, but I still viewed myself and life from the same perspective. The process of letting go just didn't seem like it was enough.

Higher Self: That is when you began to use the word surrender. What was it about that word that caused you resistance earlier?

Ego: It signified giving up and I didn't view myself as giving up in that way.

Higher Self: Some people feel that the word surrender has a religious connotation.

Ego: I didn't care about that. I don't know enough about religion for that to have any effect on me. I had no feelings about that one way or the other.

Higher Self: So why did you turn to that word?

Ego: It felt stronger, more potent and I had come to grips with the fact that in a sense I actually needed to give up.

Higher Self: Why?

Ego: I felt as though I had reached the end of the road. I didn't feel as if I could go any further on my path without giving myself up in the process.

Higher Self: Why?

Ego: Because I came to believe that I was trying to get to a place that the egoic self simply cannot go.

Higher Self: What was it that you needed to surrender?

Ego: I had to surrender myself.

Higher Self: How do you do that?

Ego: It's a bit of a strange concept.

Higher Self: It seems like a form of suicide from your perspective.

Ego: It is and it isn't. On the one hand my ego performs some necessary functions that keep me safe and feeling

300

secure. On the other hand there's a lot of baggage that I've collected over my lifetime that doesn't help and in fact prevents me from seeing beyond my egoic self. As long as I use my egoic filters to perceive myself and the world around me I won't see the truth. In a sense it's like suicide in that I need to allow my filters to die off and fall away, but in truth those are just beliefs that condition my perceptions. There is no person that is dying in this process.

Higher Self: It appears that you have made the mental leap in understanding that you and I are one. All that separates us is your filters.

Ego: Conceptually I agree. However, I am still having some difficulty in truly self-identifying with you as I have been unable to experience life from your perspective.

Higher Self: Your inability stems from trying to experience life from my perspective while retaining your ego's beliefs, which act as filters on our awareness. Only after you surrender those filters which significantly impact your awareness can you perceive from my vantage point.

Ego: That's the problem. Surrendering in that way does feel a bit like suicide.

Considerations

It would be nice if the notion of letting go or surrendering was as simple as falling asleep at night. Falling asleep for many of us is like turning off a light switch. We are awake one moment and then typically after seconds or minutes we are asleep. We may become drowsy in the process, but that is usually only a brief transitional phase. Surrendering, on the other hand, is done in increments. It seems as though it is a never ending series of small steps with a hard-to-reach endpoint that is difficult to ascertain.

We can surrender a little and feel more relaxed. As we surrender more we become more still and we may become aware of our breathing or pulse. Our thoughts may intrude and over time we can learn to let them go as well. The more we surrender our will the less our egoic self is in control. When we have surrendered sufficiently we exist in a state of being. We are not thinking or doing. We are simply being.

While in this state of being our egoic self can observe our relaxed body breathing regularly. It can sense our subtle vibrations. It can remember what these sensations feel like and recreate them later. Our egoic self can be awake and aware during this time.

What happens when we surrender the egoic self entirely? It no longer exists. It is not awake nor does it filter our awareness. Yet awareness still exists, as what we truly are, still is. We never stop being. When does that awareness become our awareness?

Ask yourself:

1. Do you prefer the term letting go or surrender? Why?

2. Which aspect of you is surrendering and what is being surrendered?

3. Do you practice letting go or surrendering during a spiritual practice such as meditation? Do you practice letting go or surrendering during any daily activities?

4. What have you been able to let go of or surrender?

5. What would you like to let go of or surrender?

Chapter 44: Intention and Prayer

Higher Self: During a session or when you meditate you used to set an intention.

Ego: Yes I used to do that with almost every session. I was always trying to accomplish something.

Higher Self: You rarely if ever set an intention these days.

Ego: In the past it was helpful for me to set an intention. I wanted to learn how to relax more deeply or lessen my need to control outcomes or understand what belief had been triggered precipitating an event the prior day. There were many things I was trying to learn or do from the perspective of my ego. It only made sense that I would set an intention and attempt to further myself in that regard.

Higher Self: The process worked well for you.

Ego: Yes I would set the intention, as my egoic self, anticipating that you would provide what was necessary in order to fulfill the request.

Higher Self: Sometimes you did not direct the intention to me.

Ego: Sometimes I broadcasted the thought or request to the universe at large, but usually I had you in mind even if I wasn't more specific. I figured that if I opened myself to develop further in a particular direction that I would move in that direction.

Higher Self: So it was a fairly willful process on your part.

Ego: Exactly. I wanted and attempted to willfully make the change or somehow have the change in me occur.

Higher Self: Why have you stopped?

Ego: I reached a certain understanding that it was likely best for me to proceed differently.

Higher Self: How so?

Ego: I had gotten to the point where I was attempting to lessen the role of my egoic self. So it seemed counterproductive to have my sessions run by my egoic self, which is what I had been doing by setting intentions.

Higher Self: How do you know that it was your egoic self setting the intentions?

Ego: Because my intentions were attempts at instigating some level of movement or change. I was always striving for something, even when the intention was simply allowing for a change, which seems more passive. Regardless of what I was intending my egoic will was directing the process.

Higher Self: It seems as though you are judging that process as being wrong.

Ego: No I'm not. It was very helpful, but it's hard for me to reconcile how to lessen the role of my egoic self using the same process going forward if I continue to drive it willfully.

Higher Self: That is why you turned to surrender.

Ego: Yes. It seemed as though I had reached a point where the best approach was to simply be, without any intending or striving.

Higher Self: Yet you initiated this process with your egoic self.

Ego: Well of course. If I wasn't going to buy into the process and get it started it wasn't going to happen.

Higher Self: Then you reached an impasse.

Ego: Ultimately I realized that I was still driving the process.

Higher Self: And so?

Ego: It finally became clear that there was only one solution for me, which was to surrender myself. Actually it was surrendering my filters, but since I was identified with my beliefs and conditioning it seemed as if I was surrendering myself or at least my personal will.

Higher Self: How has that worked for you?

Ego: I couldn't find a way to do it. No matter how I tried it was still me initiating the attempts and monitoring myself for progress. I finally turned to prayer.

Higher Self: Who did you pray to?

Ego: I prayed to God or All That Is or the Source of All That Is.

Higher Self: What did you pray for?

Ego: I prayed for help. I realized I couldn't do this on my own.

Higher Self: How did prayer differ from intention?

Ego: The intentions were self-motivated and based upon what I would allow. When I prayed I realized that I had to give up control completely. The outcomes were no longer based on what I wanted. I was praying to be released from the bondage of self. I wanted Source to surrender my egoic self for me, as I was unable to do it for myself.

Higher Self: How did you come upon this method?

Ego: A friend of mine suggested I read the book that is used by Alcoholics Anonymous. The founders of that movement wrote the book in 1935. I hadn't realized that there were such strong spiritual underpinnings to that movement. My friend, who is an addiction professional, bemoans the fact that many AA chapters have moved away from those spiritual roots. He claims that is why AA and addiction treatment centers at large are less successful now as compared to the past.

Higher Self: Reading that book helped you to realize that you were addicted to your ego.

Ego: It caused me to realize that we are all addicted to our ego and that is the root of all addictions. All of those other addictions are just further manifestations of our primary addiction. When I read in the AA book, "Relieve me of the bondage of self, that I may better do Thy will," I realized the problem they were addressing wasn't alcohol. The addiction to alcohol was just another symptom. It is the deeper problem of self, the egoic self that requires remedy.

Higher Self: But you recognize that the egoic self is actually your unfiltered or authentic self moving through the filters of the ego. The ego is nothing more than your beliefs and conditioning. It is not a real person.

Ego: I get it. However it seems like a real person because we identify with it.

Higher Self: So the issue is less about the egoic self and more about the ego and our identification with it.

Ego: It all gets back to the demon standing on my left shoulder. It is simply the ego whispering in my ear. It is whispering to that which I truly am. I don't have to listen to it and I certainly need not identify with it.

Higher Self: Yes I hear it too.

Ego: Of course you do, as you and I are the same.

Higher Self: Your experiences in your more recent sessions have now allowed you to perceive that this is so.

Ego: When I pray and ask that my egoic filters be suspended and that I experience only that which I truly am I actually do experience you to a greater extent.

Higher Self: There was a time when that prayer would cause you to lose conscious awareness.

Ego: Now it does not. I'm not sure if it was just a transitional phase during which I adapted to that state of being or whether it was facilitated by a shift in my self-identity. Either way it does not matter.

Higher Self: The reasons for it are less important than the experience of it.

Considerations

Often the word intention rather than prayer is used when teaching a spiritual practice. Sometimes this is done to avoid offending the student in case of any religious sensitivity. Is that necessary? Almost everyone on a spiritual quest acknowledges a higher power. If not, what are they attempting to realize they are in union with?

If the student is going to direct their intention to that higher power, then why not simply call it prayer? What is the resistance? The reason most often is that there is a fundamental difference between the two processes. Intention is ego-based. It is, I intending this or that. I am in control. Prayer is often asking for this or that or being in dialogue with what is often considered a higher power. The process of prayer typically subordinates the personal will.

Shifting from intention to prayer is an acknowledgment that our ego cannot do what our higher self intends. Many that pray take it one step further. They end their prayer with, thy will be done. With that the ego relinquishes its sense of control. It is accepting of any outcome. In this circumstance it is no longer the ego that is driving the process. If done with great sincerity, the higher self is guiding this vehicle.

Ask yourself:

1. Do you perceive a difference between setting an intention and praying?

2. Do you prefer to set an intention or pray? Do you do both?

3. When you set an intention who or what are you directing it to? When you pray, who or what are you praying to?

4. Do you relinquish your free will when you set an intention? Do you relinquish your free will when you pray?

5. Do you retain an attachment to outcomes when you set an intention? Do you retain an attachment to outcomes when you pray?

6. Which process feels more potent to you?

7. Have your intentions become manifest? Have your prayers been answered?

Chapter 45: Gratitude and Grace

Ego: I've been in a bit of a funk lately.

Higher Self: Yes, I have noticed.

Ego: All of this striving to achieve my goal is getting to me.

Higher Self: Actually, you have been striving less. That is not what is principally impacting you.

Ego: Well then, what is?

Higher Self: Your prayers are being answered.

Ego: What prayers?

Higher Self: You have been asking to suspend your egoic self and that has been occurring.

Ego: I don't feel the enthusiasm for life that I did.

Higher Self: You are not getting high like you used to. The addiction to your ego has greatly diminished. The egoic excitement associated with your plans and expectations has dramatically lessened as a result of letting go of your attachment to many outcomes.

Ego: I didn't consider that this would happen. It's left me feeling a bit flat. I'm not depressed, just not feeling as excited as I was. Why hasn't the rest of what I've asked for happened? Why aren't I experiencing more of what I truly am?

Higher Self: It is coming.

Ego: I've heard that before. When is it going to get here?

Higher Self: When it arrives.

Ego: That makes me feel like a five year old in the backseat of a car on a family trip asking when we're going to get to our destination.

Higher Self: Being impatient will not hasten what you seek.

Ego: Underneath all of my good intentions and prayer, I'm still trying to drive this process.

Higher Self: To an extent you are, but you are much less ego-motivated than you were.

Ego: So what do I need to do in order to get there?

Higher Self: Do nothing, which is obviously difficult for you.

Ego: You bet it is. I'm not good at doing nothing.

Higher Self: Take some time off. Have some fun for a change.

Ego: Bruce and I went out for dinner last night. We had a really nice time. Jen and I spend a lot of time together. I haven't exactly been focusing on this matter exclusively.

Higher Self: That is true.

Ego: Do you have any other suggestions?

Higher Self: Let it be.

Ego: Something doesn't make sense to me.

Higher Self: What are you referring to?

Ego: Three years ago when I was stopped at that red light at Pioneer Trail and Flying Cloud Drive and I was told that I was done I lost all attachment to outcomes. At that time I felt great. Now I just feel neutral.

Higher Self: That process allowed you to feel unburdened. A great weight lifted off your shoulders and you were very relieved. You felt free of the task at hand.

Ego: Why don't I feel free now?

Higher Self: You still remain somewhat burdened by the need to achieve, although it is not entirely ego-driven. However the part of it that is, causes you to feel shackled to the need to do and accomplish. You are growing weary of this task and that feeling. It would be best if you could let that go and even further lessen your attachment to outcomes.

Ego: I really liked the feeling that I had three years ago and it lasted for about a year.

Higher Self: You have not lost that way of being. You are much more like that now than you were prior to that event.

Ego: Why do you call it an event?

Higher Self: Because it happened suddenly. It was an occurrence.

Ego: An occurrence of what?

Higher Self: The concept that best describes it is called grace.

Ego: I don't understand what grace is.

Higher Self: Consider it a gift.

Ego: It was a sudden dramatic shift in how I felt after hearing that I was done. That's when we closed the office and stopped the project.

Higher Self: Even after resurrecting the project you do not have the same attachment to the outcome that you once did.

Ego: I wonder why that is.

Higher Self: There was a fundamental change in you that occurred that day.

Ego: I don't remember doing anything.

Higher Self: You cried out to God. You said, "God what do you want from me?" You were in considerable distress.

Ego: Yes I was quite distraught and then when I heard the message that I was done I felt remarkably better.

Higher Self: You have received many messages in the past and you have never felt like that as a result of any of them. You were given more than the message you heard.

Ego: What else?

Higher Self: With that message came a divine influence, which was why you felt so much better immediately and thereafter. You did not even fully understand the message. The message alone was not responsible for the change in how you felt.

Ego: I see your point. It did have a great influence on me and in looking back, it continues to. Even though I continue to work on this project I fully realize that I'm not in control of the outcome department. I'm much more comfortable with that position and I have much more trust that everything will work out for the best.

Higher Self: Why?

Ego: That's a funny question for you to ask.

Higher Self: Not at all. Do you understand why you have less need for control and greater trust?

Ego: In the past concepts like trust and attachment to outcomes were just mental constructs. I understood what they meant. However I couldn't feel any difference when I would consider these concepts from only a mental perspective in an effort to calm my fears.

Higher Self: How is it different now?

Ego: Now I can feel greater trust and feel that everything will be okay. I know I don't have total control and I can't drive every outcome the way my ego would prefer, but since I trust that everything will be fine I no longer need to. I am very grateful for being able to feel this way as I don't worry about the future as I once did.

Higher Self: It was a gift, but you had readied yourself to receive the gift.

Ego: By asking.

Higher Self: That was important too, but you had already significantly changed your feeling nature such that the influence you received that day could have the intended results.

Ego: All of my sessions and mindfulness practices had significantly changed my ability to feel.

Higher Self: It is your feeling nature which allows you to experience me so much more easily and often. Otherwise it is more difficult to effectively communicate through your filters.

Ego: That has allowed me to shift my beliefs to a sense of knowing based upon personal experience. In the past I only had beliefs about you, but now I have had sufficient experiences to know rather than simply believe.

Higher Self: Yet you continue to seek more experience so that you can know more. Why?

Ego: I want to know what I am.

Higher Self: You realize that any answer I attempt to communicate to you will be inadequate.

Ego: Yes I realize that you communicating through my filters will not allow me to perceive you.

Higher Self: You can only know what you are through direct experience.

Ego: Yes. I have been asking for my egoic filters to be suspended and to only perceive through the consciousness of what I truly am.

Higher Self: And since you cannot willfully make that happen you have no control in this process.

Ego: Yes I realize that I have no control and as a result I can't drive the outcome I desire.

Higher Self: Yet you persist in attempting.

Ego: What are you talking about?

Higher Self: You want to know what you are and you are attached to that knowing.

Ego: Oh.

Higher Self: It was only through grace that you lost the attachment to an outcome you had been previously preoccupied with. Once you lost that attachment the path opened up to you.

Ego: That's why you said to let it be.

Higher Self: Yes. You cannot confer this knowledge upon yourself or go outside of yourself and acquire it. This knowledge is gained through direct experience. You have done what you can and now it is time to let it happen in the timeframe of its choosing. Trust that it will work out as it needs to.

Ego: I guess I don't have a choice.

Higher Self: You do not. It is beyond your control, capability and comprehension. You have done your part.

Ego: So in other words, I'm done.

Higher Self: You have prepared yourself well.

Ego: I am grateful for all of the support I have had.

Higher Self: You have had support in life and from what you call the spiritual realm. You are never alone.

Ego: Many people have helped me along the way and I can only imagine how many helpers have participated on your side.

Higher Self: Everyone receives much support, but for most people it is difficult to perceive, which is why many people have lost faith.

Ego: We are not taught to remain open to these influences and so they don't seem real to us. I have been fortunate. I have been guided through this process. The guidance I've received from you and other people have allowed us to develop technology which has aided us greatly in our development. The messages I've received over the years have kept me moving forward on my path. The people that have been and are in my life have made all of this come to life.

Higher Self: Yes, all of these support mechanisms are very important. You have also done your part.

Ego: Thank you.

Considerations

The phrase, it takes a village, is often used to express the sentiment that many people are needed to fulfill a task. The same is true for living one's life. Even the process of birthing typically involves more than the mother and child. Raising the child involves an army of support and continued human support usually occurs in many different forms throughout life. The involvement of other human beings is essential and for many of us, is what life is all about. Most of us are very grateful for the relationships and support that has surrounded us in life, although sometimes we forget to acknowledge our gratitude.

If we could witness the support we receive from the spiritual realm our lives would be transformed in an instant. Humility would reign supreme after realizing all of the love and assistance that is bestowed upon us. Even our core egoic belief of, I'm not good enough or I'm unworthy of love, could not be maintained in the light of that love and support. This is the state of grace that always embraces us, but rarely is appreciated.

Why don't we perceive it? As long as we retain our egoic filters we cannot perceive the truth of what we are and what surrounds us. Our addiction fuels our misperceptions and keeps us wanting.

Take a moment and express your gratitude for what you have been given in this life. During this moment open yourself to the possibility that all of the love and support imaginable is here for you. Lay down your defenses and receive what is being offered to you always.

Ask yourself:

1. Do you generally express gratitude? How often do you express gratitude? Is it something that naturally flows from you every day?

2. What are you grateful for?

3. Are you grateful for your life?

4. Have you ever experienced grace?

5. Are you open to experiencing grace?

6. Do you believe that you have to earn grace?

7. Do you believe that your ego stands between you and grace? If so, what can you do about that?

Part V – The Technology, Applications and Instructions for Use

Chapter 46: Technology

Some people think that using technology for relaxation or spiritual development is somewhat contradictory. Why would anyone use man-made technology to effect a change in one's degree of relaxation or spirituality? In this case, the technology is simply a way of stimulating an individual with natural phenomena. The sound, vibration and magnetic fields are coordinated in a manner to suppress the egoic functions that maintain vigilance and maximize spiritual embodiment. Both of these changes facilitate profound relaxation and greater spiritual development.

The technology consists of an amplifier and transducers built into a comfortable delivery platform, which uses layered music to induce synchronized sounds, vibrations and magnetic fields.

The seating portion of the chair contains the back and seat transducers. Due to the fiberglass construction the entire seating structure vibrates homogeneously. It also emits sound. The ambient sound level is independently adjustable and headphones can be used if desired. Headphone usage is generally recommended to block out any extraneous noise or if one wishes to run the chair more quietly. Otherwise headphone usage is not necessary and generally not recommended.

The seat transducer is the workhorse of the technology. The mass-loaded cone (1 pound of aluminum) moves up and down creating some sound, but a lot of vibration. That motion and the manner in which it is attached to the fiberglass, causes the whole transducer to move, including the large magnet at the bottom. This motion creates a dynamic magnetic field containing bass and midrange frequencies. That field also transmits faster frequencies from the smaller magnetic field created by the voice coil.

Music has been specifically designed for use with technology. The music is layered – multiple melodies play simultaneously so that it becomes tiresome to follow the music. The intention is to have the user not be listening to the music and instead to develop an inattentive state of mind. There is also bass and midrange frequencies throughout most of the music track to maintain the integrity of the magnetic fields.

Commercial music can be used with the technology. However it is recommended that any music used have a significant amount of bass and low midrange frequencies throughout the soundtrack. Another reason that the music provided is layered is to provide a broad spectrum of frequency content in order to stimulate the entire range of the energy system.

More can be learned about the technology as well as new features being added to the technology by visiting the website, www.ToolsToAwaken.com.

Chapter 47: Stress Reduction

Stress and stress related illnesses are at epidemic proportions. However, our reaction to stressors can actually be one of relaxation. It's all a matter of learning how to generate a healthy response in the face of stress and to learn how to routinely exist in this state. And everyone can learn.

When we experience fear-based emotions associated with stress we tend to shut down or act out in order to reduce our feelings of fear. Doing so disconnects us from our feelings, literally taking us away from our body. The key to feeling relaxed in the face of stress is to learn what it feels like to be fully present and relaxed in our bodies.

The technology induces a relaxed and present state of being that you can easily feel provided you allow yourself to feel. The more you feel relaxed, the easier it becomes to recreate these feelings. With greater use these relaxed feelings intensify making you more resistant to feeling the effects of stress and making it easier to recreate feelings of relaxation and presence even after you allow stress to get the better of you.

Using music, the technology produces pleasant sound and vibrations, which induces a very deep state of relaxed drowsiness. This occurs as the relative constancy of the sound and vibratory stimuli induce brain changes that reduce the sympathetic fight or flight response. In addition, the synchronized magnetic field induces a much greater state of presence as a result of its interaction with the human energy system.

During your session, you are also instructed to fall asleep, which promotes the development of drowsiness. However, the intermittent changes in the intensity of the sound and vibration from the music, typically keeps you from falling into a deep sleep.

As a result of the induced brain changes and greater presence you become profoundly relaxed, but over time you learn to remain aware. This produces a mind-aware, body-asleep or nearly asleep state of being, which is the state of maximal relaxation. You learn to appreciate how relaxed and present you can feel, which then allows you to recreate these feelings anytime.

Chapter 48: Awakening

Are you a spiritual seeker on a quest for authentic spiritual awakening? If so, you probably realize that despite your best intentions and all of your efforts you cannot willfully mandate this transition. Why? Typically, the path requires a degree of egoic surrender that presently eludes you. Fortunately, it is easier to surrender more completely when your self-identity is less tied to your ego and there is a process that can assist you – facilitated spiritual experience leading to a shift your self-identity. This makes it easier to unconditionally surrender.

Those seeking awakening, when successful, generally experience awakening in a non-abiding fashion. After variable periods of time in an awakened state, they re-experience ego-identification, albeit they have had a tremendously valuable experience that shifts their self-identity. Unfortunately they are not sufficiently free of limiting beliefs to remain in a sustained awakened state. This occurs as they haven't fully worked through those beliefs and blocks.

The spiritual progression chart has been developed in part to illustrate another step in the process that is typically bypassed in the awakening process – the soul embodied state of being. This is a transitional spiritual stage where self-identity is shared between ego and spiritual self. It is a stage where you can much more easily work through your limiting beliefs and accommodate to a shifting self-identity. The technology and associated course work facilitates this process and this is a state of being, unlike Source Awakened that you can mandate.

While you are on your quest for awakening it's nice to get a head start on the clean-up process or better still, avoid the need to do so afterwards. And during this process you will enjoy the transition each step of the way.

Chapter 49: Recovery

Our biggest obstacle, individually and collectively, is our addiction to our ego. This addiction prevents us from shifting our self-identity. The founders of Alcoholics Anonymous understood this; that's why the foundation of the Twelve Steps is built on:

Step 1: We admitted we were powerless over alcohol – that our lives had become unmanageable.

Step 2: Came to believe that a Power greater than ourselves could restore us to sanity, and

Step 3: Made a decision to turn our will and our lives over to the care of God as we understood Him.

It is a blessing when an alcoholic or drug addict hits rock bottom, as he or she realizes that there is no future in addiction, just a shameful, regrettable, and guilt ridden past that keeps repeating itself over and over again; leaving them stuck on the relapse roller coaster ride. AA literature states that alcoholics who are motivated to change and are willing to, "go to any lengths to find a spiritual experience."

Those of us that aren't alcoholics are typically not as strongly motivated. We feel as though with a few changes we can fix ourselves and our circumstances and our lives will be better, but that is no different than the delusional thinking of an alcoholic or drug addict. As long as we are striving to fix our ego we will never recover from the delusion that we are nothing more than our ego.

The key to making a shift away from our ego is the same whether you are addicted to a substance or to your ego. It is the "vital spiritual experience" referred to in the book Alcoholics Anonymous. "We have found much of heaven and we have been rocketed into a fourth (spiritual) dimension of existence of which we have not even dreamed. We have had deep and effective spiritual experiences which have revolutionized our whole attitude toward life, toward our fellows and toward God's universe."

Would you like to have a deep and effective spiritual experience that will revolutionize your whole attitude toward life, toward your fellows, and toward God? That is the purpose of our technology.

Chapter 50: Energy Alignment

Every aspect of us is energy vibrating at varying rates. Simplistically, we are composed of energy vibrating slower (matter), more quickly (subtle energies) and faster (Source). The field of Energy Alignment concerns itself with the harmonization of our energetic identities, resulting in unity consciousness and becoming Source manifest in our material plane of existence. The fundamental aspects of Energy Alignment are presence, flow and identity.

Presence: Increasing our spiritual presence throughout our body is fundamental to this process. We are spiritual beings and as such our spiritual self/Source is rooted at our core. However, our spiritual presence throughout our entire body is limited by fear and it is also masked and distorted by energetic blocks. In general, when we as our spiritual selves are ego-identified and fearful, we do not manifest fully throughout our bodies. In addition, our limiting egoic beliefs form the basis of energetic blocks, which further mask and distort our spiritual energy system. When we are less fearful, the greater presence of our spiritual self promotes releasing or transforming blocks.

Flow: Our entire energy system is very dynamic. It has the potential for great fluidity as it is designed for the expression of Source throughout our material plane of existence. As beings with free will, we can and do conceive of and impose structures and blocks that limit the fluidity and expression of Source energy throughout our energy system. As we allow greater energy flow from Source throughout our entire system there becomes a greater incompatibility between Source energy and the limited egoic beliefs that form the basis of our energetic blocks. As such, the blocks are transformed or are released.

Identity: The act of self-identification represents the manner in which we manifest and express ourselves in totality (our current state of being), including how we feel and behave, not just believe, as beliefs are solely ego-based. Self-identifying as Source in this manner affirms and expresses what we truly are. Self-identifying in any way other than Source, our authentic Self, is a denial of what we are, thus masking our spirituality and our complete energy system. Self-identifying as anything other than Source creates our most fundamental, limiting belief.

How does the human energy system change as a result of Energy Alignment? Although all of our energy system is derived from Source it is our belief that the Spirit or Hara line represents Source energy directly and that what we term the personal spiritual self or soul, chakras and auric bodies all represent aspects of our energetic self that emanate from the spirit line and are more personal to this life.

As energy blocks clear (limiting beliefs are released or transform) the chakras reveal themselves as balanced with a symmetrical spin and the auric bodies appear more expanded. The individual's personal spiritual self also is shown to be more integrated with the physical body. In addition, the spirit line appears straight, not broken, fragmented or curved.

With the transition to the Source Awakened state of being and greater self-identification with Source, the chakras appear white with a faster spin rate and white light radiates from the individual. See the Spiritual Progression Chart for more information.

How does our technology facilitate Energy Alignment? Using music, the technology produces pleasant sound and vibrations, which induces a very deep state of relaxed drowsiness. During your session, you are instructed to fall asleep, which promotes the development of drowsiness, but the intermittent changes in the intensity of the sound and vibration from the music typically keeps you from falling into a deep sleep. As a result of the changing intensity and greater presence you become profoundly relaxed, but over time you remain aware.

Our observations (including observations from an out-of-body observer and a second gifted psychic observer during the past 17 years) and subjective reports indicate that the synchronized magnetic fields stimulate the human energy system. Specifically, the root chakra is stimulated creating greater feelings of safety and security, thereby reducing fear. Additionally, the Hara line is stimulated, which allows for greater expression of our spiritual self throughout the body. Individuals that can perceive the stimulation of their energy systems report that they feel greater spiritual energy activity and flow. This activity can be perceived as a pleasant sensation of subtle vibration felt throughout the body, although typically first experienced in the hands and feet.

In this relaxed and more energetically present state the person's ego is far less engaged and they are more receptive to change. We believe that this represents an overall state of higher spiritual vibration. A higher state of vibration facilitates the release and transformation of energetic blocks.

What are the effects of Energy Alignment on any given individual? It is our belief that individuals that are profoundly relaxed with a less engaged ego and functioning at a higher spiritual vibration are more predisposed to releasing energetic blocks (limiting beliefs). They also more readily self-identify as a spiritual being as in these higher states they begin to have varied spiritual experiences. Therefore during sessions they manifest a more spiritually expressed energy system, as witnessed by our observers. However, if after their sessions, they maintain their old beliefs and self-identification, their energy system will soon return to its previous state.

On the other hand, if they intend to release limiting beliefs and intend to self-identify as a spiritual being and they are successful, their energy state is more likely to shift and remain that way. Therefore, ultimately it is the individual that dictates any change in themselves and the permanence of that change.

Chapter 51: Instructions for use

Instructions for the initial sessions are:
1. Fall asleep and let the technology wake you up.
2. Focus on what your body is feeling – feel the vibrations.
3. Every time you begin to have thoughts feel your body.
4. Just let go and experience it.

Using this technology is a very fast way of learning how to shift your state of consciousness and increase your power of observation. But, like any process, it is not instantaneous and requires some practice. However, in our experience this technology tends to bring about results more quickly and produce a more profound level of physiologic relaxation than other methods for many users. This is very helpful for stress reduction and provides an excellent foundation for spiritual development.

The first goal is to observe and learn what your sleeping body or nearly asleep body feels like. In this way you can recreate this maximal level of physiologic relaxation any time you choose. You can become far more relaxed much more of the time and are less likely to be triggered by stressful events. The second goal, which takes longer to achieve is to learn what your higher mind is like in this state, unfettered by your ego or conditioning. Your higher mind is actually your energetic, authentic or spiritual self. It is who you truly are.

Although you will learn to dramatically shift your state of consciousness, you do so by focusing mainly on your body. It's fairly simple. With the help of this technology you can allow yourself to deeply relax or fall asleep and then the technology will stimulate you enough to cause an increase in your awareness. You will find that your state of consciousness oscillates between drowsiness or sleep and more alert wakefulness. Your consciousness will shift up and down and down and up in your initial sessions.

What you are trying to achieve on a consistent basis is a state of consciousness in which your body is very deeply relaxed or even asleep, while you retain enough awareness to observe how heavy and relaxed your body feels and how rhythmic and automatic your body breathes. You want to achieve this state of consciousness because the first goal is being aware of what your very relaxed or sleeping body feels like. Once you learn what it feels like you can much more easily recreate this relaxed state by simply recreating how that feels.

With repeated achievement of that state during sessions your level of awareness will slowly increase, while you maintain your body in a very relaxed state. Don't force the increased awareness; just let it happen.

The second goal is achieved when your level of awareness increases such that you are able to realize the difference between your higher mind and your egoic or lower mind. Your higher mind emerges when you become more aware while your body remains asleep or nearly so. When your body and brain are asleep so is your ego because your ego is a product of the brain. Your higher mind is your energetic or spiritual self and is not a product of the brain.

As a result, when your brain is nearly asleep or asleep, your ego is rendered less or non-functional. In this way, your higher mind, which is truly who you are, is no longer influenced by your ego or your conditioning. Your conditioning, part of your ego, results in the subconscious reactive patterns of your coping strategies. That is what so often influences your emotions and behaviors, particularly in response to a stressful event. Your higher mind is truly independent of these coping strategies.

It's helpful to use the bathroom to avoid any disruption during your session. Assume a nice comfortable position in the chair and just like when you go to sleep, use a blanket and get comfortable. The lights will be turned off and feel free to close your eyes.

The music that is typically played through the chair is layered. Multiple melodies are played simultaneously. This is done to provide full spectrum audio frequencies to your body and also to aid you in ignoring the music, as it is difficult to follow. The lack of visual stimuli and the relative constancy of the sound and vibration produce a brain state of inattention, which aids you in becoming drowsy. The intermittent fluctuations in the sound and vibration will aid you in becoming more aware, once you have become drowsy or fallen asleep so that you can seek that level of consciousness where your body is very relaxed or even asleep and your higher mind is awake.

Early in this process, your state of consciousness will drift between wakefulness and sleep. When you notice that you are alert or thinking, direct your attention to your body. Try to feel the vibrations throughout your body and more importantly feel how heavy and relaxed your entire body, neck, face and head are becoming. Learn what that feels like. Once you have learned what this feels like you will have the ability to recreate this state during your normal daily activities. Since being relaxed feels good, you will likely become this way more of the time.

Note that this technology is not a medical device or a medical treatment. Due to the vibrational stimulus if you have a pacemaker, please consult your physician before use. Also recognize that this technology is new and may have effects that are currently unknown to us.

This technology is a form of energy work. Since it facilitates a deeply relaxed state, realize that certain emotions may emerge. Allow your emotions to manifest without trying to contain or suppress them. They will typically have less of an effect on you if you have already

333

become more relaxed. Sometimes, emotions may manifest hours or even a day after the session. Pay attention to them and try to understand their significance in your life. Also to the extent they need to be expressed, please do so safely.

Because this technique focuses on the body and we sometimes are not all that well in touch with our bodies you may notice some pain during your session. Our advice is to move into or breathe into that pain and allow it to intensify. Typically, if it does intensify it will release or fade away. If it doesn't intensify, simply continue the process of deepening your level of relaxation and note what happens with the pain.

While these sessions may feel therapeutic in nature they are not provided under the context of traditional medical/mental health treatment. Sessions are not intended to be used as or to replace medical/mental health treatment.

Conclusion

Our egos are quite clever and they wear many disguises. We call the disguise of addiction by various names including alcoholism, workaholic and by another twenty or so names. Whatever it is called, at its root is our addiction to the ego itself. As such the only way to effectively cure the problem is to treat that root cause, our addiction to ego.

At the core of our ego is a flawed belief, that we are not good enough or worthy of love. Most of us have been performing for love our entire lives. There is no way to break this cycle until we realize that we are not the beliefs that comprise our ego. We are more primary and of a spiritual nature. That is the center of a human being.

The spiritual path is heart-centered. Although our journey may begin in our head with a thought it must continue with an opening of our heart. It is our feelings that carry us on this journey. For that there is no substitute.

An opening of our heart doesn't signify the end to the journey and in fact there is likely no end. Regardless, the further we progress the greater we distance ourselves from the constraints of our ego. Ultimately however, at some point in the journey we are no longer ego-identified. At that point we are no longer the person that struggles to be good enough or worthy of love. We are no longer addicted to our ego.

Postscript

It has been several weeks since I have completed this book. Have I had the kind of spiritual awakening I have read about? The answer is no, however I believe the process of awakening has continued in me.

I am fortunate in that I am surrounded by extraordinary people that can witness the subtle events that underlie more obvious events that we have given labels to. Jennifer has seen that the seals or filters of my lower four chakras are now open and my Hara line at those levels is very different in its appearance. This process had begun about seven weeks ago, starting in my first chakra.

During this process my heart has opened more substantially. My emotions deepened considerably, which initially brought emotional pain that quickly yielded to a deepening of love-based emotions. A number of energetic phenomena have also occurred, but at this time they seem more like technical details that are less noteworthy.

My ego had wanted to report to you that I had reached a new plateau in my spiritual journey. I can report however, that with every small step I take I become less addicted to my ego.

For follow-on information when available please visit www.AddictedToMyEgo.com.

Appendix

Tips on writing one's story

First and foremost, why are you considering doing this? What do you hope to gain from this process? My primary goal in writing my story was to better understand myself. I spent more time in reflection and feeling past moments in my life than I did writing. The process was fun at times, but often painful. The pain lingered some days and past memories that I had thought I had worked through caused me to feel sad and irritable, but those were the days I learned the most about myself.

Don't embark on this path unless you wish to revisit and re-experience past trauma and emotional upheaval. In addition, don't waste your time unless you plan to be brutally honest with yourself, completely vulnerable and willing to perceive all you can about yourself. Have a box of tissues next to you and more in reserve. You will need them.

If you do not feel you are ready to revisit certain past episodes in your life or be completely honest and vulnerable, leave this task for another time in your life. If you do embark on this path and you find that it is too painful or causing you too much distress, then seek friends or professional help for guidance and assistance.

ALWAYS REMEMBER that you are not your story, you are not your ego and you are never alone.

Write from your heart not your head. If you find yourself thinking, stop writing and feel your way back to your story or stop writing for that day. Write everything you feel. Don't write too much in any one day unless the words are literally pouring out of you. This is not a race. There is no correct timeframe for writing one's story. Don't worry about chronology. Feel free to skip around as different emotional themes have played out many times in your life. Take your time and dive deep. This is your life. Explore it completely.

If you plan to show it to others or publish it, then at some point it may require editing. Remember that editing is done from the head and not typically from the heart. Please do not attempt to edit while writing from your heart. If you do edit your story, please consider being kind to those you have written about. If the purpose for you, in writing your story, is to help yourself, please do not harm anyone else in the process. That doesn't mean you shouldn't write the truth, but after doing so, edit accordingly from the head and heart, with compassion.

In writing your story be open to receiving new insights about yourself. Push your boundaries of openness and open-mindedness. If a strange idea pops into your head, don't dismiss it. Start writing and see where it takes you. Insights are typically provided to you and not generated by brain-based thought processes. They will lead you to new levels of understanding. These are the pearls of wisdom you are most likely in search of.

On a practical note, it is better to write a little every day or most days rather than forcing yourself to write a lot during one or two days per week, as it is easy to lose continuity. You will likely be surprised at how much writing you can accomplish in thirty minutes when you are writing from your heart. There is usually a time during the day that is best for you. For me, it was sometime between 3am and 6am, after awakening, when it was deathly still and there was very little chance of interruption. I felt as if a buffer of material had been prepared for me during sleep and all I did was wake up and empty it through my fingers. Then I would read it to see what I had written.

In writing one's story there are so many life-based topics to consider that perusing a list would actually be a distraction from getting to what is most important for each of us. Your soul doesn't need a list of life-based topics to consider. Having just stated this please let me ask you to consider certain topics that have been set out separately in this book.

These topics have a more global influence on our lives and are vital to moving beyond the ego. These considerations in Parts II and IV are so important in understanding what we truly are that they have been given additional emphasis in this process. These chapters have also been written using an inner dialogue format to encourage an alternative approach to writing one's story.

If you already have an active inner dialogue this approach will come quite naturally for you. If you do not, don't let that stop you from trying, as it may work as well for you as it has for me. In either case, write from the vantage point of your ego and challenge your higher self to provide the answer. In all of my years of writing this way I have never been successful at boxing my higher self into a corner. It has always provided an answer that surprised and usually delighted me.

If you proceed with writing your story I wish you all the best. I am reminded of my mother while in hospice care with Jen psychically observing her in dialogue with her higher self working through her issues. I can only imagine how much better her life would have been if she had accomplished this task earlier in life.

May the rest of your life be better as a result of this process!

44089337R00197

Made in the USA
Middletown, DE
27 May 2017